As If!

THEORY Q

A series edited by
Lee Edelman,
Benjamin Kahan, and
Christina Sharpe

As If!

QUEER CRITICISM ACROSS DIFFERENCE

Chase Gregory

DUKE UNIVERSITY PRESS
Durham and London 2025

© 2025 DUKE UNIVERSITY PRESS

All rights reserved
Project Editor: Liz Smith
Designed by Dave Rainey
Typeset in Portrait Text, SangBleu Sunrise, and Open Sans
by Copperline Book Services

Library of Congress Cataloging-in-Publication Data
Names: Gregory, Chase, [date] author.
Title: As if! : queer criticism across difference / Chase Gregory.
Other titles: Queer criticism across difference | Theory Q.
Description: Durham : Duke University Press, 2025. | Series:
Theory Q | Includes bibliographical references and index.
Identifiers: LCCN 2025004848 (print)
LCCN 2025004849 (ebook)
ISBN 9781478032120 (paperback)
ISBN 9781478028895 (hardcover)
ISBN 9781478061113 (ebook)
Subjects: LCSH: Gay authors—United States—History and
criticism. | Lesbian authors—History and criticism. | Criticism. |
Queer theory. | Homosexuality and literature. | Identity
(Psychology) in literature. | Deconstruction. | Literature and
race. | Gender identity in literature.
Classification: LCC PS153.G38 G74 2025 (print) | LCC PS153.G38 (ebook) |
DDC 810.9/35266—dc23/eng/20250528
LC record available at https://lccn.loc.gov/2025004848
LC ebook record available at https://lccn.loc.gov/2025004849

CONTENTS

Acknowledgments

So many people helped me write this book.

Perhaps most obviously, *As If! Queer Criticism Across Difference* would not have happened were it not for the team at Duke University Press. Thank you, all, for expertly and patiently guiding me through the publication process. Thank you to James Moore for helping me secure subvention grants. A huge thank you to Ryan Kendall for instructing me through each step of the journey, from contract acceptance to physical book. Thank you to my manuscript's three anonymous readers (please tell me it was you if we ever meet), whose generous feedback challenged me in generative, exciting, and compelling ways. Special gratitude to Kenneth Wissoker and to the Theory Q editorial collective—Lee Edelman, Benjy Kahan, and Christina Sharpe—for believing in this project and for taking a chance on someone who is still a relative greenhorn to academic publishing.

This book only exists because of the mentorship of Robyn Wiegman, Wahneema Lubiano, Antonio Viego, and Rey Chow. Robyn, especially, thank you for countless forms of pedagogical coaching: long office-hour discussions, meticulous quotation-mark formatting edits, frantic email back-and-forths that felt like tennis matches, intense publication seminars, an Intro to Queer Theory course, many dramatic Feminist Theory Workshops, the trip to Ann Arbor, and so many other instances of intellectual aid and personal support. Thank you also to Ranjana Khanna, Kimberly Lamm, Ara Wilson, Priscilla Wald, Anne Garréta, and Tiwonda Johnson-Blount, whose presence affected my time at Duke in a myriad of helpful ways.

As If! Queer Criticism Across Difference benefited from multiple workshopping opportunities, both formal and informal. Thank you to Valerie Traub and Sue Lanser for organizing the "Lesbian Studies in Queer Times" workshop at the University of Michigan in April 2016 and to Toril Moi and the Center for Philosophy, Arts, and Literature at Duke University for organizing the 2018 "Character: Identification, Ethics, Ontology" Young Scholars Workshop. Many thanks also to Rachel Moss for organizing the Oxford University "Beyond *Between Men*: Homosociality Across Time" conference and to Omari Weekes and Mary Zaborskis for inviting me to their "Reading for Filth: Gross Methods in Literary Studies" American Comparative Literature Association (ACLA) roundtable; both these occasions allowed me to test out an early version of chapter 3. Thank you to Allen Jones for inviting me to present an early version of chapter 2 at the "Subversive Punctuation: Coding Silenced Voices" Modern Language Association (MLA) panel. I am also grateful to Brian McGrath for inviting me to read at the "Style, in Theory" MLA panel and to Carolyn Laubender for organizing the "Pedagogy, in Theory" ACLA roundtable; both events helped hone what became chapter 4. Thanks are further due to Annabel Kim for including me in the MLA panel "Citation, Otherwise," which inspired parts of this book's conclusion (and for being an engaging and helpful interlocutor for me during her time at Duke).

Several organizations also allowed me to work on this project. Funds from the Howard Whitaker Jr. Summer Research Fellowship; a 2018–19 dissertation fellowship; various travel awards from Duke University's Program in Literature and Program in Gender, Sexuality, and Feminist Studies; startup funds from the C. Graydon and Mary E. Rogers Faculty Fellowship; and subvention funds from Bucknell University's Office of the Provost were all instrumental in getting *As If!* across the finish line. Thank you to the Duke Graduate Students Union and to all the people involved in the effort to unionize (both times). Thank you also to the Thompson Writing Center, the Pinhook, the House of Coxx, Surf Club, Cocoa Cinnamon, the Scrap Exchange, the Durham Literacy Center, Siphon Coffee, Amami Kitchen and Espresso Bar, the Sawhorse Café, Alees Café, CommunityAid Thrift, Engle's Farm and Greenhouses, ONE Health and Wellness, the Lewisburg Community Garden, the American Association of University Professors, and the Union County Library.

Thank you to the people who got me through graduate school, including Cameron Awkward-Rich, Hannah Bornstein, Morgan Browning, Bennett Carpenter, Nick Clarkson, Kendyl Cole, Kate Costello, Annu Dahiya, I. Augustus Durham, Jessica Gokhberg, Aaron Goldsman, Jamie Gonzalez, Rachel Greenspan, Jay Hammond, Caoimhe Harlock, Dustin Huber, Calvin Hui, Carla Hung, Laura Jaramillo, Annabel Kim, Mark Kushner, Jackie Molyneaux, Mitchell Murtagh, Sonia Nayak, Claire Ravenscroft, Mandy Rizki, Yair Rubenstein, and Jake Soule. Many of you read early parts of this manuscript, either in formal workshops or in casual writing swaps. Thank you especially to Rushi—John Stadler, Cory Lown, Jake Silver, Jess Quick Stark, Daniel Stark, Katie Jane Fernelius, Paul Cox, and Austin Hopkins—for sushi, for RuPaul, and for providing a grounding, silly counterpoint to the disorienting, too-serious grind of postgraduate education.

Thank you to Julie Morris for indomitable verve, board games, delicious mixed drinks, Rubber Peacock, and the water/fire basketball pillow; thank you to Julien Fischer for consistently on-point commentary, for an obsession with queer theory gossip that rivals my own, for razzing me about being more Lacanian than I'd care to admit, and for providing the biting Scorpio spirit that my grade-grubbing Virgo sun desperately craved. Thank you to Shannan Hayes for radical honesty, whip-smart questions, and a shared lust for Alan Cumming. Thank you to Cole Rizki for the many times you had to jokingly remind me I had a body to attend to, both in theory and in real life—for feeding me fresh honey and eggs, for cleansing sage scrubs, for smoothies and tinctures, for the stretch breaks and strong hugs. Thank you to Nick Huber for a thousand things (D&D, excellent playlists, *Adventure Time* recaps, firepit gatherings, absolutely devastating jokes ... conversations that cut me to my core, a deep and abiding humanity, etc.) and to Corinne Huber for a thousand more (Brogden Middle School reading days, canasta tutorials, choral concerts, softball games, wicked humor, friendship that left me grounded, an infectious and generous zeal, etc.).

Jake Silver, thank you for that one time you recited the entire *Survivor* snake monologue (it was inspiring) and for the time you sang "Orinoco Flow" word for word without looking once at the karaoke screen for guidance (it was equally inspiring). Thank you also for letting me inherit several of your least-important succulents, two life-sized pet statues, one bust of Abraham Lincoln in drag, and an unopened glass bottle of 1995 Coke when you left for fieldwork in Palestine; they are totems that have no doubt kept me strong during long hours writing at home.

John Stadler, thank you for goofy conversations and for serious conversations, for a shrewd editorial eye and an always-available ear, for Big Gay Writing Group and Queer Cinema Night. Thank you for several delicious pies, one waterpizzamelon, twenty Duke Graduate Student Union bake sales, twelve or so writer's workshops, two Harry Potters, six unhinged Halloween outfits, one shared appreciation of Sufjan Stevens, one strangely moving trip to the Liberty Bell, and one freezing, angry day of protest in Washington, DC. Thank you also for letting me claim that *101 Dalmatians* counts as queer cinema and for being that rare someone with whom I feel v, v simpatico.

I have too much to thank Jess Issacharoff and Carolyn Laubender for. Sorry guys.

I wrote the last part of this book in Lewisburg. So many people helped me find my footing in the bizarre place that is central Pennsylvania, among them Elinam Agbo, Maria Antonaccio, Saul Arber, Josie Barth, Benae Beamon, Rebecca Beichner, Morgan Benowitz-Fredericks, Kate Birmingham, Juliana Brafa, Adam Burgos, Kenton Butcher, Jordi Comas, Brianne Croteau, Rafe Dalleo, Katie Daly, Sanjay Dharmavaram, Gabby Diego, Michael Drexler, Elizabeth Durden, Ken Eisenstein, Kim Faulk, Abby Fite, Winnie Foreman, Cymone Fourshey, Bix Gabriel, Bob Gainer, Kristin Gibson, Ted Hamilton, Mitch Hart, Katie Hayes, Ellen Herman, Mai Linh Hong, John Hunter, Diane Jakacki, Christopher Johnson, Susan Jordan, Kelly Knox, Weijia Li, Laura Libert, Taylor Lightman, Joe Malherek, Bill McCoy, Ghislaine McDayter, Rebecca Meyers, Billy Miller, Darakhshan Mir, Daniel Neinhuis, Carl Nelson, Deirdre O'Connor, Caitlyn Olsen, Cassie Osei, Jim Pearson, John Penniman, Jean Peterson, Carrie Pirmann, Ian Proud, Lynne Ragusea, Tony Ragusea, Ellen Robinson, Roger Rothman, Marcus Scales, Joe Scapellato, Eric Schwartz, Jocelyne Scott, Chet'la Sebree, Deborah Sills, Bonnie Smith, Paul Smith, Yvonne Smith, Jason Snyder, Carrie Sterling, Anthony Stewart, Andrew Stuhl, Katie Tardio, Alan Tran, Julie Vandivere, Kathi Venios, Margot Vigeant, Austin Wadle, G. C. Waldrep, Carol White, Jaye Austin Williams, Ally Wood, Nikki Young, and Farida Zaid.

Thank you to Erica Delsandro for unbeatable cookies, fabulous feminist ferocity, and for being, just in general, a beautiful big ball of light all the time. Thank you to Julie Hagenbuch and Eddy Lopez for cultural dinner exchange, excellent backyard hangouts, and letting us love Vincent. Thank you to Elena Machado for next-level hugs, Vaughn Lit hallway laughter, and Durham road trip company. Thank you to Virginia Zimmerman for pub sing harmonies. Thank you to Bryan Vandevender for Gram's brunches, Knoebels trips, and "How to Be Queer in Central PA." Thank you to Stephan Lefebvre for excursions to the last remaining Hot Topic, for introducing me to Boscov's, and for classical-music-writing dates. Thank you to Jennifer Thomson for always being the rare voice of fucking reason.

Thank you to Bret Leraul for several garden parties, two spectacularly catastrophic IP courses, and one beautiful friendship; thank you also for being an inspiring organizer and for speaking both theory and Californian with me. Thank you to Ellen Chamberlain and Deepak Iyer for teaching me all about birds, for letting me tag along with new binoculars, and for modeling a patient queer gentleness that I really admire—and that often makes me wish I were a scientist. Thank you to Jesse Pouchet for whoopie pie appreciation, Zephyr snuggles, Culture Coffee Cookie Club, and lending me the bird book; thank you also, sincerely, for a roommatehood that got me through a tough year. Thank you to Sarajane Snyder for Mondragón Books, for teaching me about garden tea, for Banned Books Week Drag Night featuring Karenheight 451, for deliberate world-building, and for the radical library. Thank you to Emily Loney for game nights, swapped students, looseleaf recommendations, and for being incurably lawful good. Thank you to Denise Lewis for organizing a chaotic department on the daily, for teasing me about the fire starters, for procuring a new toilet, for axe throwing, and for literally every conversation I have ever had with you—I am not sure you know how much I needed them all.

Thank you to Meenakshi Ponnuswami for more things than I can count but especially for being a constant source of snark, encouragement, commiseration, comedy, and generosity of spirit. (Thank you also for the speech you made at the Diwali party in your backyard in 2022, which I truly think about all the time.) Thank you to Rick Reinhart and Sanh Tran for every gay invitation: for karaoke, for LGBTQ faculty and staff happy hour, for "Cocktails & Vinyl" nights, for trips out to antiques and momo dumplings, for gossip, for "Anti Mame," for generational hot takes, and for fully welcoming me into the Lavender Mafia.

Jeremy Chow: Your care, advocacy, wit, and friendship have pulled me through first-day-of-school jitters, administrative tomfoolery, a pandemic, and countless other trials and tribulations. Thank you for surprise office Rice Krispie treats, for speaking out, for calling in, for four trips to Reptiland (one of which I'd rather forget), for *Bee Movie* viewing parties, and for the "Shrek Fans Only/Shrek OnlyFans" text thread. I would not have survived my first five years at Bucknell without you. Eloise Stevens: Thank you for so much, but specifically for the cold plunges, sauna conversations, orange and banana couple observation, Instagram poetry, Taurus Moon Craft Nights, campus walks, luxurious robes, Bucknell greenhouse visits, Western Massachusetts nostalgia, and shared avuncular proclivities. Thank you also for letting me third wheel with you and your wife, the moon.

There are many others whose contributions to this book's creation might not be as obvious but that are no less instrumental in its completion. I am beholden to these teachers, who I hope remember me: Lauren Berlant, William Brown, Shawn Chen, Lisa Coleman, Ian Drummond, Bill Fauver, Lisa Gold, Sonari Glinton, Sonia Hofkosh, Mike McAvin, Stephan Pennington, Sandra Robinson, Modhumita Roy, Jed Rucker, Katherine Whittaker-Scott, Bianca Vasquez Torres, and Jean Wu. Huge thanks are also due to Leslie Dvorshock for her insight and for letting me text her crayon drawings after every therapy session. Thank you to Toka Beech, Kathleen Cohen, Tori Eliot, Scott Istvan, Kevin McDonald, and Lorrayne Shen for several years of sustaining friendship, both in person and in my DMs.

Thank you to Garrett Gilmore for a decade of interlocution, for having absolutely the right takes every time, and for more years than that of college radio/critical theory comradery. Thank you to Devin Toohey for comic store tours of Los Angeles, hot leftist takes, and the many encouraging (mostly C-3PO-related) texts. Thank you to Niki Krieg, whose steadfast companionship and collegiality kept me on my grind through Northeast Modern Language Association sessions and New York City coffee meetups, and to Sigourney Norman for being the best roommate I've ever had. Thank you to Chris Stoj for gay bachelor apartment days, for watching Barbara Johnson's entire memorial service with me when you found it on YouTube in 2013, and for watching "*Brokeback Mountain* but without any of the sad parts" with me at your parent's house that same year. Thank you to Katie Kent for, inexplicably, always understanding.

Thank you to Chloe Pelletier and Will Cover for years of parallel-city friendship and to Rob Chamberlain for opening your Atlanta home and heart to us on more than one occasion. Thank you to Jess Bailey for the indie bookstore tours of London, the expat companionship, and for a wedding gift that brought me to tears; thank you to Alex Nussbacher for the delicious meals and excellent company. Thank you to Arielle Harris and Jacob Waters for everything but especially for Sandy and Pepper, for endless hours of Philadelphia hospitality, and for the phrase "chocolate cunks." Howie Levine, Leah Reiss, Esti Bernstein, Zara Fishkin, Will Vaughn, and Laurie Rabin, thank you for babka taste test parties, for blueberry picking, and for the most entertaining WhatsApp thread I've ever been a part of; thank you also for welcoming me into your lives with enthusiasm when I started dating your Quidditch captain many years ago. Hayley Bisceglia-Martin, Zoë Bollinger, Rachel Bracker, Tyler Breisacher, Erin Burns, Will Hollingsworth, Scott Humbarger, Jordan Navarrette, Greg Nemes, Amy Schellenbaum, and Sarah Verity, thank you for Thinking You're Fancy. Robbie McCracken, thank you for being the fourth Gregory. Paige Breisacher, thank you for the decades of nerdy collaboration, friendship, and silliness and for your singular personhood—you are, I'm convinced, an incandescent and certifiable genius.

Thank you to Pat Wright for being an example of life lived weirdly and with relish and for treating me like an intellectual from the moment I could talk; thank you to Alyce Gregory for cassette tapes, canned olives, peacock sounds, and poetry. Thank you to Lisa, Matt, and Rachel Boxer for innumerable acts of kindness but especially for taking me in as one of your own; this book would not have happened without you. Thank you to Teresa John, Thomas Murphy, and Chad LaTourette for being such excellent additions. Thank you to Lauren, Rick, Brent, and Evan Rossin and to Scott, Blake, Colby, and Dillon Case for the many, many good adventures and to Lenna Elliot for the good adventures to come. Meagan Rossin, thank you for teaching me, both literally and figuratively, how to lift my head.

Kasha and Izzy, thank you for being warm and good, always.

Paul Gregory, thank you for every single music recommendation, for Greek food, for warm bread, for papier-mâché, for modeling soft Cat Stevens masculinity, for teaching me how to plant pansies, and for so many other things. Chris Gregory: When I was in kindergarten, I told you I wanted to be a writer, and rather than talk me out of it, you made me promise to dedicate the first book I published to you. Thank you for the uncountable ways you helped me finally fulfill that promise. To my radiant and hilarious siblings, Avery Gregory and Duncan Gregory, thank you both for wholly getting me. I love you a ridiculous amount. "Butt-Butt Saves the Zoo" forever.

When they came into my life very early on in my collegiate career, Lee Edelman, Joe Litvak, and Christina Sharpe changed me as a person and made me desperately want to become a critic. Their fingerprints are all over this project and (I hope they know this) all over my heart.

Two more people have had an immeasurable impact on this book. Those two people are Coorain Devin and Keith Ashley. To Keith I owe twenty years of mentorship, fifteen years of pen pal correspondence, and, I suspect, an eternity of *saṃsāra* traveling. Thank you for THINK!, for letting me be your loyal T.A., and for texting multiple videos of your friendly neighborhood javelina. Thank you also for one important night in Tucson when—cross-faded on mezcal and weed, listening to Judy Garland and the Proclaimers, lying on the floor looking at your freshwater aquarium—we figured out the thesis of this book. To Coorain I owe years of friendship and creative collaboration that have made life weird, glittery, and bursting with love. Thank you for "Outbound to Wonderland," for Jamaica Plain co-op overnights, for frozen Maine rhubarb, for chickens named Clorox, for mutual comings-out, and for perfect art. To both of you, I owe my first and most powerful understandings of queer recognition.

Finally, thank you to Carly B. Boxer, for all the right reasons.

Introduction
Reading and Writing *As If!*

In the weeks and months following George Floyd's murder and the subsequent up-risings of 2020, I noticed a common refrain from many well-meaning white people. Over and over, in Instagram posts, tweets, Facebook statuses, and sometimes even on in-person protest signs, I saw repeated the looping, milquetoast sentiment: "I understand that I can never understand." The more I saw this phrase, the more it irked me, and I was relieved to find after a few weeks that I was not the only person to notice the sudden virality of this slogan, nor the first to be annoyed by it. Hunter Harris, in a blog post about the experience of watching white Americans "reckon with a reckoning," describes her own encounter with a version of the same mantra: "One friend went to a protest and shared a photo of a neon sign that read 'I understand that I'll never understand, but I'll stand.' Soon, I started seeing the signs everywhere. At first, it was a red flag, then it became its own joke in my mind: *I understand that I'll never understand. But I'll stand' is what I say when I don't like my friend's boyfriend,* I thought, *but he did just put his card down for all our drinks.*"[1] I, too, am perplexed and annoyed by the ubiquity of this phrase and this specific mode of posturing. Why is this the slogan of choice among a certain set of white allies? What work is it doing? What does it assume? And why do I feel, like Harris, that this phrase is a red flag?

"I understand that I can never understand" takes as axiomatic the fact that the speaker is incapable of fully grasping something. In the most obvious interpretation of this sign, that something is the experience of being Black in America—an experience that, it is true, the white person wielding the sign would not have experienced.

In another read, though, the experience that the speaker is purportedly incapable of understanding is the experience of existing in an anti-Black world. If this is indeed the case, the phrase "I understand that I can never understand" is nothing more than a cloying cop-out; that is, "I understand that I can never understand" takes the inevitability of misunderstanding as an alibi to claim extrication from the very systems of anti-Blackness it purports to protest, as if it were possible to opt out. Perhaps, then, what I find irritating is the implicit suggestion that white supremacy cannot be understood by white people. At its most sinister pitch, this phrase positions white allies as ignorant of structural oppression in ways that end up enforcing those oppressive structures. Eve Kosofsky Sedgwick, in her formative queer theoretical work *Epistemology of the Closet*, calls this the "ignorance effect"—that is, mobilizing one's own claim to ignorance as a mode of maintaining and enforcing power.[2]

The sentence reminds me of other well-worn phrases. "I understand that I'll never understand" also rubs me the wrong way because it gratingly echoes another response to a different type of reckoning: The statement sounds uncannily like the well-meaning family member who, on the occasion of your coming out, responds, "I don't understand it, but whatever makes you happy." It recalls the "Straight but Not Narrow" buttons that still occasionally grace the backpacks and lapels of well-meaning heterosexual allies. Both acts of linguistic acrobatics read like updated versions of "love the sinner, hate the sin." Such phrases do their best to avoid any identification with the target of their address because of the contamination that such identification risks (Sedgwick calls this risk "the double-edged potential for injury in the scene of gay coming out").[3] It is hard not to squirm at the backhanded allyship at work in assertions like these, which take great pains to distance the identity of the utterer from that of the addressee. At its most insidious, the wedding of identity and understanding is not only reductive, controlling, and hermetic; it is also antithetical to political coalition.

My hunch is that "I understand that I can never understand" in particular touches a nerve with me because its popularity is symptomatic of a related tendency in queer studies, the field in which I work. This tendency—likely as well-intentioned as the white allies posting on Facebook—links knowledge to identity in ways that delimit how theory is produced, valued, and read. The idea that someone's positionality informs their knowledge is not a new idea, nor is it, at this point, as controversial and world-shattering as it once was. Under this logic, it follows that different subject positions might produce different kinds of knowledge(s). Ushered in by groundbreaking work by Sandra Harding, Patricia Hill Collins, and others, feminist standpoint theory of the 1980s placed new emphasis on positionality in an effort to resist hegemonic philosophies that posited an androcentric, white supremacist, or heterosexist universal.[4] But despite the noble goals of identity-rooted scholarship, previously radical efforts to democratize the academy have been ruthlessly co-opted by a neoliberal understanding of identity. In this ideological climate, individual persons come to represent whole categories of people, ideas, politics, or modes of knowledge. In the wake of this neoliberal turn, "the university's management of racialized and gendered *bodies* occurs through its management of racialized and gendered *knowledge*."[5] As such, it often behooves academics working in particular arenas to speak "as" a particular and recognizable identity. This trend is most prevalent within what Robyn Wiegman helpfully labels "identity knowledge" fields—that is, academic areas that specifically tackle issues regarding race, gender, or sexuality.[6] Among these is queer studies, the field with which this book is most concerned.[7]

With knowing irony, early queer studies mobilizes identity in the service of an intellectual project that is later defined by its deconstructionist suspicion of identity. Consider, for example, queer theorist Judith Butler's bemused discovery, early on in their career, that "being" a lesbian was both a result and a requirement of their entrance into the academic professional scene: "The professionalization of gayness requires a certain performance and production of a 'self' which is the *constituted effect* of a discourse that nevertheless claims to 'represent' that self as a prior truth. When I spoke at the conference on homosexuality in 1989, I found myself telling my friends beforehand that I was off to Yale to be a lesbian, which of course didn't mean that I wasn't one before, but that somehow then, as I spoke in that context, I *was* one in some more thorough and totalizing way, at least for the time being."[8] The privilege of the claimed identity "lesbian" that Butler encounters at the conference on homosexuality shores up Butler's academic credibility and therefore, ironically, lends credibility to their critique of identity. By this account— fittingly titled "Imitation and Gender Insubordination"—it is only because Butler theorizes as a lesbian that they can credibly dismantle the very category "lesbian" as a stable or knowable identity from which to write and speak. As Butler quips in the same article: "To write or speak *as a lesbian* appears a paradoxical appearance of this 'I,' one which feels neither true nor false."[9] With the melancholic ambivalence typical of Butler's larger oeuvre, their anecdote admits both the ever-present danger and the intermittent necessity of claiming identity.

As If! Queer Criticism Across Difference advocates for queer studies to more boldly claim its poststructuralist, ironic, literary-critical genealogies. In the thirty years since Butler penned "Imitation and Gender Insubordination," the paradox of this relation has dropped away.[10] In this process of identity idealization, identities proliferate and calcify into stable political entities. In other words, the imperative to treat identity as a felt truth rather than as a social position reduces a complex concept to a question of knowable tautology, instead of relational ambivalence.

I am interested in modes of queer study that resist this imperative. *As If! Queer Criticism Across Difference* examines literary criticism from the first decade of queer theory's entry into the academic scene, 1990–2000. Often, this queer literary criticism is produced within the humanistic disciplinary shelter of English departments; usually, it takes as its critical object literary work such as novels or poetry; always, it is interested in the ways in which identity (particularly sexuality, race, and gender) intersects with cultural production and reception. Specifically, this book revisits queer literary criticism of the 1990s. All of the authors who pop up in the chapters to come are trained in English or comparative literature departments, and their methodology consists of close reading on the level of the word, phrase, or sentence.

I turn to these authors as examples not merely to give them their queer theoretical due or to expand our understanding of the contributors to queer theory beyond a few major players—although I'm happy if that's an accidental side effect. I also do so to draw attention to queer studies' literary inheritance. In a world where academic scholarship is increasingly being funded insofar as it has deliverable sociological correlates, the humanistic or literary aspects of early queer studies have dropped out, along with the modes of writing in which the authors I examine are invested. To be sure, queer literary criticism is but one piece of a complicated queer theory genealogy: Since the term *queer theory* came into common academic parlance, scholars have sought to expand and complicate the presumed genealogies of the field, adding much-needed nuance and depth to the discipline's multiple lineages.[11] Queer studies now extends its methods far beyond those of its literary-critical past; moreover, as many have by now pointed out, the genealogy of queer studies does not begin with English departments alone or with the identities purportedly manning those departments. David L. Eng, Jack Halberstam, and José Esteban Muñoz, for example, lament queer studies' "conventional relationship to francophone and Anglo-American literatures and literary studies" on the grounds that such conventions limit queer inquiry to "presumed white masculine subjects."[12] Despite the conventionalities of the average English department, however, I have found that it is precisely at the site of reading that identity breaks down in productive and interesting ways. For this reason, the ease with which Eng, Halberstam, and Muñoz yolk "literatures and literary studies" to a particular and limited identity makes me bristle with suspicion.

Here's what is interesting, to me, about the queer critical writing coming out of English departments in this era: Unlike other facets of queer or gay and lesbian studies, early queer literary criticism is rife with cross-identification. In much of the early work of queer studies scholars studying literature, authors perform cross-identifications that seem improbable, inappropriate, or impossible to the authors who enact them—moreover, they do so with flamboyant relish. It is important that this tendency occurs most often when the authors are writing about literature. Whether it is because the act of reading literature can engender weird and complicated strains of empathy or because the act of writing affords greater anonymity to its authors than the act of physically delivering a paper, there is something about the literary that encourages this kind of identificatory leap. On the contrary, these cross-identifications revel in the messiness of identity, reminding readers of the negativity structuring social relations and challenging the neoliberal idea of identity as coherent, knowable, or a true source of knowledge. I call this writing practice *as if!* criticism.

As If! Queer Criticism Across Difference examines the work of four critics: Deborah E. McDowell, a straight Black feminist writing about lesbian desire; Barbara Johnson, a white lesbian writing about and through Black-authored texts; Robert Reid-Pharr, a gay Black man identifying as part of a community of Black lesbian friends and critics; and Eve Kosofsky Sedgwick, a straight white woman writing about gay men. McDowell, Johnson, Reid-Pharr, and Sedgwick are not the only authors in whose work I find this rhetorical mode, but they do offer some of the best examples of *as if!* criticism. They are exemplary but not exceptional. Taken together, these authors reflect a moment in queer literary criticism that—while not a free-for-all when it comes to cross-identificatory writing—was nonetheless a time where such cross-identifications were more permissible or considered intellectually worthwhile.

The proliferation of cross-identification in the work of McDowell, Johnson, Reid-Pharr, and Sedgwick reflects the moment at which these four writers write. *As if!* criticism is in vogue in the academy between 1989 and 2000. In this moment, identity knowledges, deconstructionist methodologies, racial anxieties, and radical activisms clash like particles in a hadron collider. Faced with the crisis of the AIDS pandemic, activist groups attempted to build solidarity among disparate identities by uniting under the very stigma that allowed for the government's dismissal of mass death, all while resisting political rhetoric implying that only certain identities were susceptible to the virus. When the critics I follow were writing, thinking, teaching, and publishing, US state neglect surrounding AIDS blatantly relied on the invocation and separation of certain identity categories (recall, for example, the Centers for Disease Control's early "Four H's" campaign, which warned that AIDS manifested primarily in the "high risk" groups "Haitians, hemophiliacs, homosexuals and heroin addicts").[13] Seeking to combat the Right's effort to label AIDS a "gay disease," groups like ACT UP strategically sidestepped identity, instead universalizing AIDS as a disease anyone, not just gay men, could contract. In the words of art critic and organizer Douglas Crimp, it was at this juncture that "new political identifications began to be made . . . across identities."[14] The term *queer*—so the story goes—proved useful for both activists and academics: As a reclaimed slur, it sided with perversion and pleasure rather than respectability and assimilation; as an uncertain descriptor, it disavowed identity categories while still invoking specific stigmatized sexualities.[15] These political experiments, including the reclamation and mobilization of *queer* as a term, inspired a generation of gay and lesbian scholars to rethink their own relation to identity.

Yet, as much as the newly rebranded signifier *queer* promised to unseat the identity politics that had been mobilized by the Right, the project of forging alliance while still grappling with and accounting for difference proved challenging. Like the authors showcased in the next four chapters, other activist-academics writing during the 1990s turned to cross-identification as a possible means of navigating a moment of various crises. Crimp, writing in 1992, observes that "a number of identities-in-conflict [exist] in ACT UP: men and women, whites and people of color, and so forth. In spite of the linguistic necessity of specifying identities with positive terms, I want to make clear that I am not speaking of identities as nonrelational. Because of the complexities of the movement, there is no predicting what identifications will be made and which side of an argument anyone might take."[16] From that same year, art critic Kobena Mercer offers one example of how the political climate under Reagan/Bush necessitated not just new forms of political alliance but also new forms of aesthetic assessment. "In the contemporary situation, the essentialist rhetoric of categorical identity politics threatens to erase the connectedness of our different struggles," he writes. "At its worst, such forms of identity politics play into the hands of the Right as the fundamentalist belief in an essential and immutable identity keeps us locked in the prisonhouse of marginality in which oppressions of race, class, and gender would have us live."[17]

Even as the alliances brought on by AIDS engendered potentially radical cross-racial identifications, such identifications were not immune to—and, in fact, were bound up in—extant systems of racial hierarchy, fetishization, and material oppression. Indeed, the 1990s United States also represents a particular moment of white cultural anxiety about the status of America's racial hierarchy. The scholarly works examined in *As If! Queer Criticism Across Difference* are examples of the decade's heightened focus on race, both by virtue of their critical object choice and by virtue of the way in which their authors frequently flirt with the color line. The 1990s mark a period in American history in which paranoia over the instability of racial categories leads to a resurgence of interest in racial passing in both narrative fiction and the real world.[18] The fact that two of the authors showcased in this book, Johnson and McDowell, write extensively about Nella Larsen's *Passing* (1929) is no small coincidence.

As If! Queer Criticism Across Difference takes as axiomatic that any invocation of *as* also entails its already-present figurative *as if*.[19] I borrow the *as if* in my title from Johnson's late-career essay "L'esthétique du mal." Johnson, in turn, borrows it from three very different sources. The first is German philosopher Hans Vaihinger's *Die Philosophie des Als Ob* (1911). The second is Andrew Boyd's tongue-in-cheek *Life's Little Deconstruction Book: Self-Help for the Post-Hip* (1998), which advises its readers to "be as if." The third is Cher Horowitz's iconic and oft-repeated exclamations of "As if!" in the gay classic *Clueless* (1995). Here, Johnson explicates the impossibility of either full belief in or full identification with the authors or texts one encounters as a critic and teacher. Riffing on the difficulties inherent in cross-cultural pedagogy, Johnson first describes "reading as if" as the suspension of disbelief necessary for theory, translation, and teaching. In Johnson's field of comparative literature, the deconstructive injunction "be as if" amounts to the "bad suture" between a word and its imperfect translation.[20] Drawing an important line from teaching to reading, Johnson emphasizes the literary and textual aspects of such a suture. "As if" reading (that is to say, all reading) constitutes "thought as a break rather than thought as a chain," because there is always a cognitive leap to be made between reading "as" oneself and inhabiting an author's objects, ideas, or position. That is to say, Johnson conceives of "reading as if" as reading that relies on a suspension of disbelief. This in turn allows for a temporary suture between one's own reading position and one's object of study. In pedagogy and in reading, "as if" can be understood as an abeyance of one's current theoretical, material, embodied, or political position in the service of another, temporarily assumed position or perspective.[21] There is no writing as; there is simply the imperative to write as, the performance of writing as, or the impulse to characterize certain forms of writing as more authentic than others.

A major claim of this book can be understood thus: When Barbara Johnson, the subject of my second chapter, writes "as a lesbian" and when Robert Reid-Pharr, the subject of my third, writes "as a lesbian," their relationships to the term *lesbian* are similarly ironic, fractured, and unresolved—this despite the fact that Johnson is a woman who fucked women and Reid-Pharr a man who fucks men. Because of how she is interpolated by and lives in the world, Johnson is ostensibly writing from an authentic position and experience. However, her so-called writing "as" becomes writing *as if!* in the moments when what should be an easy identification becomes difficult. Because it stages Johnson's not-quite-successful identifications with the categories into which she has been hailed (white, lesbian, woman), Johnson's prose reveals the myth of easy identification. Reid-Pharr employs a different and complementary tactic, explicitly adopting identity categories that are counterintuitive to the assumptions of his audience. In his book of autobiographically inflected criticism titled *Black Gay Man,* Reid-Pharr's sudden claim that he some-times lives, reads, and thinks "as a lesbian" may seem purely ironic—if not for the fact that Reid-Pharr's insistence on his own lesbianism is also, simultaneously, deeply sincere.[22] This tension, never fully resolved in his book, foregrounds the difficulty of his own (and, indeed, of any) identification. As such, he too writes *as if!*

In each of these examples, cross-identification becomes the mechanism by which the text productively problematizes identity's relationship to authorship. When an author's presumed identity does not align with their avowed identifica-tions, the illusion of identity is thrown into stark relief. The awkward ruptures that result from the chasms that both Johnson and Reid-Pharr must cross to identify as lesbian reveal the awkwardness of the identity category itself. Identity, then, is open-ended rather than a completed entity with definitive actions, behaviors, and interiorities: When someone tries to write according to one script, this mode of writing pulls the rug out from under, objecting, "As if that's the only way!"

Because it blurs the line between self and other, and between desire and recog-nition, identification is never a straightforward affair. Following Sigmund Freud and his interlocutors, identification is neither the same as identity nor identity's opposite. Rather, as Diana Fuss cogently argues: "Identification inhabits, organizes, instantiates identity. It operates as a mark of self-difference, opening up a space for the self to relate to itself as a self, a self that is perpetually other. Identification, understood throughout this book as the play of difference and similitude in self-other relations, does not, strictly speaking, stand against identity but aids and abets it. . . . In perhaps its simplest formulation, identification is the detour through the other that defines a self."[23] If, as Sedgwick writes in her introduction to *Epistemol-ogy of the Closet,* "to identify *as* must always include multiple processes of identifica-tion *with,"* it may not make sense to speak of "cross-identification" at all.[24] To quote Biddy Martin and Butler in their introduction to a special "Cross-Identifications" issue of *Diacritics,* "The notion of 'cross-identification' may seem paradoxical, for every identification presumes a crossing of sorts, a movement toward some other site with which or by which an identification is said to take place."[25] In this way, identification "prevents identity from ever approximating the status of an ontolog-ical given, even as it makes possible the formation of an *illusion* of identity as imme-diate, secure, totalizable."[26] The relationship between identification and identity is paradoxical: Identification cannot occur without some concept of fixed identity, but the act of identification highlights the constructedness of identity.

This school of thought—one to which I also adhere—takes *cross-identification* and *identification* to be nearly, if not totally, synonymous. More recently, Kadji Amin argues for a return to a more capacious and difficult understanding of identification. "It is all but impossible to feel entirely unambivalent about, entirely described by, a social identity category," he writes. "The question, then, is whether we can develop a tolerance for contamination and for the inevitable misfit of identity categories, rather than continually kicking the bucket further down the road, generating ever more terms in pursuit of an impossible dream—that of social categories capable of matching the uniqueness of individual psyches."[27] My project is similarly opposed to an understanding of identification that stitches it seamlessly to identity, insofar as identity is understood as "a personal, felt, and thereby highly phantasmic and labile relation to . . . categories."[28]

Insofar as *as if!* criticism, in its style and method, makes visible displacements, defamiliarizations, and misrecognitions, it shares an affinity with the "disidentification" most famously theorized by José Esteban Muñoz. Muñoz moves away from earlier understandings of identity that reduce subjectivity to "either a social constructivist model or what has been called an essentialist understanding of the self."[29] He notes that "identification . . . is never a simple project. Identifying with an object, person, lifestyle, history, political ideology, religious orientation, and so on, means also simultaneously and partially counteridentifying, as well as only partially identifying, with different aspects of the social and psychic world."[30] Focusing on artists of color whose performed identities and identifications "emerge from a failed interpellation within the dominant public sphere," Muñoz convincingly argues that practice of this difficult and incomplete identification is a queer critical and cultural survival strategy.[31]

The type of writing I explore in *As If! Queer Criticism Across Difference* is thus unlike other versions of autotheoretical writing that have a more straightforward relationship to identity. Nancy K. Miller observes that the posited links between knowledge and identity have long helped foster a style of personally inflected criticism, which she calls "reading as."[32] Tracing this trend within the postseventies academic scene in women's studies, Miller hypothesizes that the proliferation of "reading as" texts is the result of new feminist imperatives to speak from one's identity position.[33] In more contemporary parlance, the type of writing that Miller and others describe might also be called "autotheory," a mode of feminist theorizing that, Lauren Fournier writes, "reveals the tenuousness of maintaining illusory separations between art and life, theory and practice, work and the self, research and motivation."[34] As Fournier and others show, there is a long tradition of feminist autotheoretical writing, a literary history that includes works by feminist authors such as Cherríe Moraga, Audre Lorde, Paul B. Preciado, and Maggie Nelson (to name but a few frequently cited examples). Thinking through and with the personal, these modes of writing align themselves with feminist efforts to resist the hegemonic production and valuation of knowledge.

By contrast, *as if!* criticism aligns itself with a wealth of poststructuralist, feminist, queer, and critical race work that seeks to rethink rigid (and often oppressive) identity frameworks and, indeed, to question the very idea of a stable identity or authentic self at all. Negotiating their own interpolation and positionality within their fields at a time when these fields were constantly self-assessing, critics writing *as if!* work both with and against the disciplining logics of the identity knowledge fields of study into which they find themselves unwillingly boxed. This intellectual promiscuity offers a clue as to why, in an era of multiple crises, cross-identificatory autotheoretical writing emerges.

Crucially, the cross-identification showcased in the work of these four authors is not smooth, complete, or easy. These authors cross-identify, certainly, but they do so with a coy insincerity that also draws attention to the differences between author and identificatory object. Wittingly or unwittingly, all four of these authors consistently stage their own identifications across race, gender, or sexuality as, variously, scenes of misstep, ridiculousness, embarrassment, bad passing, drag, breakdown, or disconnect. These messy, interrupted, embarrassing, often gleeful identifications across difference draw attention to the material power structures that police subjecthood inside and outside the academy while also standing in defiance of them. Indeed, the publicness of these cross-identifications alone makes them remarkable. As Fuss notes, "While we tend to experience our identities as part of our public personas . . . we experience our identifications as more private, guarded, evasive."[35] *As if!* criticism, however, performatively stages identification for its readers. In fact, here, problematic scenes of cross-identification serve as a jumping-off point for queer critical inquiry.

The type of criticism I explore in *As If! Queer Criticism Across Difference* is also unlike the social phenomenon of "passing" as it is traditionally understood. In conventional understandings of passing, a person of one group is recognized or perceived as a member of another group. Instead, the routes of identification I trace here have much more in common with Pamela L. Caughie's definition of *passing* as a postmodern phenomenon. In Caughie's revised definition, passing comes to represent "double logic" rather than "the binary logic that governs its common use."[36] Passing, understood in this unorthodox way,

> necessarily figures that always slippery difference between standing *for* something (having a firm position) and passing *as* something (having no position or a fraudulent one), between the strategic adoption of a politically empowering identity (as when blacks pass as white or homosexuals pass as heterosexual) and the disempowering appropriation of a potentially threatening difference (as when men pass as feminist or whites rep-

resent blacks), and between what one professes as a writer or a teacher (the positions one assumes in an article or a classroom, often as a spokesperson for another's position) and how one is actually positioned in a society, institution, discourse, or classroom. Marked by a discrepancy between what one professes to be (and what one professes) and how one is positioned, passing is a risky business, whether one risks being *exposed* as passing or being *accused* of passing.[37]

McDowell, Johnson, Reid-Pharr, and Sedgwick embrace this risk, theatrically exposing themselves as bad passers throughout their critical oeuvres. In so doing, they take up Caughie's charge to confront "the difficulties of one's own performance as a way of understanding the difficulties of others" as well as Mercer's charge to interrogate "not an essentialist argument that the ethnic identity of the artist guarantees the aesthetic or political value of a text, but on the contrary, how commonsense conceptions of authorship and readership are challenged by practices that acknowledge the diversity and heterogeneity of the relations in which identities are socially constructed."[38] Staging attachments that rarely read as appropriate, *as if!* criticism ambivalently raises the question of difference.

As such, *as if!* criticism is more analogous to drag than it is to other types of gender expression and more akin to blackface than it is to other types of racial performance. While there is a vast contrast in the theorized political effect of these performance practices (drag, by and large, as a helpful cultural tool for critiquing gender-oppressive systems; blackface, almost always, as an insidious cultural tool for maintaining white supremacy), both provoke political outrage, albeit from different sides of the aisle. How these two analogies—drag and blackface—register in contemporary discourse speaks to *as if!* criticism's power to both disrupt rigid structures of identity and unabashedly make use of those same racist, sexist structures. Though they stem from different histories and politics, in both practices, the obvious masquerade of blackface and drag brings the performer into intimate proximity with the race and gender markers to which their makeup refers, while at the same time cultivating a calculated gap between performer and referent. Writing on gay men's attachment to female divas, David M. Halperin questions whether "identification" is the right name for this relation at all: "What we may be dealing with, in the end, is a specific kind of engagement that somehow mobilizes complex relations of similarity and difference—but without constituting subjects or objects in the usual ways. Instead, that mobilization produces fields of practice and feeling that map out possibilities for contact or interrelation among cultural forms and their audiences, consumers, or publics, and that get transmitted from one generation to another. We simply have no good languages for that phenomenon—only a variety of critical vernaculars (such as 'identification'), all of them misleading or harmful or inexact."[39] Glossing the history of blackface in Hollywood as it relates to the racial fetishism present in Robert Mapplethorpe's *Black Book*, Mercer writes that the image of the blackface minstrel "concerns a deeply ambivalent mixture of othering and identification."[40] He goes on to lay out the many different intersecting vectors of power and desire at work in this ambivalence.[41] Writing knowingly and performatively across identity enacts a similar contradiction: Much as the "unbearable" social relation is paradoxically structured around the failure of the social, so too is these authors' identification across difference structured and propelled by the contradictory forces of "at once . . . incapacity and creativity."[42]

Like a lot of self-conscious performance, *as if!* criticism both reinforces the status quo and undermines it, leaving audiences to wonder if these critics' performative self-awareness saves them from reproducing the very structures of identity they mock.[43] Simultaneously repulsive and attractive, the identifications laid bare in *as if!* criticism reveal both a tenacious insincerity and a desperate will toward connection. The political ambivalence of *as if!* criticism recalls what Lauren Berlant calls "that muddled middle where survival and threats to it engender social forms that transform the habitation of negativity's multiplicity."[44] In so doing, this type of performance opens new avenues of cross-, dis-, or self-identification.

As if! criticism, in other words, is criticism whose flamboyant exhibitionism operates as camp—that is, as both a disavowal and an embrace. In "Paranoid Reading and Reparative Reading," Sedgwick offers two ways to read camp (one paranoid, one reparative). On the one hand, camp is "most often understood as uniquely appropriate to the projects of parody, denaturalization, demystification, and mocking exposure of the elements and assumptions of a dominant culture"; on the other, camp might be understood as motivated by an impulse that it "wants to assemble and confer plenitude on an object that will then have resources to offer to an inchoate self." Significantly, while explaining camp as a sensibility both paranoid and reparative, Sedgwick names many of the strategies and affects consistent with *as if!* criticism, including "startling, juicy displays of excess erudition," "prodigal production of alternative historiographies," "rich, highly interruptive affective variety," "disorienting juxtapositions of present with past, and popular with high culture," and, perhaps most tellingly, "the irrepressible fascination with ventriloquistic experimentation."[45]

Among the identity categories *as if!* productively camps is class. Because of the ways in which class fails to materialize as one of the identities taken up by the rise in identity studies in the 1980s, an exploration of class as identity becomes tricky in the context of the history of the US academy.[46] Nonetheless, class also functions as a category of identity and identification in the United States. This is particularly important to note because much of early queer literary criticism appears in the work of scholars who are for the most part working at rich coastal universities. As Matt Brim cogently notes: "If queer theory happened, it happened at the places that are most notable for having the resources to hyperinject intellectual vitality into faculty labor and that are, as a result, the only places where queer theory could have been noticed as having happened. And that class-based spectacularity makes all the difference."[47] The authors showcased in this book are, in large part, no exception to this rule, and we might position them as identifying with a classed elite as well.[48] Like preppy SoCal socialite Cher Horowitz, these critics, for the most part, operate adjacent to the economic elite and avail themselves of the privileges granted to them by their status and institutional access.

At the same time, Brim's choice of "spectacularity" reveals that the performance of class as identity is more complicated than the material realities of a university job would initially suggest. While these theorists are all writing from rich institutions that traditionally serve the ruling class, they are all writing as people who came from decidedly middle-class backgrounds and who are all, in a way, "passing" as people who belong in these institutions. Joseph Litvak, writing in 1997, diagnoses the right-wing anti-intellectualism of the era as one of upper-class repulsion, brought on by the rise of "middle-class sophistication" that "vulgarizes mere (i.e. aristocratic) sophistication and sophisticates mere (i.e. lower-class) vulgarity."[49] For Litvak and others, this repulsion stamped the literary criticism of the 1990s with a specifically queer stigma. Political rhetoric of the time linked an anti-intellectual agenda to an antigay agenda via debates about what and how critics should write and what and how they should read. Leaning into this stigma, cross-class identification in early queer criticism might constitute a kind of sophisticate drag, a bad class passing that camps the stylistic and identificatory restrictions of academia.

As it stands, McDowell, Johnson, Reid-Pharr, and Sedgwick grapple with class as identity in various ways. McDowell's identifications with and "as" lesbian flirt with the regulatory class formations of the post–civil rights era that positioned both lesbians and "bad" (single or "failed") mothers outside of and opposed to the heteronormative middle-class Black subject.[50] Johnson, despite her whiteness, might be said to grapple with the struggle within Black feminist criticism that her contemporary Hortense J. Spillers lays out a few years earlier, when Spillers writes that "*within* genders, the black intellectual class is establishing few models of conduct and social responsibility."[51] In his interruptive interludes, Reid-Parr not only relies on the underclass status of his white partners as a means of eliciting scandal; he also manipulates the classed expectations of academic publishers, "passing" as polite, middle-class, and respectable before using language that refuses to genuflect to these expectations for ultimate shock effect. The culture wars that form the background of Sedgwick's productively unsuccessful demonstration capitalize on class resentment of the elite institutions from which she (and, indeed, all these authors) writes. These various cross-identificatory engagements with class constitute another way in which *as if!*'s resists neoliberalism, in which class falls away as a category of consciousness. Here, Cher Horowitz again serves as an example, this time not as a member of the elite but as a figure outrageously aping it (a parodic performance even more obvious when one recalls her Georgian precursor, Emma Woodhouse). Camp, rather than being the sensibility of the ruling class, is instead—crucially—a histrionic adoption of ruling-class sensibilities to comedic or otherwise subversive effect. These authors thus invoke camp's long history of mocking the propriety and seriousness enforced by class-inflected standards of decorum.

The *!* at the end of *as if!* signals, among other things, a camp sensibility. In English, an exclamation point can denote many different things—among them interjection, surprise, shock, emphasis, strong feeling, the shrieking that might accompany said feelings, a warning of risk or danger, and (in stage directions) sarcasm.[52] I retain the exclamation point in both my book title and my reference to the type of criticism I seek to name and explore, to distinguish this mode of writing as ironic, theatrical, and on purpose. The punctuation at the end of *as if!* is meant to convey the shock one experiences at an improper identificatory attachment; that rush, what Corey McEleney (writing about Johnson) elsewhere calls "astonishment," shocks us out of our readerly revery and, potentially, shakes things up enough to resist those quotidian categories in which oppressive systems traffic.[53] Another word for this astonishment, perhaps, is *punctum*, a word whose root recalls the punctuation mark at the end of my own title, the *!* meant to signal the kind of incredulity that throws one off balance. Kathryn Bond Stockton, before telling her readers to "go punctuate" themselves, writes that "queers are experts in self-punctuation, self-penetration."[54] It is my hope to describe and reproduce the shock of the punctum, highlighting moments of disorientation and recalibration—what Johnson calls, in a moment of great wisdom, "the surprise of otherness . . . that moment when a new form of ignorance is suddenly activated as an imperative."[55]

Ultimately, the trite white allyship slogan showcased at the start of this introduction continues to bother me not because I disagree with it but because it functions as a justification for inaction rather than an attempt to acknowledge and value the messy intersection of nonproprietary identities and identifications. The critics whom I examine in the following chapters also understand that they can never understand. But unlike the well-meaning Instagrammers of this introduction's opening anecdote, that conclusion is not based on a belief in the inherent truth of lived experience, nor is it based on a belief in one's access to an essential identity. Trained in a poststructuralist mode in which "understanding" is neither the goal of analysis nor fully possible, these writers provide an example of how we might find the limits of understanding liberatory rather than immobilizing. Like the authors showcased in this book, I do not believe that it is possible for one person to ever understand another. I do not believe in the inherent progressive political potential of intimate understanding, because I know how monstrous those intimacies can be and often are.[56] As a lapsed Lacanian, I still cringe at the idea that one can ever fully know the other in any situation (or the self, for that matter). As a gay white person teaching and writing about anti-Blackness in the United States, I know that scenes meant to elicit white empathy more often than not end up creating a fantasy in which the body of the oppressor is merely substituted for the body of the oppressed, effecting yet another violent erasure.[57] As a queer theorist and as a teacher, ostensibly, of queer theory, I am well aware that understanding sexuality or subjecthood is a fantasy; that in the classroom, this fantasy becomes a laughable learning goal that, by definition, we can never achieve; that "queerness, wherever it shows itself (in the form of a catachresis), effects a counterpedagogy."[58] Misunderstanding is an inevitability that is built into every social interaction between subjects.

For most of their careers, these authors approach the problem of identity and identification differently at different times; they are not always writing in the mode highlighted in this book. They do, however, often employ elements of style that are integral to *as if!* writing. The four chapters of this book illustrate four typical characteristics of *as if!* criticism. In order, these are dissatisfaction, intimacy, interruption, and embarrassment. Each chapter uncovers these elements as they crop up throughout a selective sample of each author's work, before turning to an actual example of *as if!* writing. It is my hope that this structure—in which I trace a stylistic pattern in an author's greater oeuvre, leading up to an instance of critical writing that exemplifies the type of cross-identification I aim to highlight—better illustrates both the evolution of this critical method and its unique properties.

Chapter 1, "Miscarrying On," focuses on dissatisfaction. Dissatisfaction in *as if!* critical writing is marked by qualification—that is, by revision, rereading, or amendment, but also prerequisite, requirement, or condition. In this chapter, I examine McDowell's "lesbian" readings and rereadings of Larsen and Toni Morrison. I read her many revisions of an article on Larsen's *Passing*, published three times between 1989 and 1991, as well as her use of postscripts in her monograph *"The Changing Same": Black Women's Literature, Criticism, and Theory* (1995) in the context of critical conversations surrounding her work, including various instances in which McDowell's person comes to stand in for various disciplinary fields. Repeatedly revising her own assertions as well as the assumptions other critics make about her based on her assumed identity, McDowell's prose fights back against the critical identity categories into which she and her work are pigeonholed.

My second chapter, "Barbara Johnson's Passing," introduces the concept of intimacy, another common aspect of *as if!* critical reading. Johnson's fifth monograph, *The Feminist Difference: Literature, Psychoanalysis, Race, and Gender* (1998), is riddled with moments of interruption or breakdown. Particularly, instances where Johnson parenthetically comes out to her readers as both a white feminist working on Black-authored texts and (later) as a lesbian who does not read "as a lesbian" are important moments of revelation; I contend that such instances highlight critical loyalties, impulses, and aptitudes that seem surprisingly unobvious, politically unsavory, or inappropriately intimate.

Chapter 3, "Shock Therapy," focuses on interruption. I examine Reid-Pharr's self-described "pornographic" writing alongside his explicit cross-identification with Black lesbian feminists, particularly Barbara Smith and Cheryl Clarke. Reading several essays from his 2001 essay collection *Black Gay Man*, I theorize that the repeated "shock" of Reid-Pharr's pornographic interludes serves to interrupt both narrative continuity and the authority of identity. Chapter 3 ends with an analysis of Reid-Pharr's short essay "Living as a Lesbian," which uses these interruptions to acknowledge material and embodied difference, while simultaneously insisting on forging new ways of identifying. I argue that these shocks allow for the possibility of a tenuous coalition based on something other than fixed identity categories—what Cathy J. Cohen calls a "queer politics of positionality."[59]

My final chapter, "Gay-Male-Oriented and Now," looks closely at staged scenes of embarrassment in Sedgwick's work. Here I read Sedgwick's identifications with gay men and gay-male-authored work in conversation with her more fraught identifications across race. I track how Sedgwick's embarrassing anecdotes signpost her own *as if!* critical strategies. Looking mostly at *Tendencies*, Sedgwick's essay collection that showcases her most notorious cross-identifications, I argue that Sedgwick's encounter with her own whiteness, staged via her exhibitionist anecdotal criticism, constitutes a moment of both impasse and connection.

What emerges in the work of McDowell, Johnson, Reid-Pharr, and Sedgwick is a Sisyphean mechanic: Forming identifications via a faith in the poststructuralist promise of identity's fiction (a queer utopia), these authors nonetheless run up against the impossible project of social relation (a queer antisocial). McDowell's defiant qualifications and revisions to her own work serve as savvy self-interruptions that cross, even as they fracture, disciplinary boundaries. Johnson's uncanny readings of Black-authored texts and spectacularly awkward attempts at "lesbian" reading reveal uncomfortable intimacies and surprising links between the author and the subjects she studies. Reid-Pharr's shocking and explicit interludes test the limits of cross-identification only to theorize that those limits constitute an unexpected point of commonality. Sedgwick's infamous cross-identifications result in "displacements" that, rather than stop her short, instead catalyze a new militancy born of difference rather than sameness.[60] As such, these identifications address the impossible dichotomy so concisely summed up in the imperative of Jewelle Gomez's polemical meditation on feminist solidarity: "Repeat After Me: We Are Different. We Are the Same."[61]

As I read McDowell, Johnson, Reid-Pharr, and Sedgwick from my own temporal vantage point—a historical moment in which these boundaries often feel impermeable and in which it is hard to imagine playing so fast and loose with something as politically charged as identity—I am fascinated by the critical cross-identificatory strategies their work so boldly flaunts. Roughly thirty years have transpired since the work I have surveyed in this book was first published, and yet I am struck by the ways in which the concerns of the 1990s continue to resonate, in different ways, today. Like many of the pieces of criticism I have examined here, this book was written at a political moment marked by powerful remix of neoliberalism, rising fascism, and anti-intellectualism; through a period of worldwide isolation, mass death, and record-breaking plague; and during an exciting, explosive moment of rupture and revolt against anti-Black and colonial systems of power. At the time of this book's final revisions, we are a year into a US-backed, unprecedentedly documented genocide; the risks of rigid identity politics have become starkly, deathly clear.

The authors showcased in this book write during a time of spectacular, state-sponsored death. All the pieces of queer literary criticism on which this book focuses were published between 1990 and 2001, a period that saw approximately 350,000 AIDS deaths in the United States.[62] Guided by the homophobia of the 1980s, it behooved the Reagan administration to insist that AIDS was a "gay disease," a policy that directly catalyzed these staggering numbers. This is a major lesson of AIDS: In moments of tragedy that break along the lines of identity, identification becomes a topic of much rhetorical and political regulation.[63] As a means of resistance, the cross-identifications on display in this book run counter to a neoliberal belief in an easy or authentic relation between identity and identification, instead producing those campy shocks that lay bare the ruse of fixed identity. As such, the writing of many early queer literary critics often presents a paradox of authenticity: It interpolates these critics into a subject position ("gay," "queer," "lesbian," etc.), but the credentials of that subject position are based on the quality of their reference, imitation, cross-identification, and drag performance. Relishing this paradox, cross-identificatory modes of writing might lead to other, more capacious ways of thinking about the personal as political. On the one hand, the contrasting affective tenors produced by these identifications produces wild whip-lash. On the other, the routes of queer identification they trace are, for me, sources of deep solace, useful disorientation, and delicious pleasure.

The work of these four critics draws attention to the difficulties of difference, enacting what Grace Kyungwon Hong helpfully calls "a cultural and epistemologi-cal practice that holds in suspension (without requiring resolution) contradictory, mutually exclusive, and negating impulses" and "an epistemological position, onto-logical condition, and political strategy that reckon[s] with the shift in the technolo-gies of power that we might as well call 'neoliberal.'"[64] Glossing Lorde's "impossible but necessary politics of 'difference,'" Hong argues that such an impossibility—here defined as that which is outside the conceptual bounds of the hegemonic or-der—poses "a question that can never be answered, but that must be continually addressed, enacting a temporality of suspension rather than a resolution."[65] I find value in remaining attentive to the ways in which this impossible simultaneity op-erates. Though it may be a doomed project, cross-identification seems to me a use-ful antidote to the kind of activisms that, in crisis, produce such pithy, distancing slogans as "I understand that I can never understand."

In short, McDowell, Johnson, Reid-Pharr, and Sedgwick showcase their qual-ified, intimate, shocking, or embarrassing identifications because they recognize that there are no clean hands in a dirty world. These critical transgressions, if nothing else, reveal the positions and categories to which we are all bound and the power structures in which we are all embroiled. Resisting the boundaries of identity upon which white supremacy and heterosexism operate through their identifications across difference, while still leaning into the inevitable fiasco that is social relation, *as if!* criticism, at its best, performs what Lauren Berlant (writing about Sedgwick) calls "the dread of admitting knowing what brokenness is while managing the rage to repair."[66] Quixotic and doomed though these identifications are, they nonetheless do important work, employing misunderstanding as the very mechanism that drives their critical inquiry.

Miscarrying On

A LONG TIME COMING

The preface to Deborah E. McDowell's debut monograph, *"The Changing Same,"* begins with a striking metaphor: "This book has been a long time coming, and has had at least two conceptions and one stillbirth."[1]

McDowell's opening analogy reflects the structure and tone of her book. Slyly alluding to the inability to "finish" both in writing and in sex ("long time coming") and defiantly figuring her book as either an aborted or a miscarried child ("two conceptions and one stillbirth"), McDowell both exploits and pokes fun at a long-standing literary tradition of analogizing motherhood, sexuality, and writing. With sardonic self-deprecation, McDowell admits to several false starts and, as its title would also suggest, foreshadows her book's larger trope of rereading, reviewing, and revising. Her highly gendered comparison, far from being arbitrary, not only disappoints expectations for a preface (readers might expect a proper beginning, not a disparaging confession) but also draws attention to the figurative and literal links between embodiment, sex, motherhood, and the literary production that she traces throughout her critical examination of Black female novelists. In doing so, this first sentence also hints at the restrictions placed on Black female authors—and, more specifically, on Black feminist critics—that *"The Changing Same"* will proceed to challenge.

Significantly, the aborted conceptions and one stillbirth that McDowell describes are the result of an encounter with what she calls "critical theory"—that is, a new wave of continental thought that was taking the American ivory tower by storm at the time of her writing. McDowell goes on to explain that the original dissertation on which her book is based could not survive the cataclysm of French-influenced poststructuralism, the arrival of which on the US academic scene catalyzed the dissertation's revision on a massive scale. By her own account, McDowell's first monograph is the result of a struggle and collaboration between three ways of doing criticism: trendy critical theory, defined as criticism driven by a desire to move from identity to difference; Black feminist criticism, which McDowell defines as criticism driven by a desire to investigate "how categories of race, gender, class, and sexuality all figure into literary analysis and critical inquiry"; and "feminist reading strategies, more generally," which she defines as criticism driven by a desire to "seek to expose ideologies of male dominance, question traditionally masculinist standards of evaluating literature, and critique the sex/gender arrangements that exclude women from symbolic activity."[2] The three academic camps that McDowell names throughout *"The Changing Same"* produce their own critical identity categories. These categories attach themselves to McDowell at various points throughout her early career, much, it would seem, to her chagrin. Employing different methods at different moments, and espousing various and varied identifications throughout her work, McDowell is nonetheless repeatedly evoked by her fellow academics as a stand-in for an entire knowledge field.

This chapter is about the strategies McDowell employs in order to counteract this tendency. The discourses surrounding McDowell's work, and her response to that discourse, illuminate how her critical strategies combat the fixity of her position as circulating referent or stand-in and complicate her all-too-easy interpellation by other academics in various fields. In much of her literary criticism, McDowell first writes as if she has one unchangeable argument only to undermine her position of authority via self-correction, false starts, or refusal of linear progression. Ironically performing various identifications for her readers and then immediately qualifying the authority these identifications might grant, McDowell's revisions and amendments both solidify her critical credentials and interrupt the fixity of the categories into which she has been placed. In this way, McDowell's prose contradicts the idea of a single critical position or intellectual identity from which one might identify and write.

A close look at McDowell's early literary criticism highlights an important general characteristic of *as if!* writing: dissatisfaction. McDowell's work is dissatisfied. On the level of the text, as well as on the level of publication, it is rife with revisions, reversals, and a sense of incompleteness. In McDowell's early career, these revisions and reversals manifest on the metalevel of publication, as when she revisits and republishes her own work multiple times in multiple forums. Within individual chapters and article-length works, McDowell's qualification disrupts her many identifications across discipline, playing fast and loose with her identifications while also staging the ways in which those identifications don't quite work via "a straightforward (and some would say shameless and unseemly) act of 'personal criticism.'"[3] In these instances, the text stages moments in which identifications are made difficult or fall short, first asserting McDowell's own academic allegiances and then undercutting or complicating them. Insofar as it allows her to identify with multiple disciplines, the first part of this strategy builds professional qualifications as a well-rounded and intersectional scholar. Insofar as it disrupts her disciplinary loyalties, the second part of this strategy qualifies both the allegiances she holds to one method or field of study and the claims any one method or field of study might make on her or her work.

Most often, McDowell employs performative qualification to convey this dissatisfaction. In everyday use, the word *qualification* carries a helpful double valance. *Qualification* can mean both "a quality or accomplishment which qualifies or fits a person for a certain position or function; (*now esp.*) the completion of a course or training programme which confers the status of a recognized practitioner of a profession or activity," and "a reservation, restriction, provision; (also) the action of modifying or limiting something; modification, limitation, restriction."[4] In line with the first definition, *qualification* names critical practices that exploit markers of legitimacy in academic fields—markers such as an advanced degree, a certain way of speaking and writing, a traceable pedigree of academic mentorship, an institutional affiliation, or publications with a well-regarded press. As its root *qualis* suggests, qualification might also include more qualitative criteria. Insofar as *qualification* is understood broadly as one's credentials, it can be both quantifiable (number of degrees, years of experience, sales made, etc.) and much more abstract (job listings that require qualifications such as "a good sense of humor" or "a team attitude," for example).

The double valence of *qualification* means that often *qualification* is a term at odds with itself. The categories of race, gender, sexuality, class, and others into which one is interpellated often serve as qualifications that grant the right to speak for a particular group, authority over certain forms of knowledge, or claims to an authentic relationship to self. By contrast, if we define *qualification* as "a statement or assertion that makes another less absolute," a writerly practice of qualification would instead revise, limit, complicate, or otherwise amend an author's authority. Within a written text, this second type of qualification can take many forms, including discursive footnotes, modifying adjectives, parenthetical asides, couched claims, asterisked phrases, or punitive edits. All have qualifying effects, and all therefore fit under this second definition. When I use *qualification*, I maintain these

attendant and contradictory associations: *Qualification* here references hiring credentials, quantifiable experience, and qualitative attributes based on one's character or identity, as well as adjustment, doubling back, and reassessment. If we hold
these two meanings of *qualification* tenuously together, we arrive at an academic
writing practice that, through repeated and performative revision, makes visible
the way identity can both discredit and authorize a critic. McDowell's prose constitutes a mode of writing that counteracts academic discourses' will to place her
and her work in one stable category.

McDowell employs various qualifying tactics on many levels in *"The Changing
Same,"* from the holistic to the singular. Most prominent among these tactics are
achronological organization, self-conscious framing, and performative revision.
McDowell presents her essays out of temporal sequence—a decision that, by her
own admission, allows her to "avoid any teleological coding, to avoid any implication that this development constitutes a progressive unfolding toward some analytical completeness or conceptual resting place." Though "taken together, [the
chapters] chronicle something of [McDowell's] own intellectual development,"
their achronological arrangement allows her to hold interpretations in tension,
as well as to avoid status as a monolithic author.[5] McDowell's qualification strategy also manifests as asides to her readers regarding the ever-changing proclivities of the academy. Frequently acknowledging that theoretical trends are prone
to change—and, moreover, that she is fully susceptible to the allure of each new
academic fashion—McDowell writes in her introduction: "I accept *this* moment's
critical axiom that self 'identity' always gives way to 'difference,' thus making difficult any easy and clear-cut identifications and alliances."[6]

Finally, *qualification* manifests as formal amendments and nonteleological chapter arrangement. Four out of nine chapters in *"The Changing Same"* include after-
words, appended in 1995. These brief amendments, distinguished by a line break
and italic formatting, address the essays to which they are attached, often voicing
McDowell's dissatisfaction with the conclusions of her younger self. In these af-
terwords, McDowell-of-1995, writing in the wake of "critical theory," revisits and
revises her claims. Each chapter ends with a beginning—that is, with a look back
that is also a springboard for other possible "new directions." These qualifying
postscripts perform McDowell's signature method of doubling back, rereading,
rewriting, and amending. Repeatedly revising her own assertions as well as the assumptions other critics make about her based on her interpolated identity (variously as Black feminist critic, nonlesbian, or critical theorist), *"The Changing Same"*
parodies the critical identity categories to which she and her work are reduced,
denaturalizing the ways in which a critic's identity informs how literary criticism
is received and classified. In other words, implementing these *as if!* strategies on

multiple registers, McDowell dryly qualifies (revises, amends, restricts) her identitarian qualifications (credentials, identifications, authorizations).

QUALIFYING *CONDITIONS*

In 1983, the editors of the lesbian feminist journal *Conditions* invited poet and critic Cheryl Clarke to curate a roundtable. The result of this invitation is a special section of *Conditions* titled "Conversations and Questions: Black Women on Black Woman Writers," in which five prominent Black feminist thinkers—Clarke, Jewelle L. Gomez, Evelynn Hammonds, Bonnie Johnson, and Linda Powell—record, transcribe, and edit a candid discussion for the *Conditions* readership. Though the language of the initial talk is later curated by its participants, the published conversation among the five women retains the cordiality and improvisation one might expect of the original: The group remains casual, informal, and intimate, and interwoven with their analysis are jokes, anecdotal asides, and the occasional awkward pause. Their wide-ranging conversation, spread out over forty-nine pages, covers a wide array of issues within the subtitle's expansive theme, among them womanist fiction, Black feminist writing, literary critique, and their own lived experience. At some point in this pentalogy, Clarke asks the group: "Is criticism merely the demand for a 'rigorous examination of the text,' as Deborah McDowell said[?]"[7]

Instead of answering the question posed, the group bristles at Clarke's citation; upon hearing Deborah McDowell's name, the group unanimously derides her scholarship as a bad example. Gomez quickly brings up one of McDowell's recently published pieces, a reading of Morrison's *Sula* (a piece that will, twelve years later, become chapter 1 of *"The Changing Same"*). This essay is subsequently panned by the group. Clarke herself offers this vicious takedown: "As much as she was trying to put down the style and approach of traditional white male criticism in her piece in relationship to Black women writers, she fell into the same trap.... She is exceedingly vituperative in espousing her views. She is hard, biting, condescending, competitive, impatient, patronizing, and homophobic!"[8]

Clearly, McDowell's piece touches a nerve. The *Conditions* roundtable effectively categorizes her as a scholar directly opposed to lesbian criticism—and therefore, for the panelists, a scholar who is also opposed to Black lesbian identity. As their conversation progresses, the group doubles down on Clarke's original assessment:

> LINDA: When I read ["New Directions for Black Feminist Criticism"], one sentence sort of leapt off the page which seemed to say, "You lesbians don't say nothing to me till you make it easy for me, till you can make

it a little easier for me to digest." And the name for that I do believe is homophobia.

JEWELLE: For McDowell any relationships drawn between criticism and lesbianism are invalid.

CHERYL: Or "reductionist."

LINDA: She said in her article that definitions of lesbianism were imprecise. She was asking for more precision of definition.

JEWELLE: She also took issue with Barbara's interpretation of *Sula* as a lesbian novel.

LINDA: Because if we say *Sula* is a "lesbian" novel, we'll have to say others are. I think it's wonderful.

CHERYL: And that's exactly what she says. She also ridicules the criteria Barbara uses for assessing a novel to be a lesbian novel. She says they are "vacuous." I have reservations about the criteria Barbara Smith sets forth in her piece and also her use of *Sula* as a lesbian novel, because I think Morrison undermines the relationship between Sula and Nel. I think she develops the relationship between Sula and Nel's husband to avoid the lesbian issue. Even so I don't think Barbara's criteria are "vacuous."

LINDA: Well, the point is that by definition lesbian is fringe. What frightened McDowell was that she sees "lesbian" can be broader than she is prepared to admit. It could be a way to talk about *Sula*. It could be a way to talk about Zora Hurston. It could be a way to talk about James Baldwin. And that's what she reacted to. She had quite an issue with the concept and term "lesbian."[9]

Clarke and her compatriots see McDowell's aversion to the potentially universal signifying power of *lesbian* as at worst homophobic and at best heterosexist. In so doing, Clarke and company dismiss McDowell's piece on the grounds that its rejection of *lesbian* stems from homophobia. This homophobia, their discussion implies, is born of McDowell's lack of lived lesbian experience. If there was a way to be a Black woman writing about Black women writers, McDowell's attempt was not it.

Voicing her own dissatisfaction with a respected foremother of Black lesbian criticism, McDowell showcases an unwillingness to identify fully with Smith that upsets and annoys others in her field. As a Black woman, and a Black critic, McDowell is supposed to identify with Smith—Smith's essay, after all, is about how to cultivate unalienated identification. Specifically, McDowell takes issue with Smith for using a hitherto specific or minoritarian term (*lesbian*) to do broad theoretical work (namely, the work of all Black feminist criticism). McDowell thus rejects Smith's call for Black feminists to read with lesbian desire. The essay so reviled by the *Conditions* group, titled "New Directions for Black Feminist Criticism," is one of McDowell's earliest forays into the critical conversation. Originally published in the *Black American Literature Forum* in 1980, McDowell's "New Directions for Black Feminist Criticism" responds to Barbara Smith's essay "Toward a Black Feminist Criticism," which was published in 1978. In a bold move, young McDowell is quite critical of Smith's powerhouse article. To be sure, the method that "Toward a Black Feminist Criticism" encourages places great importance on the life experience and desire of the critic; Smith writes, for example, that the type of criticism for which she is advocating would explore "how both sexual and racial politics and Black and female identity are inextricable elements in Black women's writings," would work "from the assumption that Black women writers constitute an identifiable literary tradition," and would "think and write out of [Black women's] own identity and not try to graft the ideas or methodology of white/male literary thought upon the precious materials of Black women's art."[10]

This is our first hint of McDowell's general iconoclasm. In her original evaluation of "Toward a Black Feminist Criticism," she criticizes Smith for her overspecificity, one she sees as antithetical to an expansive Black feminist project. *Lesbian*, at least in Smith's work, presents a power problem for McDowell: The particularity of the signifier *lesbian* means it has the power to enact reductive violence on the text it reads by virtue of a kind of critical tunnel vision; at the same time, it is so ill-defined that it forfeits its explanatory power and, therefore, the critical descriptive power that would connect it to real-world sexual practices, structures of desire, or identities associated with lesbianism. Noting the slippage between *lesbian* and *Black feminist* in Smith's critical performance, McDowell sees Smith's "lesbian aesthetic" as both an "individual political persuasion" and "ideology," though not as a sexuality or even as a category of identity as such.[11] Arguing that the term *lesbian* loses its specific descriptive and critical power when Smith attempts to graft lesbian structures of desire onto a narrative that does not explicitly name itself as lesbian, McDowell contends that this specificity limits Black feminist criticism rather than allowing for critical openness. Strangely, even as McDowell casts lesbian readings as overly specific, she worries that Smith's definition of *lesbian* "is vague and imprecise; it is, oddly, a desexualized sensibility that subsumed far more Black women writers, particularly contemporary ones, than not into the canon of lesbian writers. Further, if we apply Smith's definition of lesbianism, there are probably a few Black male writers who qualify as well."[12] Smith's own Black feminist criticism fails because it is, by virtue of its self-avowed desires, at once too specific and too general, too political and too personal.

In a moment of striking similarity between the *Conditions* panelists and their critical target, the five participants of the *Conditions* roundtable themselves take seriously the concern that *lesbian* might be an inadequate term for either theoretical approach or political mobilization. Significantly, the panel's rubric for legitimacy relies mostly on an author's lived experience, but at the same time, the questions raised in McDowell's critique of Smith are not very different from the questions raised by the panelists in the last part of their documented discussion. In the final section of "Conversations and Questions," Clarke et al. focus on the distinction, made famous by novelist and critic Alice Walker, between "lesbian" and "womanist" theory and practice. Walker prefers the later as a rubric for Black feminist thought, a position that Clarke and her compatriots find suspicious. The roundtable's debate involves the same problems of capacity, specificity, and political efficacy addressed in McDowell's read of Smith. Like McDowell, Walker's ostensible straightness makes her dismissal of the term *lesbian* suspect. Clarke remarks: "If Audre Lorde said, 'I don't want to call myself a lesbian anymore, I want to rename myself "womanist,"' I might feel differently. Audre has been out for years. She's lived as a lesbian. . . . But Alice—I love her, I think she's fabulous—but I don't think she should be telling me, as a Black lesbian, to call myself womanist."[13] This unease is not enough, ultimately, for the women to dismiss the term *womanist*; the productive generality of *womanist* is also intellectually seductive, and for Clarke, *womanist* is politically productive and politically ambivalent. Nonetheless, living as a lesbian provides the only acceptable credentials for being able to reject or modify the term.[14]

Ironically, the women in the *Conditions* roundtable dismiss McDowell because she does not identify as a lesbian, in much the same way Smith is dismissed because she does. Like McDowell, Smith, too, fought an uphill battle against reductive identity-based receptions of her own work. In an interview from 2014, Smith recalls the reaction she received when she first gave a partial reading of the paper at Howard University in 1978:

> I read excerpts from "Toward a Black Feminist Criticism." I also had written some specific remarks for a Black audience, because the piece had been written for *Conditions*, which was a primarily white lesbian feminist literary journal that was very anti-racist in its perspective. I wanted to say some specific things aimed at the Black community and Black writers. The first comment was from Dr. Frances Cress Welsing and she basically said, "I feel sorry for the sister. It's too bad that you're a lesbian,

because homosexuality will be the death of the race." ... When I went to the back of the auditorium there was a Black male literary critic who wrote for mainstream publications like *The New York Times*. I was saying to him how horrible this experience had been, how devastating this was, how bad I felt. You know what he said to me? He said, "At least you weren't lynched."[15]

Smith's story speaks to the potential and actual effects of critical reception on her own body ("at least you weren't lynched") but also to how her own identity position as a Black lesbian, in addition to her critical method, argument, and object, figures into her work's overall reception. It is easy to understand the defensiveness of the *Conditions* panelists. The panel participants who so vocally oppose McDowell's rejoinder to Smith do so out of a heartfelt appreciation for the groundbreaking work of "Toward a Black Feminist Criticism," which itself is a classic example of identity knowledge criticism—that is, criticism informed by personal position and experience. In this famous piece, Smith suggests and performs an experiential and erotic lesbian critical reading practice.[16] Smith's essay is a game changer; her intervention, at the time of its debut and afterward, proved both influential and controversial within Black literary-critical and feminist circles, and its thesis met with both outrage and appreciation.[17] The conversation in *Conditions* was published at a time when identity knowledges were still vying for legitimacy and recognition within the academy, and McDowell's refusal to grant *lesbian* the critical power and purchase it wields in Smith's original essay might easily be read as a sinister attempt to destroy the small gains that identity-based criticism had won in the previous decade—gains that these critics were still struggling to make permanent.

Hung up on McDowell's lack of lesbian qualifications and setting her up as a straight straw woman, the published *Conditions* conversation misses the more interesting work performed in McDowell's quarrel with Smith. The argumentative moves in "New Directions in Feminist Criticism" betray McDowell's underlying queer sensibility, even as her argument (and she herself) is misread as homophobic. McDowell's understanding of *lesbian* as at once too specific and too general echoes discussions surrounding the political value of *queer* that would reach their zenith around the publication of *"The Changing Same."* As Judith Butler argues, the term *queer* is both specific and general:

> As expansive as the term "queer" is meant to be, it is used in ways that enforce a set of overlapping divisions: in some contexts, the term appeals to a younger generation who want to resist the more institutionalized and reformist politics sometimes signified by "lesbian and gay"; in some contexts, sometimes the same, it has marked a predominantly white move-

ment that has not fully addressed the way in which "queer" plays—or fails to play—within non-white communities; and whereas in some instances it has mobilized a lesbian activism, in others the term represents a false unity of women and men.[18]

For Butler, the signifier *queer*—like the signifier *lesbian* for McDowell—proves both too all-inclusive and too limited to be a proper analytical framework. For all their melancholic hesitation around the term, Butler ultimately does not abandon *queer*, whereas McDowell seems much more willing to reject *lesbian* on similar grounds: Where Butler finds promise and possibility in the transitory power of *queer*, McDowell dislikes the imprecision of *lesbian* as Smith employs it.[19] Nonetheless, in her analysis of "Toward a Black Feminist Criticism," McDowell rightly reads Smith as deploying *lesbian* in precisely this way. As such, "New Directions in Black Feminist Criticism" articulates the very paradoxes with which much of early queer theory is also grappling.

Despite her surface-level opposition to Smith's project, McDowell's read shares much in common with later scholarly efforts to incorporate "Toward a Black Feminist Criticism" into the queer theoretical canon. Smith's personal and detailed essay predates the advent of the term *queer theory* by a good fifteen years, but many queer theorists have since noted that Smith's method, choice of object, and style often correspond with the methods, objects, and styles of queer literary criticism. Roderick A. Ferguson, for example, goes so far as to argue that Smith's Black lesbian criticism serves as an early example of the "queer of color critique" for which his book advocates (to be sure, his book's full title, *Aberrations in Black: Toward a Queer of Color Critique*, points readers in the direction of Smith from the start, echoing the *toward* in the title of her famous essay). By his read, Smith's criticism positions itself against restrictive orthodoxies espoused by both the capitalist state and liberal liberation politics, and his book helpfully situates the emergence of Black lesbian feminism such as Smith's within a moment marked by polarization as well as a racial discourse that "inherited the normative ideologies of civil rights, canonical sociology, and national liberation."[20] The emergent regulatory class formation of the civil rights era positioned lesbians and "bad" (single or "failed") mothers outside of and opposed to the heteronormative middle-class Black subject.[21] McDowell, writing nearly twenty-five years before the publication of *Aberrations*, recognizes this same anti-identity politics in Smith, but with much more pronounced ambivalence.

When "New Directions in Black Feminist Criticism" reappears in *"The Changing Same,"* McDowell makes her dissatisfaction clear via a lengthy italicized amendment at the end of the chapter. Both the very idea of the postchapter amendment and the sentiments said amendment explicitly registers qualify her previous work. Spanning eight and a half pages, the 1995 amendment that follows McDowell's 1980 essay is nearly as long as the text it appends. Crucially, McDowell does not use the majority of the italicized text to double down or defend her early work, nor does she use it to definitely correct her previously held sentiments. Instead, most of Mc-Dowell's postscript focuses on the fragmented, ever-shifting, and hard-to-define field of Black feminist criticism, devoting several paragraphs to an extended meditation on what, if anything, *Black feminist criticism* means. Employing a repeating formula in which she offers a possible definition only to find it falls short, McDowell nears, but never arrives at, a capacious and indeterminate understanding of Black feminist criticism more based on what it is not than on what it is.

SULA, TAKE TWO

Clarke et al.'s critical reproach would be unremarkable—disagreement is, after all, a quotidian mechanism by which academic discourse operates—were it not for two other quite different critical conversations in which McDowell's name once again crops up. Six years after the special issue of *Conditions*, McDowell's lukewarm-to-hostile reception within prominent Black lesbian feminist circles prompts and informs her return to *Sula* when she writes an article titled "Boundaries: Or Distant Relations and Close Kin" for Houston A. Baker Jr. and Patricia Redmond's edited collection *Afro-American Literary Study in the 1990s* (1989). In a response published in the same volume, literary critic Michael Awkward takes McDowell to task for reasons similar to those of the *Conditions* group. "For me, the two most troubling aspects of McDowell's arguments are their virtual erasure of race and culture in her reading of *Sula* and the striking difference her statements here about Afro-American female characters from even her most recently published assertions written before her apparent wholehearted adoption of contemporary critical theory," he writes.[22] Once again, McDowell is chastised for her dalliance with critical theory; Awkward, too, finds that McDowell falls into the same traps as "traditional white male criticism."[23]

Rather than repeat the structure of her 1983 essay—in which she responds directly to the imposing figure of Smith in a one-to-one relation reminiscent of the structure hypothesized in Harold Bloom's *The Anxiety of Influence* (1973)—in her 1989 essay on *Sula*, McDowell's text qualifies her earlier argument. In a revision that again aligns her work with anti-identitarian queer literary criticism, McDowell arrives at her conclusions via a discussion of how sexuality functions in Morrison's novel. In her article, McDowell sees the sex in *Sula* as primarily autoerotic: *Sula* is first and foremost about the sex Sula has in relation to herself. As if to unconsciously reinforce this queer vein, a telling typo halfway through McDowell's chapter on *Sula* further supports McDowell's connection between sexuality, reading, and the relationship of self: "The narrative is neither an apology for Sula's destruction nor an unsympathetic critique of Nel's smug conformity. It does not reduce a complex sex [*sic*] of dynamics to a simple opposition or choice between two 'pure' alternatives."[24] The seeming misprint in the *Changing Same* reprint, in which *sex* subs in for *set* in the intended phrase "complex set of dynamics," highlights the way in which *sex* remains, for McDowell, a principal way of thinking through *Sula*'s ideological and narrative complexity.

Here, McDowell celebrates *Sula* for not subscribing to traditional evaluative rubrics traditionally employed by African American literary criticism at the time of her writing. These rubrics, for McDowell, focus too much on an idealized Black "SELF" (a term McDowell leaves capitalized each time), relying on a model of reading and identification that is too static, and thus fail to resist binary categories of "positive" or "negative," leaving no space for what McDowell promotes as a productive or complicating ambiguity. For McDowell, *Sula* thus succeeds as a generative creative opus precisely because it "glories in paradox and ambiguity."[25] McDowell tries again, revising her own argument about *Sula* and lauding the way the novel complicates stable formations of self. Her text implicitly performs the failure of its author to autoidentify, while simultaneously performing the autoerotic return to the self that she outlines in Morrison's novel. Like much of McDowell's work, "Boundaries: Or Distant Relations and Close Kin" blends a close reading of the novel with more far-reaching commentary about the state of Black criticism. Initially evoking and ultimately rejecting W. E. B. Du Bois's call for what she terms "idealized literary representation" in Black literature, McDowell praises Morrison's prose for complicating and resisting easy, positive, or whole idealizations.[26] Ultimately, McDowell argues that, just as *Sula* "complicates the process of identification in the reading process, denying the conventional Afro-American critic a reflection of her or his ego ideal," so too does critical theory.[27] "Falling in step with recent developments in contemporary critical theory, some critics of African American literature have usefully complicated many unexamined, common assumptions about the SELF and about race as a meaningful category in literary study and critical theory," she writes. "These recent developments have made it difficult, if not impossible, to posit with any assurance a 'positive' Black SELF, always already unified, coherent, stable, and known."[28] This, for McDowell, is the value of Morrison's work and its Black feminist project.

This argument is, ultimately, what gets McDowell in trouble again. Like the women of the *Conditions* panel, Awkward invokes McDowell as an example of a Black literary critic whose dalliance with (white) critical theory discredits her authority. Unlike the *Conditions* critics, Awkward more specifically names white French poststructuralism as a seductive, corrupting force: McDowell's proximity to French theory threatens the perceived political authenticity of identity-based critical work. More importantly, Awkward's critical anxiety comes from the fact that McDowell is not content to stay in her identificatory lane. McDowell, again, finds herself positioned as a critical theory boogeyman; her methodological loyalties work to the detriment of not just her criticism but African American literary criticism more broadly. Awkward's critique positions white-coded critical theory as a poison to their respectable fields, to which a more authentic Black criticism serves as an antidote. Awkward, in his response to "Boundaries," chastises McDowell for abandoning the Blackness of Black-authored literature, naming critical theory as the reason for McDowell's unfortunate turn.[29] For McDowell, both the critical turn and Black feminist theory prove helpful tools for pushing against representational ideals of Black womanhood—ideals tied to traditional sexist and heterosexist ideas about the woman's place at hearth and home, representational ideals that stem not only from the stereotypes of dismissive white theorists but from Black male critics as well.

Rather than deny the critical promiscuity Awkward condemns, McDowell plays up the metaphor in her response, published six years later in *"The Changing Same"* in the form of an italicized postessay amendment. Here, McDowell links Awkward's accusation to a greater anxiety surrounding "bad" mothering. Writing that "metaphors of 'family,' 'kinship,' and 'community' structured these attacks [on Black women novelists] that bordered on calls for censorship and attempted to demand that Black women writers meet a representational ideal in the name of creating racial unity and wholeness," McDowell goes as far as to compare the conservative admonishments of Black male literary critics to "injunctions . . . that seemed to echo those that the German National Socialists (Nazis) held for 'their' women—*kinder, kirche, kuche* (children, church, and kitchen)."[30] Needless to say, McDowell's comparison between Nazis and the Black male critical literati might well give her readers pause. But it also might elicit a scandalized guffaw at McDowell's dark joke—one that lays bare the hyperbolic nature of these debates and mocks the deep seriousness with which Awkward lays out the stakes of academic inquiry. Indeed, McDowell's response to Awkward's reaction suggests that the world of heterosexual marriage and reproductive motherhood is threatened not only by "critical theory" (and specifically critical theories of reading that she applies to *Sula*) but also by the complex sexual dynamics that Morrison explores in her novel; these parallel assertions hint at a deviant sexuality underpinning the act of criticism itself. In her response to Awkward's response to "Boundaries," Black feminist criticism is positioned as a disruptive force within the Black literary-critical tradition and the Black community as a whole. "Because the writings of contemporary Black women indeed seemed to hold little sacred about pietistic views of family," McDowell writes, "they were read and loudly proclaimed to be threats to a unified Black community, healthy and whole."[31]

While McDowell vehemently denounces Awkward's attacks as sexist and limiting, she does not dispute the verity of their accusations. McDowell argues that Sula's sexual self-pleasure disregards traditional kinship structures, writing that Sula's narrative "strongly suggests that one cannot belong to the community and preserve the imagination, for the orthodox vocations of motherhood—marriage and motherhood—restrict, if not preclude, imaginative expression."[32] Significantly, other examples of nonreproductive deviance beyond Sula's autoeroticism also crop up in "Boundaries." There, McDowell notes that the bond between Sula and Nel is strengthened by the occasion of the death of Chicken Little: Linking the same-sex friendship of Nel and Sula (friendship that Smith calls "lesbian" but that McDowell hesitates to name by such specific terms) to the death of a child in their care, McDowell positions the two main characters in a "queer" position relative to reproduction, "good" motherhood, and the traditionally valued kinship structures of the old critics. By her account, McDowell's status as a Black woman and Black feminist critic (the slippage here, again, is indicative of how her person comes to naturally stand in for her assumed critical practice) threatens a male-dominated tradition of African American literary criticism, often personified in her work via the figure of Awkward. For both theorists, Black feminist criticism has the potential to upset the bonds and obligations of Black kinship and community both inside and outside the academy. McDowell's theatrical exasperation with the figure of Awkward not only counteracts his punishing and hyperserious tone; it also mocks the stakes of his censure.

"FOR MCDOWELL . . . READ BLACK FEMINIST CRITIC"

The qualifications McDowell employs also kick back against the totalizing impulses of another related literary-critical trend: that of white feminists attempting to account for "race" by invoking a figural Black feminist critic. Once again, in *"The Changing Same,"* McDowell's tendency to revise, qualify, and ambivalently respond comes in the form of an explicit response to a critical conversation in which she is invoked but not invited. In the final chapter of Marianne Hirsch and Evelyn Fox Keller's edited collection *Conflicts in Feminism* (1990), three white feminist critics (Jane Gallop, Hirsch, and Nancy K. Miller) participate in a roundtable titled "Criticizing Feminist Criticism." The issue on the table is the personal and political consequences of internal debate within feminist circles. In a seemingly offhand comment about her own evolution as a feminist scholar, Gallop tells the following anecdote:

> I was telling this guy in Syracuse that I thought in *Reading Lacan* I had worked through my transference both onto Lacan and onto things French in general. And he asked, "So who do you transfer onto now?" My first thought was to say "no one." And then one of the things I thought of was a non-encounter with Deborah McDowell. I read work from my book last February at the University of Virginia. I had hoped Deborah McDowell would come to my talk: she was there, she was the one person in the audience that I was really hoping to please. Somebody in the audience asked if I was writing about a Black anthology. I answered no and tried to justify it, but my justifications rang false in my ears. Some weeks later a friend of mine showed me a letter from McDowell which mentioned my talk and said that I was just doing the same old thing, citing that I was not talking about any books edited by Black women. I obsessed over McDowell's comment until I decided to add a chapter on Pryse and Spiller's *Conjuring*. As powerful as my fear of not finishing is, it was not as strong as my wish for McDowell's approval. For McDowell, whom I do not know, read Black feminist critic. I realize that the set of feelings that I used to have about French men I now have about African-American women. Those are the people I feel inadequate in relation to and try to please in my writing. It strikes me that this is not just idiosyncratic. This shift, for me, passed through a short stage when I felt like what I was saying was OK. The way McDowell has come to occupy the place of Lacan in my psyche does seem to correspond to the way that emphasis on race has replaced for me something like French vs. American feminism.[33]

While Clarke and Awkward both invoke McDowell as a symbol of French theory's unwelcome incursion onto the Black literary-critical scene, Gallop does the opposite: For her, the name (and visible presence) of "Deborah McDowell" stands in for a more general figure, the "Black feminist critic" positioned in Gallop's anecdote as the antidotal alternative to French theory rather than its suspicious purveyor. Instructing the roundtable and its imagined audience to read McDowell as "Black feminist critic," Gallop explicitly names "Deborah McDowell" as the figure that catalyzes her critical and psychological attention shift from theory written by "French men" to theory written by "African-American women."

Gallop's casual assertion "I realize that the set of feelings that I used to have about French men I now have about African-American women" has come to live in infamy in feminist literary-critical circles, and the provocative sound bite continues to circulate widely in texts of feminist literary criticism.[34] The quote's recurrent citation, especially in the five years immediately after the publication of *Conflicts in Feminism,* indicates that Gallop's claim illuminated—with striking candor—something important about the trajectory of feminist criticism at the turn of the decade. Unlike the other writers who reflect on this rather infamous quote, McDowell has more reason to take it personally, although her involvement is only clear if Gallop's line is situated in the larger anecdote in which it appears. Gallop, in her story, describes feeling the same about both "French men" and "African-American women" and her subsequent description of her anxieties and attachments in her two periods of academic consciousness in starkly different, nearly oppositional terms.[35] In an example par excellence of a disciplinary habit that Jennifer C. Nash and others will later describe, Gallop positions Black feminist criticism as the opposite of Parisian sophistication so that it might serve as its practical antidote, a corrective to an overly white, overly Francophilic women's studies.

Seizing on the occasion for her own meditations on identity and identification in the academy, McDowell devotes a chapter of *"The Changing Same,"* "Transferences: Black Feminist Discourse; The 'Practice' of 'Theory,'" to unpacking this anecdote. As the term *transference* suggests, the "pre-fabrication of Blackness" McDowell names in Gallop is an erotically charged fantasy. In naming her own desire, Gallop describes a structure of same-sex desire that repeats another legacy: that of a sentimental relation to scenes of Black suffering but also an eroticized relation to scenes of Black suffering. Indeed, these stakes might be why McDowell's critical methodology and stylistic strategy are deeply invested in precisely the two questions of who gets to be or identify as a reader of literature and what (or, in the case of Gallop's anecdote, who) is the literature to be read. Gallop's invocation of McDowell as figure is strikingly negative, framed in terms of a "non-encounter," a phrase that echoes Gallop's remark that "my first thought was to say 'no one.'" To McDowell, Gallop's formula is depressingly familiar. She notes the ways in which the sound bite "For McDowell, whom I do not know, read Black feminist critic" recalls a longer history of "non-encounters" between Black and white feminists in the United States, writing that "the identity of Black feminist criticism has so far been anything but fluctuating. It has been solidly fixed to a reference schemata and a racial stigmata in a history we've read before."[36] In setting up McDowell as someone she does not know but whose presence nonetheless arouses an entire set of associations related to the figure "Black feminist critic," Gallop precludes any option for McDowell to read as anything else. McDowell's analysis arrives at the relation of reader/spectator to scenes of sexual or physical violence against Black people and the ethical and political consequences of consuming circulating and repeated scenes of racial violence. Specifically, she compares Gallop's remark to one made a

century earlier by white abolitionist and novelist Harriet Beecher Stowe in reference to Black abolitionist activist and author Sojourner Truth: "I had myself often
remarked the name, having never met the individual."[37] Though McDowell does
not name sentimentalism specifically in her critique of Gallop, her specific mention
of Stowe, coupled with her invocation of reading in the phrase "history we've read
before," obliquely conjures *Uncle Tom's Cabin* (1852), the sentimental novel for which
Stowe is most famous. *Uncle Tom's Cabin*, like other white-authored abolitionist
texts before it, appeals to a white readership with scenes of Black suffering meant
to evoke feelings of deep sympathy. As Saidiya Hartman argues, these feelings—
brought on as they are by the spectacle of Black suffering—are born out of the
power dynamics of slavery and so are undivorced from the violence of white supremacy that they claim to combat.[38] The sentimental, characterized by a sincere
appeal to white readerly emotion, thus becomes an indirect target of McDowell's
critique. What is the antidote, then, to this brand of white sincerity and sentimentalism? In contrast to other texts that take up this quote, McDowell's response does
not emphasize "I realize that the set of feelings that I used to have about French
men I now have about African-American women" in her own reprint of Gallop's
story. Instead, she lingers on the line "For McDowell, whom I do not know, read
Black feminist critic."

McDowell names the subheading under which Gallop's anecdote appears "Rememories," a title that hearkens both to the section's doubly anecdotal structure
(McDowell is recalling a story about Gallop recalling a story) and to the history
of racial sentimentalism that, according to McDowell, Gallop's own anecdote repeats. The subheading also functions as an implicit citation of another literary
giant, Toni Morrison, as the neologism *rememory* features prominently in Morrison's *Beloved* (1987). In case her audience doesn't quite grasp the connection, Mc-
Dowell makes it doubly obvious, quoting *Beloved* directly in the epigraph to the
section: "It was not a story to pass on."[39] When McDowell uses Morrison's term in
her section header, she also invokes a long history of Black feminist thinkers and
writers with whom her work engages. In naming her nonencounter with Gallop
a "rememory," McDowell rereads the traumatic reverberations of slavery into the
mechanisms by which McDowell gets "read" by Gallop as a Black feminist theorist.
For Hartman, Johnson, and others, to repeat these patterns is to rely on a structure of violence with its roots in transatlantic slavery. In Morrison's work, *rememory* functions as both a noun ("Some things go. Pass on. Some things stay. I used
to think it was my rememory. You know"; "Paul D dug it up, gave her back her
body, kissed her divided back, stirred her rememory") and as a verb ("I don't 'spect
you rememory this, but Howard got in the milk pile and Red Cora I believe it was
mashed his hand"; "Thank God I don't have to rememory or say a thing because

you know it").⁴⁰ In each case, *rememory* recalls the trauma of slavery while more generally describing the trauma of a repeated past that continues to return. At the same time, the text steers clear of disciplinary dourness, wary that deep seriousness might ring dangerously close in affect to the stony-faced sentimentalizing impulse of white authors like Stowe (and her inheritors). Almost immediately, at the beginning of her response to Gallop, McDowell qualifies the impulse to take historical knowledge as an identity-based given. "To speak of 'historical knowledge' at all is to stage or enter a vigorous debate between those who see 'history' and 'knowledge' as ontological givens and those who don't. I identify with those who don't," she writes.⁴¹ Here McDowell's quip works to undercut her own authority as a subject who "knows" history.

The turn to the literary also brings attention, crucially, to the word *read* in "For McDowell . . . read Black feminist critic." Such attention not only brings questions of language to the fore but also implicitly alerts readers to the ambiguity of Gallop's phrase. The phrase "For McDowell . . . read Black feminist critic" is a command to Gallop's listeners/readers: Read McDowell this way, the way I read her. In this case *for* means "in place of." If we are to interpret the phrase this way, Gallop commands her readers to read "McDowell," as she herself has done, as a metaphorical and figurative stand-in for the figure of the "Black feminist critic" understood reductively. But Gallop's demand and desire are undermined by the very verb she employs. In print, both the word *for* and the word *read* become frustratingly polysemous: Because readers of *Conflicts in Feminism* cannot easily discern Gallop's pronunciation, they cannot easily distinguish whether she says *read* in the imperative present or *read* in the active past. If we take *for* as meaning "because," then Gallop's sentence is not an imperative but an explanation. In other words, "For McDowell, whom I did not know, read Black feminist critic" could also mean "For you see, I read McDowell to be a Black feminist critic" with *read* working as a transitive verb taking *McDowell* as its object. Gallop's confession does more than just blur the line between her object and her method (both are something like "feminist literary theory"); it also, rhetorically, lumps object and method together with two distinct identity categories. The directive "For McDowell . . . read Black feminist critic" all at once collapses McDowell into one knowable category, makes McDowell stand in for the category at large, and as such makes McDowell's name and person interchangeable with any other Black feminist.

The surprise of the singular *critic* retroactively changes the verb from transitive to intransitive, effectively making "McDowell" into a work of literature to be read rather than a reader of literature. *Read* can also be intransitive: If *McDowell* is the subject of *read*, then Gallop uses a construction that the *Oxford English Dictionary* tells us is primarily reserved for cases when the subject is a text. The definitions for *read* used as an intransitive verb include: "To be readable; to be pleasing to read; to make clear sense when read. Now rare"; "To have a specified character or quality when read; to produce a certain impression on readers; to give rise to a particular interpretation"; "Of a language, piece of text, etc.: to admit of or require reading in a particular direction or sequence; to be understood by reading in a particular order"; "To be able to be interpreted (in a particular way)."[42] Because *read* can be both transitive and intransitive, and because McDowell is a reader herself, *read* can also be a verb in the past tense, with *McDowell* as the acting subject, so that the phrase "McDowell . . . read Black feminist critic" could mean something like "McDowell has read Black feminist criticism" or "McDowell has read Black feminist critics."

The counter to sentimentalism, perhaps, is inauthenticity. As we might expect from a critic writing *as if!*, any easy identification is temporary, mocking, and partial: Stylistically, McDowell aligns herself with "Black feminists" but also with the "poststructuralist" Gallop. Her text is written with an ironic promiscuity. But McDowell's occasional jabs (another *read* entirely: *read* as in a cleverly deployed insult) are not merely a takedown of Gallop; they are, instead, a clever way of aligning herself with the very feminists she critiques. In the sections before "Rememories," during a discussion of the various ways "theory" and "practice" are gendered and raced within the academy, McDowell mimics the very turn of phrase she will later call out in Gallop's anecdote: "I must rush to add that race (here, read *black*) and gender (here, read *female*) are not only the stigmatized markers on the practice/ politics side of the border, for they trade places in a fluid system in which differences of nationality, sexuality, and class are interchangeable."[43] In repeating Gallop's patterns of speech—namely, her parenthetical instructions to "read" certain words as stand-ins for other words—McDowell both impersonates and identifies with the target of her critique. In so doing, she highlights the ambiguity of "Black feminist theorist" as a position and identity that is both text (someone to be "read") and reader, implementing and advocating a methodology informed both by critical theory's suspicion of an ontological past and by Black feminist theory's suspicion of a dehistoricized present.

PASSING FANCIES

The piece of McDowell's writing most associated with queer literary criticism is, as it happens, also the piece in which her performative dissatisfaction is most on display. Chastised in *Conditions* for not giving enough evaluative power to sexuality, McDowell tries again: In 1986, she pens an introduction to a new edition of Nella Larsen's *"Quicksand" and "Passing"* published in the Rutgers University Press American Women Writers series.[44] Titled simply "Introduction," the essay highlights the sexual politics hidden beneath the overt racial politics of both works of fiction. But that is just the beginning of the story. In fact, three versions of Mc-Dowell's *Passing* essay exist. It makes its second appearance in 1993 as an article in Henry Abelove, Michèle Aina Barale, and David M. Halperin's edited collection *The Lesbian and Gay Studies Reader* (there, under the alias "'It's Not Safe. Not Safe at All': Sexuality in Nella Larsen's *Passing*") and then finally reappears in 1995 in *"The Changing Same"* (now sporting the title "The 'Nameless . . . Shameful Impulse': Sexuality in Nella Larsen's *Quicksand* and *Passing*").[45] In its many qualitative republications, McDowell's *Passing* essay proves to be a crossover hit, enjoying a readership across disciplines. The differences in each version of the *Passing* essay betray Mc-Dowell's careful tailoring: In each piece, her critical identifications shift according to the audience she addresses, and her editorial choices qualify her for each publication. Because of this, comparing the multiple iterations of this essay offers a unique opportunity to explore how a critical strategy of revising and qualifying brings to light the specific demands of each discipline in which the essay circulates. Each iteration of the *Passing* essay reveals the possible alliances and difficult gaps between critical theory, Black feminist theory, and gay and lesbian theory at the time of McDowell's early writing.

Because it is an early piece of critical writing that explicitly reads lesbian desire into a nonexplicitly lesbian text, McDowell's essay on lesbian structures of desire in *Passing* frequently crops up in queer critical citations.[46] As such, her essay remains a crucial part of early queer theoretical thought. As we have now seen, this is also true of much of McDowell's other work, including especially her second reading of *Sula* (wherein sexuality troubles ideas of selfhood, reproductive futurism, and heterosexual marriage). Even Clarke, whose *Conditions* roundtable chastised Mc-Dowell for homophobia, later acknowledges that McDowell's later work reflects a more nuanced and effective understanding of sexuality. Recalling her original dismissal of McDowell's work, Clarke diagnoses the original anger expressed by her and her fellow discussion participants as a manifestation of the radical political lesbianism of the moment. In a footnote to this anecdote, Clarke registers her happy surprise at McDowell's later pivot toward a lesbian reading of Larsen: "In 'The "Nameless . . . Shameful Impulse": Sexuality in Nella Larsen's *Quicksand* and *Passing*,' McDowell (1995) writes a trenchant article on Larsen's novels. Yet the part on *Passing* is particularly stunning. What many of us had interpreted as a novel of racial passing, McDowell reinterprets as a novel of sexual passing."[47] McDowell's renewed attempt to recognize lesbian desire in *Passing*, and the trenchant close read it produces, legitimizes her in the eyes of her Black feminist peers. In "The 'Nameless . . . Shameful Impulse,'" McDowell runs into the same ambiguous entanglement of sexuality, identity, and reading that she encounters in her second reading of *Sula*, but despite her previous rejection of Smith's argument about lesbian relationships in Morrison's *Sula*, her new piece argues that *Passing* is a narrative of covert same-sex desire. This time, through an attentive and engaged reading method, McDowell earns her queer diploma.

McDowell's own aversion to neat and tidy endings, and her related affinity for qualification and revision, is key to the *as if!* critical strategy on display in her multiple rewrites of the *Passing* essay. In the introduction to *"The Changing Same,"* McDowell foregrounds Larsen's trouble with endings—a telling focus, and one that draws attention to McDowell's own performative revision. "The 'Nameless... Shameful Impulse'" begins by discussing Larsen's trouble with endings, a discussion made deliciously ironic in the context of McDowell's own seeming inability to conclude: "While critics have commended these features of Larsen's writing since the beginning of her career, they have constantly criticized the endings of *Quicksand* and *Passing*."[48] In "The 'Nameless... Shameful Impulse,'" McDowell writes that though both *Passing* and *Quicksand* "feature daring and unconventional heroines, in the end, they sacrifice these heroines to the most conventional fates of narrative history: marriage and death, respectively."[49] Via her own assessment and her gloss on the assessment of other critics, McDowell argues that Larsen's failure to suitably end her novels results from a tension between ideology and form. According to McDowell's explanation, Larsen finds endings difficult because she feels constrained by "the more acceptable demands of literary and social history," relegating her otherwise "independent," "strong," female protagonists to socially allowable fates.[50]

The nonteleological arrangement of the chapters in *"The Changing Same,"* accompanied by each chapter's after-the-fact amendments, not only draws attention to McDowell's identification with Larsen but also constitutes another way in which the text performs the inconsistency of identification and critical loyalties, further unsettling McDowell's endings. McDowell's critical investments exist in tension with one another, and her own unsettled endings betray a "tension between ideology and form" that is different from, but similar to, the tension between ideology and form she notices in Larsen's work.[51] Remarking on the "unsatisfactory and unsettling" endings of *Quicksand* and *Passing*, McDowell writes as if she is a feminist critic (who might condemn Larsen's failure to save her characters from marital gender subordination or death) or as if she is an African American literary critic (who might lament the limited radical potential of Larsen's middle-class respectability politics). McDowell's efforts also are a rejoinder to the limited "feminist perspective" that would take Larsen's endings at face value:

> It is little wonder that critics of Larsen have been perplexed by those abrupt and contradictory endings. But if examined through the prism of

Black female sexuality, not only are these resolutions more understand-able, they also illuminate the peculiar pressures on Larsen as a woman writer during the male-dominated Harlem Renaissance. They show her grappling with the conflicting demands of her racial and sexual identities and the contradictions of a Black and feminine aesthetic. Although the endings of *Quicksand* and *Passing*, like the resolution of *Plum Bun*, seem to be concessions to the dominant ideology of romance—marriage and motherhood—viewed from a feminist perspective, they are much more radical and original efforts to acknowledge a female sexual experience most often repressed in both literary and social realms.[52]

How are readers of *"The Changing Same"* to know to whom "unsettling" refers? It is unclear which readers are unsettled here. If Larsen accedes to the conventional ending to assuage her contemporary reading public, it is unlikely that they will find the ending unsettling. It seems unlikely that the critics of African American literature that McDowell has previously discussed—those champions of familial racial unity—will find Clare's death particularly objectionable. Is it feminists, then, examining Larsen from "a feminist perspective," who might find the end of *Passing* unsettling? Is it Black women, examining Larsen "through the prism of Black female sexuality"? Are either of these McDowell herself, or are they her imagined audience? Like the novels she investigates, McDowell's criticism may leave us with more questions than answers. Such questions parallel the semantic trouble of the word itself: the very descriptor *unsettling* unsettles its referent.

The most notable difference between "The 'Nameless ... Shameful Impulse'" and "'It's Not Safe'" is that both the 1986 introduction and "The 'Nameless ... Shameful Impulse'" include an analysis of another Larsen novel, *Quicksand* (1928). In contrast to *Quicksand* (in which Larsen uses marriage as a safe space for her female characters to explore otherwise unsanctioned sexual appetites), *Passing* uncou-ples marriage and sexuality, opening alternative routes for female desire. Because they are no longer contained within the marriage plot, Larsen must hint at the erotic lives of her characters rather than name their desires explicitly. *Passing*, for McDowell, thus illustrates the "dialectics of desire and fear, pleasure and danger that define women's sexual experiences in male-dominated societies"—dialectics that Larsen disguises as the dynamics of racial passing.[53] Choosing to focus on the "pleasure and danger" negotiated by Black women and the negotiations of il-licit sexuality necessitated by the conflicting discourses of the Jazz Age, McDow-ell omits *Quicksand* entirely in "'It's Not Safe'" and thus omits her analysis of the failures of heterosexual marriage. Instead, she reserves her more detailed critique of marriage for publications and fields outside of lesbian and gay studies, another sign of her shifting and slippery loyalties. McDowell's choice to not address the problem of heterosexual marriage from "'It's Not Safe'" strategically highlights a disciplinary gap between Black feminist criticism and gay and lesbian studies: In gay and lesbian studies, antinormativity is much more easily theorized through same-sex desire.

The fact that "The 'Nameless . . . Shameful Impulse'" is McDowell's third attempt at a finished product further speaks to the fact that she, like Larsen, can't seem to properly end her analysis. It also performs the author's identification with Larsen herself. This identification is made particularly clear in the first and final versions of her essay, in which a series of rhetorical questions (ostensibly about Larsen) frame McDowell's discussion: "To be writing about Black female sexuality within this conflicted context, then, posed particular problems for Larsen. . . . We might say that Larsen wanted to tell the story of Black women with sexual desires, but was constrained by a competing desire to establish Black women as respectable in Black middle-class terms. The latter desire committed her to exploring Black female sexuality obliquely and, inevitably, to permitting it only within the context of marriage, despite the strangling effects of that choice both on her characters and on her narratives."[54] We can easily imagine that McDowell, a Black woman writer writing for a middle-class, college-educated audience, also asks these questions of her own work. At times, McDowell's text invites readers to mark a parallel between the era and the author she studies (the Harlem Renaissance, Larsen) with her present moment (i.e., the moment of the "turn to theory"). Along with the Reconstruction era and the 1920s, she cites the last decade of the twentieth century as one of three periods in American history where the resurgence of texts about racial passing is evident.[55]

McDowell's sometimes-identification with the "repressed" Larsen also winkingly explains some of the hang-ups for which she herself was so roundly criticized. McDowell is much more willing to make her own identification with Larsen clear in the introduction and "The 'Nameless . . . Shameful Impulse.'" The introduction begins with a discussion of Larsen's relative obscurity: "Why a career with such auspicious beginnings had such an inauspicious ending has continued to perplex students of the Harlem Renaissance," writes McDowell. "Many have searched for answers in the scattered fragments of Larsen's biography, which reveal a delicate and unstable person."[56] She again links Larsen's alleged instability with her notorious problems with finishing. As McDowell notes in the introduction, "Since the beginning of Larsen's career, critics have praised her as a 'gifted writer,' commending her skill at the craft of fiction. . . . However, they have constantly criticized the endings of her novels *Quicksand* and *Passing*, which reveal her difficulty with rounding off stories convincingly."[57] Notably, McDowell's choice of object for when she does attempt to read lesbian desire into a work of fiction—*Passing*—sits firmly in the world of the Harlem Renaissance's Black middle class. In McDowell's later readings, rather than fully capitulating to the few acceptable female narratives available to a Black woman writer in 1928, Larsen "wanted to tell the story of a Black woman with sexual desires, but was constrained by a competing desire to establish Black women as respectable in Black middle-class terms," sneaking in sexuality "obliquely" while still remaining dedicated to a 1920s standard of "racial uplift" that hinged on a certain kind of sexual respectability that precluded other nonmarital or same-sex forms of desire.[58]

Ventriloquizing her own critics via an ironic read of Larsen's failure to end things properly, McDowell slips from critical identity to critical identity, unwilling to stick to one identification for long. Her tone shifts throughout her analysis. At times, she is cool and distant, paraphrasing other critics ("While critics have commended these features of Larsen's writing since the beginning of her career, they have consistently criticized the endings of *Quicksand* (1928) and *Passing* (1929)").[59] At others, she directly ranks the texts she reviews, not quoting or glossing others but reporting a personal appraisal of what she finds obvious about a text. McDowell's criticism often sounds like narration; by her account, Larsen's novels anthropomorphically interact with readers or ideas, taking on a character life of their own. The novel itself becomes desiring, flirtatious, and active: "It is no accident that critics have failed to notice the novel's flirtation with this idea"; "To be sure, her novels only flirt with the idea of sexual passion."[60] Furthermore, for McDowell, both racial and sexual passing rely on each woman's ability to read the other: "From the very beginning of their reencounter, Irene is drawn to Clare like a moth to a flame. . . . Into Clare's 'arresting eyes' 'there came a smile and over Irene the sense of being petted and caressed.' At the end of this chance encounter, 'standing there under the appeal, the caress, of Clare's eyes, Irene had the desire, the hope, that this parting wouldn't be the last.'"[61] In her repeated use of flirtation as a rubric for understanding the way Larsen's novels operate, McDowell also conflates author and text: "Having established the absence of sex from the marriages of these two women, Larsen can flirt, if only obliquely, with the idea of a lesbian relationship between them."[62] Like the oblique and unsettling queer relationships in *Passing*, this flirtation has no stable actor or referent, and yet it propels the mechanisms of plot.

WHAT CAN MCDOWELL TEACH US ABOUT *X*?

McDowell's cross-identificatory attempt occasions a final, fourth instance of critical name-dropping: Four years after Gallop invokes McDowell as a stand-in for all Black feminist criticism, deconstructionist feminist Barbara Johnson cites Mc-

Dowell as the inspiration for a piece titled "Lesbian Spectacles," published in *The Feminist Difference* in 1998. In this short essay, Johnson attempts to "read as a lesbian," breaking from her usual deconstructive style to (parodically) attempt to write literary criticism from a lesbian vantage point. In the first few paragraphs of her essay, Johnson writes: "I took my inspiration for such a textual category from two readings of literary texts: Barbara Smith's reading of Toni Morrison's *Sula* and Deborah McDowell's reading of Nella Larsen's novel *Passing*. I cite these critics not because they offer me examples of the act of 'reading as a lesbian' (Smith does; McDowell does not) but because of the nature of the texts they read." In her pithy parenthetical, Johnson refuses McDowell the same kind of erotic relation to the text that the project of "Lesbian Spectacles" itself ironically attempts to claim. As such, she distinguishes between "writing as a lesbian" and being a "decoder of lesbian structures" in her reference to McDowell, whose name once again is invoked as a stand-in for a more capacious idea.[63]

The allusion to authorial identity, deposited in Johnson's brief parenthetical "Smith does; McDowell does not," is out of line with the refusals of Authorship we might expect of the post-Barthes literary criticism with which Johnson is most often associated. Another high-profile citation of McDowell, Barbara Johnson's decisive parenthetical "(Smith does; McDowell does not)" dismisses the possibility that "The 'Nameless . . . Shameful Impulse'" is an example of reading as a lesbian. In Johnson's short foray into lesbian reading, McDowell's work is paradoxically hailed as an inspiring example and as an instructive antiexample: "I took my inspiration for such a textual category from two readings of literary texts: Barbara Smith's reading of Toni Morrison's *Sula* and Deborah McDowell's reading of Nella Larsen's novel *Passing*. I cite these critics not because they offer me examples of the act of 'reading as a lesbian' (Smith does; McDowell does not) but because of the nature of the texts they read."[64] This could be due to a simple matter of self-declaration: Johnson is merely acknowledging that Smith openly claims a lesbian identity and therefore reads "as" one; McDowell does not explicitly identify herself as a lesbian and therefore doesn't read "as" one. Read this way, Johnson's comment serves as an example of a moment of identity policing in which material experience and self-identification disqualify an author from certain critical identifications. Then again, though Johnson might have a stronger case for her own lesbian credentials, the entire point of her analysis is that she is not fully able to identify or read as one. In other words, if McDowell "does not" read as a lesbian, neither, ultimately, does Johnson—by her own analysis. Something about McDowell's repeated attempts to write about *Passing* as a lesbian text prompts the question: Is it possible to read as a lesbian at all?

As these instances of critical calling-out illustrate, even though McDowell is consistently interpellated by her fellow theorists, her nonallegiance to any one methodology means that she is rarely interpellated the same way. In the above examples, McDowell is at once "homophobic" (Clarke), a traitorous adopter of French critical theory (Awkward), a Black feminist theorist par excellence (Gallop), and a "decoder of lesbian structures of desire" (Johnson) who nonetheless does not read as a lesbian. The seeming arbitrariness with which McDowell's name is thrown into various camps speaks to the complicated ways in which identity is working in her oeuvre, as well as to how critical identity is as much determined by audience as it is by avowed authorial identification. How is it possible for McDowell's name to stand in for so many different schools of thought, some of which are placed in direct opposition to one another by her critics? What to do with all these citational scenes in which McDowell is variously quisling, savior, or impostor?

In the preface to *"The Changing Same,"* McDowell chronicles her experience as a young academic during the academy's critical theory sea change. Retelling the story of her book's multiple false starts, she writes: "While I have held on to the subject, nothing of the dissertation remains, for between its completion and the product you now hold in your hand, literary studies underwent a wrenching upheaval, or, as we are now wont to say, à la Thomas Kuhn, a 'paradigm shift' from the 'Age of Criticism' to the 'Age of Theory.'"[65] From the beginning of *"The Changing Same,"* McDowell's text plays fast and loose with critical methods. At first, she positions critical theory as an outside force, one that disrupted the validity of her original dissertation project (proving generational influence and thematic continuity for novels authored by Black women). In doing so, she places her own experience in the context of a conflict and collaboration between Black feminist criticism and critical theory (more specifically, between Black feminist criticism and the post-structuralist theory employed by white feminists). On the one hand, McDowell finds in critical theory new, useful rubrics for understanding "that self 'identity' always gives way to 'difference,' thus making difficult any easy and clear-cut identifications and alliances."[66] On the other, McDowell performs and recounts her anxiety, even physical discomfort, with this paradigm shift, writing in the preface that the academy's turn to theory was for her a mixed blessing, one that also occasioned "convulsions and, quiet as it was kept, occasional paroxysms of rage."[67] McDowell's anxieties and deliberations surrounding the status of her work mirror the anxieties of the larger academic climate during the so-called culture wars; in this way, her preface speaks to a generation of critical theorists who completed graduate school in the late 1970s and received tenure in the late 1980s and early 1990s. These theorists experienced the rapid rise of, and successive backlash against, critical theory in the academic sphere.

The visceral force of "wrenching" and "convulsions" cannot help but remind readers that there are both physical and mental costs to being a Black woman in the academy. Tongue-in-cheek though a phrase like "two conceptions and one stillbirth" may be, the figurative language in McDowell's preface indicates that academic authorship is personal, even painful. It is also formidably risky: "The costs of 'doing' literary studies in the 1980s—the historical frame of the following essays—were often high: retooling as the 'parts' of the critical machinery were changing by the day and while the professionalization of literary studies seemed to accelerate to the point of near collapse," she writes. "The stakes were nothing less than the rights and privileges of academic life."[68] As Barbara Christian saliently reminds her readers around the time of McDowell's writing, Black feminist academics labor in "environments which often are not only nonsupportive but, at times, outright hostile. They (we) are expected to perform mightily—with little reward—and to be grateful that we are allowed in the halls of learning. Overworked and underrecognized, we are forced to cope with office and university politics as well as the racism, sexism, and homophobia inherent in these environments and the larger society."[69] With "wrenching" and "convulsions," implicitly, McDowell raises the question of what Grace Kyungwon Hong calls "the ethics of deploying woman of color feminism and Black feminism as analytics in the context of an academy in which such deployments sometimes legitimate epistemic and physical violence toward Black feminists."[70] The continued specter of bodily violence done to McDowell's person, conjured by McDowell's figurative speech, attunes her audience to the stakes of her identification games.

There is, of course, a way to read McDowell's dissatisfaction as merely defensive. Jennifer C. Nash argues that "defensiveness" has been a characteristic effect of Black feminist thought since its fraught incorporation into women's studies departments beginning in the late sixties.[71] If, as Nash points out, the impulse toward defensiveness relies on the "constant invocation of the malicious critic as a pernicious outsider" as a figure "through which Black feminists reassert their territorial claim to intersectionality and perform their collective desire to shield intersectionality from violent criticism," then the relentless qualifying tendencies of *"The Changing Same"* are nothing more than a symptom of McDowell's paranoid impulse to never be wrong.[72] Response is, after all, a way of maintaining correctness. But a closer look at McDowell's style—in particular, her penchant for in-text revision—reveals a mode of writing more akin to the *as if!* critical stylings of contemporaneous queer literary critics. Countering fixity with playful amendment, McDowell's qualifications to her own previous statements align her work with Nash's call for a Black feminist theoretical practice that "lets go" rather than "holds on," where "'letting go' represents . . . a vision of Black feminist theory that is not invested in making property of knowledge."[73] Whereas Nash argues that defensiveness "traps and limits Black feminists and Black women academics who continue to be conscripted into performing and embodying their intellectual investments," McDowell's writing resists such territorialism.[74] On more than one occasion, promiscuous and shifting identifications enact Nash's countercall to imagine "what Black feminists can garner from sitting with, sitting *beside* [the] disavowed figure" of the critic.[75]

The metaphors of coming/cumming, abortion, conception, and stillbirth that open *"The Changing Same"* hint that these "convulsions" might also carry with them a particularly queer valence. And yet, McDowell is seldom if ever read as a queer critic.[76] Nonetheless, McDowell's continual riff on the "wrenching upheaval" occasioned by the turn to theory and the professional pressures to write and theorize along poststructuralist lines suggests a possible connection between McDowell's work and the work of critics who were, at around the same time of her writing, just beginning to articulate queer theory as an academic field.[77] The gerundive adjective *wrenching* here operates in an ambiguous relation to life and death, birth and rejection.

The ambiguous violence implied by *wrenching* in the sentence "literary studies underwent a wrenching upheaval" is not unlike the ambiguous violence Johnson describes in her work on Walter Benjamin's use of *Wehen*, in which she points out that "the proper translation of 'Wehen' would be neither 'birth pangs' nor 'death pangs,' but, rather, 'pains.'"[78] Marking *Wehen* as aligned with neither birth nor death, Johnson blurs the line between the two, complicating metaphors of translation and motherhood, playing with the violence in both. McDowell's invocation of "at least two conceptions and one stillbirth" also reinforces what Johnson and many queer and feminist theorists argue is a heterosexist and sexist idea of motherhood as unquestionably on the side of life, of good, of children, and of the future. In their polemical "What Does Queer Theory Teach Us About *X*?" (also written in 1995), Lauren Berlant and Michael Warner use *wrenching* not once but twice to describe the effect of queer theory in the academy, writing in two separate instances: "Part of the point of using the word *queer* in the first place was the wrenching sense of recontextualization it gave, and queer commentary has tried hard to sustain awareness of diverse context boundaries," and later "What does queer theory teach us about *x*? As difficult as it would be to spell out programmatic content for an answer, this simple question still has the power to wrench frames."[79] *Wrenching* along with its many associated synonyms (*spraining, twisting, pulling, injuring, ricking, turning, tugging, jerking*) and near-homophones (*retching, wrecking*) evokes, among other things, the etymology of *queer*—from the Middle High German root **terkw-* "to turn, twist, wind" along with the German *Wehen*.[80] The powerful "wrenching" force of the critical turn that McDowell describes, then, simultaneously connotes the pangs of a painful birth, the violent sway of academic sea change, and the throes of a gag reflex.

Why are queer theorists so reluctant to claim *"The Changing Same"*? To follow Sharon Patricia Holland, it might be that white queer theory seems unable to acknowledge the diversity of Black feminist thought, a pattern that no doubt speaks to its lingering attachment to racialized identity.[81] As Nash explains, women's studies is largely "organized around the symbol of Black woman even as [it] retains little interest in the materiality of Black women's bodies, the complexity of Black women's experiences, or the heterogeneity of Black women's intellectual and creative production."[82] When McDowell identifies as a Black female critic, she most often finds her work characterized in ways that erase her multidisciplined approach and rob her work of its capacity to speak to and across various theoretical frameworks. McDowell finds herself trapped in a system in which "Black women are imagined as both saviors and world-ending figures, and where intersectionality is both peril and promise."[83] She writes from the overdetermined identity position "Black woman" and therefore is constituted as a "Black feminist critic"; her name and work might all too easily stand in for the mythical monolith of "Black feminist criticism," especially within such fields as women's studies. Interpellated as a Black woman writer, McDowell must grapple with the peril and promise of her own role in the academy, in which her identifications as both Black and a woman are already overdetermined, even as they remain integral to her work and method. In other words, the identities "Black feminist critic" and "Black woman writer" overlap; McDowell's identifications are often assumed to be straightforward and therefore limited in their critical capacity to think differently or contradictorily.

Responding and revising, McDowell writes as a Black feminist critic, as a lesbian critic, as a white poststructuralist. In doing so, she not only performs her suspicion of a complete and consistent SELF but also attempts to reclaim—even showcase—what Holland calls the "saliency of Black feminist disagreement."[84] Theorizing difference within marginalized groups that are often politically or theoretically flattened into homogeneous entities, McDowell avoids the trap of neoliberal identity politics and makes us laugh in the meantime. With each qualifying move, McDowell's work wrenches her readers out of their easy assumptions. It is this perpetual motion that propels her literary criticism. Throughout *"The Changing Same"* and elsewhere, her text remains hyperconscious not only of the ways in which literary criticism restricts and relegates the authors and works she discusses to one reductive category ("Black women's fiction") but also of the similarly limiting disciplinary regulation of her own categorical position (namely, as a writer of "Black feminist criticism"). McDowell, relentlessly revising, throws a wrench into the gears of the academic identity knowledge machine.

2

Barbara Johnson's Passing

DOUBLE MOURNING IN THE ACADEMIC SPHERE

Barbara Johnson died on August 27, 2009, after eight years of battling cerebellar ataxia. Her entire memorial service is on YouTube. The video, shot with one tripod camera facing a small Harvard stage, features seventeen speakers, one previously recorded lecture on *Walden*, two slideshows of family photographs, and one live musical performance. Watching this video now, having been absent for the actual occasion, feels like interloping on an intimate space of mourning. It also feels like virtually attending a critical theory conference: The two-hour, publicly uploaded recording documents a production that is equal parts eulogy, academic panel, and revue. The event, according to an introduction by Johnson's colleague James Engell, follows Johnson's wishes "as closely as possible," down to the program illustrations.[1] But despite Johnson's careful planning, at the start of the ceremony, the detailed schedule suffers a slight hiccup. As the noise in the auditorium dies down and people take their seats, Engell informs the audience that the first slated speaker, Henry Louis Gates Jr., cannot attend. Smiling slightly, Engell asks the audience, "Please try to do something quite impossible: Yes, imagine that I am Skip." Engell, who is white, proceeds to read a letter previously penned by Gates, who is Black.

What is striking about this moment is not only the "quite impossible" cross-racial imagining Engell asks of his audience but also that such a context frames a second cross-racial imagining, as the content of Gates's letter soon makes clear.

Gates (that is, Gates as voiced by Engell) begins his remarks with a parallel meditation: "Let me begin with something light. I don't know if Barbara ever realized how many people thought that she was Black. And many students encountering her work for the first time still think that she must be a Black person." In his eulogy, Gates gives two reasons for the "confusion" surrounding Johnson's race: that her surname is among the most common for Black Americans and that her reading of metaphor and metonymy in Zora Neale Hurston's *Their Eyes Were Watching God* (1937) was so "stunning in subtlety and nuance" that readers simply could not imagine her as white. Speaking through Engell, Gates elaborates a difference between the Johnson readers did not personally know and the Johnson they felt they knew:

> It was not only her untangling of the words on the page that brought a number of readers—incoming graduate students and colleagues familiar with her work but not familiar with her personally—to the conclusion that she must be Black but also her deep and intimate sense of Hurston's language that left no question about who she was for these readers, leading them inevitably to the inevitable conclusion that this "Dr. Johnson" was most Black indeed. If Barbara didn't know that, I wish she had. For Barbara, not only are we all constituted by language, but also language is constituted by us, and perhaps she would have accepted the invitation. "If my language says I'm Black," she may have thought, "then Black I may be." Or, more appropriately, she would have stated: "then Black I be."[2]

By Gates's account, it is Johnson's "deep and intimate sense" of Hurston's language —a language that, the audience is meant to infer, typically does not get such nuanced and intimate attention from white critics—that leads students and professors alike to assume that she is a Black person. For Gates, Johnson's own Blackness comes not only from the way she sounds when she writes but also from the way her reading attends to Black authorial voice. It is this intimate attachment to and knowledge of her objects of study that allows Johnson, in Gates's estimation, not only to pass as Black but also to become, effectively, Black as well. So intimate is Johnson's knowledge that—at least for Gates—it grants her not only an attuned critical ear but also a Black writerly voice (not "then Black I may be" but "then Black I be").

Gates is far from the only critic to note that readers who had not met Johnson often assumed she was a Black woman, nor is he the first to comment on her critical affinity for Black-authored texts. Elizabeth Abel, also discussing Johnson's work on Hurston, writes that Johnson "becomes, in the course of her argument, figuratively Black."[3] Mary Helen Washington, writing in a special tribute to Johnson in *differences*, notes that "the chapters in *The Feminist Difference* on race, that is, the ones on

African American literary texts and African American authors...comprise, I am surprised to discover, about seventy-five percent of the book."[4] In a perhaps less-than-credible thirdhand anecdote found in the same *differences* issue, Avital Ronell tells another story of misrecognition: "In the gym, Phil Harper told me that Skip Gates was told by Ishmael Reed on a flight to somewhere that Barbara Johnson, whom he had never met, was probably one of his preferred Black critical minds."[5]

Another tribute to Johnson, D. A. Miller's essay "Call for Papers: In Memoriam Barbara Johnson" (2011), also meditates on her critical identity, albeit from another angle. Here, Miller discusses Johnson's lived lesbianism in conjunction with critical considerations of her work, which largely fail to read Johnson as a desiring sexual subject herself. Miller wants critics to take seriously the connotative language in Johnson's critical writing, language that might betray a more ambiguous, erotic, or linguistic Johnson—in a word, a queerer Johnson: "In acknowledging no rhetoric that could contaminate her knowledge, no connotations that might unsteady her denotations, we effectively deprived her of *language*. Nor were we any closer to heeding the stubborn presence in her writing of what Barthes would have called 'grain,' the irreducibly individual *body* in a voice as it speaks language."[6] Like the eulogies featured in the recorded Harvard memorial service, Miller's eulogy is part personal tribute, part critical paper. "Call for Papers" turns Johnson's method of close reading back on her own work, interpreting her essay "Bringing Out D. A. Miller" (2002), itself a close read of Miller's book *Bringing Out Roland Barthes* (1992), as an implicit request to be "brought out" herself as an embodied, sexual person. Miller positions Johnson's work in marked contrast to his own, in which he makes his own "gay writing position" very explicit.[7] Contextualizing Johnson's lesbian desire within its seemingly tangential relation to her work, Miller chastises the many scholarly readers of Johnson who sidestep the "queerness" of her critical style.

This is the crux of Miller's expressed frustration: Despite all of Johnson's listening, no one is listening to *her*. "And so we muted that finely orchestrated erotic friction between language *and* body—and between the given and chosen elements within each—which is what we mean by a writer's *style*," he writes.[8] To see Johnson as a lesbian, critics must hear her as one. In Miller's formulation, the queerness of Johnson is, regrettably, "muted" and therefore unseen—unseen because, for Miller, one is "brought out" like a color or complexion. Both sound and hue can be "muted." As such, Johnson's language, praised by critics for its "brilliance" but ultimately abstracted from its style and voice, becomes effectively transparent, rendering her own body invisible. By contrast: Engell's joke and Gates's story work because Engell's and Johnson's whiteness, to those who have met them, is able to be plainly seen and known. Partially due to Johnson's biographical lesbianism, Miller continually runs the risk of having his "call for papers" misheard as a call to "out" rather than "bring out." Miller is aware of this risk. "There is hardly a procedure for bringing out this meaning that doesn't itself look or feel like just more police entrapment," he writes in *Bringing Out Roland Barthes*. "(Unless such [a procedure], perhaps, were a *folie a deux*—where 'two' stands for the possibility of community—that would bring it out in as subtle and flattering a fashion as, say, the color of a garment is said to bring out a complexion.)"[9] In "Call for Papers," the mutual recognition Miller offers Johnson is one of cross-gender critical collaboration based on a shared homosexual identity. Here, "bringing out" is a meeting of two mad minds, a structure that again recalls the formula "it takes one to know one."

The similarities between Gates's and Miller's eulogies are striking. Both men exemplify her as a scholar among scholars. Both men knew Johnson when they were graduate students at Yale. As such, both of their eulogies circulate within tight webs of academic association, and both are, also, performatively conscious of their place within those intimate insider networks of reference and citation: The circumstances of Gates's address immediately mark it as already embroiled in such a network, while Miller's article is first published in the 2011 "Queer Bonds" issue of *GLQ: A Journal of Lesbian and Gay Studies*, an issue largely devoted to the potent networks of friendship and familiarity that tend to permeate US queer and feminist criticism. Both Gates and Miller imagine themselves in conversation with the late Johnson, even if neither eulogist addresses her outright. Both pieces, in different ways, are thus structured around a man speaking to a dead woman; as such, both enact scenes that themselves ask the same questions that Johnson asks in her theoretical explorations of voice, gender, and apostrophic elegy. Like Gates, Miller focuses on Johnson's use of language. For Miller, too, it is Johnson's language that allows an audience to recognize identity.

Perhaps most importantly, both Gates and Miller name intimacy as either a feature or a lacuna of Johnson's prose. In Miller's article, Johnson's writing reveals her desire to be intimately read:

> Though Barbara would certainly have welcomed being read with her own kind of rigor, her wish in "Bringing Out D. A. Miller" is not a wish to be deconstructed; it is a wish to be brought out, to be disclosed as an embodied (sexed) author rather than an abstracted (neutered) analyst. Barbara wanted this, I think, not because she believed that her lesbianism was the key to her writing (she didn't) or because she was personally or politically in the closet (she wasn't). She wanted it because she felt that "bringing out" might elicit, along with her already overt sexual orientation, an additional, more genuinely secret intimacy.[10]

In Gates's eulogy, Johnson's subtle and attentive readings of Black-authored literature allow her to pass as a Black feminist critic with a "deep and intimate sense" of African American vernacular and language. Miller's phrase "more genuinely secret intimacy" echoes Gates's phrase "intimate sense." But while Miller says Johnson longs for intimacy, Gates says it is the thing she is known for. For Gates, it is not only Johnson's way of reading but also her way of writing that enable her to pass as Black to those readers who have not met her in person; for Miller, Johnson's clear style and "abstracted" voice obscure the queer or lesbian sexuality in her work (and, Miller makes sure to note, in her day-to-day life). Given that Johnson was a white woman, and gay, we might expect that her critical interpellation as a Black feminist to be more fraught than her interpellation as a lesbian, but these two eulogies, read side by side, suggest more complicated routes of identification in Johnson's work. Just as it might be "quite impossible" for audiences to imagine Engell as Gates, so it seems, by Miller's account, quite impossible for critics to imagine Johnson as a lesbian. Indeed, if we take these two men at their word, it seems easier for audiences to imagine Johnson as Black.

Intimacy might denote insider knowledge, sexual activity, or an ease of association formed by quotidian habit; it can mean erotic desire, close friendship, or a complicated combination of these things. *Intimacy* also implies attachment (the intimate attachments a critic has with her object of study, for example). As Christina Sharpe writes, "Intimacy is always about desire—perhaps specifically about what Ann Laura Stoler calls the 'education of desire'—and the structures that organize and constitute the relationships between past and present and possible futures."[11] Sharpe is talking specifically about the desire bound up in what she terms the "monstrous intimacies" that are the result of transatlantic slavery—that is, the systems of rape and incest that sustained an economy based on human chattel. Such intimacies show how the "fundamental, familiar, sexual violence of slavery and racialized subjugation have continued to shape Black and white subjectivities into the present."[12] Sharon Patricia Holland names this familiar violence "the quotidian." Later, she explains how the "intimacy" of the racist encounter allows us to understand intimacy in the academy as it relates to literary object choice: "The turn towards the quotidian is not one that focuses on the prejudice but rather on the discretionary acts and, yes, racist practices that each of us make in everyday decisions such as choosing someone to sit beside on the subway, selecting a mate or a sperm donor, or developing a list of subjects for an academic study."[13] Intimacy here moves beyond the simple rubric of unproblematic attachment, denoting closeness that in different instances can register variously as familial, erotic, discomfiting, monstrous, banal, extraordinary, and so on.

If intimacy is "always about desire," and desire is structured by vectors of history and power, it is impossible to separate textual obsessions and the racial voyeurism at work in the literary analysis performed in Johnson's work. What does it mean to take Johnson's desire for intimacy with Black-authored texts seriously as an ambivalent motivator of her literary-critical project? What do Gates and Miller mean when they evoke the "intimacy" that Johnson either exemplified or desired? While Gates doesn't address Johnson's queerness, his invocation of the intimate relations of reading leaves the question of sexuality lurking underneath his praise. While Miller's analysis of Johnson's style doesn't address her race specifically, the rhetoric of Miller's essay nonetheless reveals the intimate relation between Johnson's whiteness, her lesbianism, and her writing style and reception. When we trace the origins of Gates's claims to Johnson's "Blackness" or follow Miller's call and bring out the erotic body of the "Deconstructionist nun," we find, like Johnson herself sometimes finds, a recurring erotic charge predicated on racial hierarchies of power.[14]

I am not interested in reproving Johnson or exposing her as motivated by racist desire. Rather, I am interested in how her writing discloses her own desire in ways that both trouble and acknowledge categories of race and sexuality within academic discourse. How does Johnson's intimacy with and desire for Black-authored texts animate her work? How, too, does her writing lay bare those intimacies, and to what end? Parenthetically coming out to her readers as both a white feminist working on Black-authored texts and a lesbian who does not read "as a lesbian," Johnson's text tactically reveals critical loyalties and aptitudes that seem inappropriate or unobvious. This chapter ultimately reads Johnson's parenthetical asides as indicators of a difficult, theatrical intimacy—that is, as moments that produce the disruptions of identification integral to the performative critical cross-identification and desire that I call *as if!* criticism.

IT TAKES ONE TO HEAR ONE

"Bringing Out D. A. Miller," the piece to which Miller's "Call for Papers" responds, is Johnson's 2002 review of Miller's 1992 book, *Bringing Out Roland Barthes*. In her review, Johnson devotes considerable attention to the first eight words of Miller's book: the short phrase "Long before I, how you say, *knew myself*."[15] Johnson's analysis nationalizes and localizes Miller's style, zeroing in on the eight-word phrase as an example of Miller's French affectation. The phrase "Long before I, how you say, *knew myself*" not only denotes gayness but also connotes a marked Frenchness, the kind of Frenchness that marks both Roland Barthes and the poststructuralist theory with which he is associated. "An English speaker would say, 'How *do* you say?' . . . The speaker is pretending to lack English, but *in a French way*," she writes.[16] "But this remains true only to the extent that he fails to say so, and does so *from the gay side*."[17] For Johnson, Miller's "knew myself" is a shibboleth, a code with sexual undertones meant to out Miller to his already in-the-know audience: "The 'how you say' would indicate that a linguistic question was passing as a code word. If you speak this language, it implies, you know what it means."[18] Johnson's privileged position as the one who knows is born of an intimate identification with her subject(s).

In other instances, Johnson's insider status is complicated by her identifications across race; these identifications are bolstered by her ability to intimately intimate a text's meaning. In an essay on Richard Wright's *Native Son* (1940) titled "The Re(a)d and the Black: Richard Wright's Blueprint," Johnson describes a scene in which protagonist Bigger Thomas pens a false ransom note to the father of the woman he killed earlier. Her argument centers on the particular "Blackness" of Bigger's rhetoric. "Like Richard Wright himself in 1940, Bigger is compelled to sign his writing 'Red,'" she writes. "Yet the note is signed 'Black' as well: '*Do what this letter say*.'"[19] The missing *s* at the end of *say*—an *s* Anglo-English readers might expect at the end of a verb with a singular subject—is the (omitted) letter that signs Bigger's letter "Black"—that is, that produces the sign of Blackness in the text. This sign is, crucially, not written; it is an elision, a blank space where the *s* might be. Johnson's language reflects this: "Hidden behind the letter's detour through communism is the unmistakable trace of its Black authorship. Yet no one in the novel seems to be able to read it. . . . Behind the sentence 'Do what this letter say' lies the possibility— and the invisibility—of a whole vernacular literature."[20] Johnson then moves to the one person in Wright's novel who is able to critically decipher the note as Bigger's own: Bessie, a Black woman and sometimes lover of Bigger, who ultimately meets a tragic fate at Bigger's hand. As Washington and others point out, Johnson's read of Wright here positions her as both insider and outsider to Black literature and literary criticism. Just as Bessie's reading of Blackness in Bigger's note depends on hearing and seeing what is not visibly obvious, so too does Johnson's reading of Wright rely on her ability to cogently read beneath the surface. Johnson, like Bessie, and unlike the unwitting white father who misreads the note in *Native Son*, also possesses a critical ear that allows her to hear the rhetorical cues that mark the text of Bigger's note as Black.[21] Johnson nonetheless passes as a Black critic by virtue of her demonstrated critical virtuosity, despite being, in Washington's words, an "outsider" to the world of the text.[22]

What is remarkable about Johnson's reading of Wright is that the reading she performs grants her in-group status to a group of which, by nearly all accounts, she is not a member. Erving Goffman, in his influential book *Stigma: Notes on the Management of Spoiled Identity* (1963), helpfully labels the person in this position "the wise."[23] Amy Robinson, writing around the same time as Johnson, calls this person the "in-group clairvoyant."[24] Expounding on the adage that "it takes one to know one," Robinson attempts to recalibrate traditional understandings of racial and sexual passing as dyadic by introducing a third actor: the person who can read the passer as passing. Refiguring passing as "a hostile encounter between two ways of reading" (that is, between the clairvoyant and the dupe), Robinson argues that identity politics is best understood as a theater of multiple intelligibilities rather than as a simple interplay between visible and invisible. The clairvoyant's knowing read typically operates via intuition, a term that itself becomes the privileged indicator of in-group status. Delinking *intuition* from its essentializing associations, Robinson instead redefines *intuition* as "a complex system of cultural literacy" masquerading as "a nostalgic 'myth of origin' that petitions the 'real' and the 'authentic' in the name of an inviolate prepassing identity."[25] Crucially for Robinson, the claim to intuition does more to shore up the in-group credentials of the knowing reader than either the passer or the dupe. In other words, Johnson's analysis of the performance of passing is, itself, performative. To again quote Robinson: "The claim to tell who is or isn't a member of one's community of identity is more important than knowing if one's suspicions are correct."[26] Here, Johnson's text positions her as neither passer nor dupe; rather, she occupies a third and powerful position: that of the knowing reader.

Importantly, the connection between the aural and the visual in Johnson's reading of Bigger's note is uncannily analogous to theorizations of sexual passing. In Johnson's *Native Son* reading, hearing the signs of a "vernacular literature" allows a knowing listener the ability to see the invisible sign of Blackness at work in Bigger's prose (and, it follows, Bigger's own Blackness). A white critic who possesses a critical ear for racial difference, Johnson's role is also not unlike the role, cogently described by Eve Kosofsky Sedgwick in *Epistemology of the Closet* (1990), of the knowing friend or foe who can name gayness even as it remains in the closet.[27] Just as, in Sedgwick's example, an outsider is wise enough to "know" that her companion is gay (that is, she is an adept enough reader that she can decode gay male structures of desire), Johnson is wise enough to know that Bigger is Black (she is an adept enough reader that she can decode Black patterns of address). Indeed, Johnson performs the role of the Sedgwickian friend-who-knows in "Bringing Out D. A. Miller." The missing *s* signs Bigger's note Black; so too does the missing *do* sign Miller's phrase French. Just as the "Red" communism that covers up Bigger's "Black" identity might also be read as covering up or making oblique reference to other stigmatized identities of the period, most notably homosexuality, so too does Miller's foreign identification mark him as gay. In both Johnson's read of Miller and Miller's knowing eulogy to Johnson, queerness, like Blackness, can be heard in a writer's style; queerness, like Blackness, also can be detected via intimate critical listening.

Knowing is not without its own dynamics of pleasure and power. Silence is not the same as an empty signifier or as its absence; following Sedgwick, we understand how silence might be delectably militarized by the knower, either with (complicity) or against (blackmail, glamorization) their closeted accomplice. "After all, the position of those who think they *know something about one that one may not know oneself* is an excited and empowered one," Sedgwick writes. "In many, if not most, relationships, coming out is a matter of crystallizing intuitions or convictions that had been in the air for a while already and had already established their own power-circuits of silent contempt, silent blackmail, silent glamorization, silent complicity."[28] Indeed, when Miller turns away from the metaphor of police entrapment and toward the gentler analogy of fashion, he attempts to wiggle out of these troubling power dynamics. But his amendment rests on a false divide between the terms it seeks to displace (the police, entrapment) and the terms it offers as alternatives (fashion, color, garment, complexion). To be sure, the existence of such historical, current, and ever-growing realities as recent drag bans, anti-cross-dressing ordinances, gang-related legal dress codes, and various other forms of systemic gender and racial police profiling indicate how sartorial presentation is still bound up in the police state.

The aural dimension of Johnson's, Miller's, and Gates's analyses—the critical listening that such analyses require—is also no less embroiled in the systems of policing outlined above. To be sure, just as Gates racializes Johnson's style in his eulogy ("then Black I be"), and just as Miller calls on critics to sexualize Johnson's style, so too does Johnson racialize Bigger's style in *Native Son*. As Nicole Brittingham Furlonge, Jennifer Lynn Stoever, and others make clear, white supremacist systems construct the Black/white binary through aural and sonic as well as visual codes. In Stoever's formulation, the white person's listening ear "drives the sonic color line. . . . Through the listening ear's surveillance, discipline, and interpretation, certain associations between race and sound come to seem normal, natural, and 'right.'"[29] Insofar as it roots out Blackness via a fixed code of racial signifiers, Johnson's analysis risks reinscribing systems of meaning-making in which, to quote Stoever, "essentialist ideas about 'Black' sounds and listening [offer] white elites a new method of grounding racial abjection in the body while cultivating white listening practices as critical, discerning, and delicate and, above all, as the standard of citizenship and personhood."[30]

Instead, insofar as she engages in a reading that remains "mindful of . . . discrepancies between the print surface and the sonic life of words," Johnson practices the kind of listening that Furlonge advocates: a mode of racially aware listening that "allows for an examination of how aural practices have generated particularly useful but sometimes limiting notions of Black racial identity over time."[31] While this may well be tied to the "white elitism" about which Stoever is rightfully suspicious, it does not necessarily follow that Johnson's critical ear results in "grounding racial abjection in the body." For one thing, Johnson's choice of text complicates a reductive understanding of her work as simply policing—if only because Johnson, in her analysis, notices what the police do not. Acting as a third-party decoder of passing, Johnson doesn't seek to prove the supposed truth of an author's identity; rather, she identifies the tells that destabilize the idea of a knowable truth. Put more bluntly, in Robinson's words, "Perverts see passing because of their familiarity with codes of deception. 'It takes one to know one' thus signifies a position that identifies a performance, not one that claims ontological knowledge of the identity of the performer."[32] Just as it would be a mistake to classify these various moments of critical intimacy as moments of complete mutual recognition or understanding, it would likewise be a mistake to dismiss them as strictly surveillance.

ADDRESSING ADDRESS

In "The Re(a)d and the Black," Johnson does not come out as white; in "Bringing Out D. A. Miller," she does not come out as gay. As such, I can't call these moments *as if!* reading proper, because her audience might read these pieces and never become aware of the cross-identification at work within them. At other points in her career, Johnson makes these cross-identifications explicit, often employing the slightly awkward approach of naming her own whiteness (and, in fewer instances, her lesbian-ness) directly. Often, these moments happen during analytical detours in which Johnson indulges in a metadiscussion about the work at hand. Preoccupied with questions of address and audience, Johnson takes time to speculate on her own positionality, as well as her readers'. While on its surface this confessional strategy might seem to shut down Johnson's cross-identifications, it instead makes the identificatory leaps in her work more obvious.

We see this strategy at work in the very piece of critical writing that Gates praises at Johnson's memorial service, an article from the *Critical Inquiry* special issue "'Race,' Writing, and Difference" titled "Thresholds of Difference: Structures of Address in Zora Neale Hurston." Johnson discusses the final unglossed folk tale recounted in Hurston's *Mules and Men* (1935), in which a daughter attempts to transcribe a letter to her father only to find there is no word for the sound he is describing. Hurston transcribes the sound as "(clucking noise)." Johnson's analysis of "(clucking noise)" as that which cannot be translated from speech to writing anticipates, though doesn't entirely match up with, later work by Fred Moten on Black performance and the sound where "words don't go."[33] Moten theorizes that certain sounds constitute resistant objects, suggesting that "words are somehow constrained by their implicit reduction to the meanings they carry—meanings inadequate to or detached from the objects or states of affairs they would envelop. What's also implied is an absence of inflection; a loss of mobility, slippage, bend; a missing accent or affect; the impossibility of a slur or crack and the excess—rather than loss—of meaning they imply."[34] The noise in the story Hurston documents might serve as another example of such a resistant object. The father, here likely a stand-in for the southern Black populations Hurston was anthropologically surveying, possesses knowledge of an oral sign that can't be captured in writing, while the literate daughter, likely a stand-in for Hurston herself, is the one for whom the joke of the story is inaccessible. The story, writes Johnson, is an indictment neither of the literate, "educated" daughter nor her illiterate father but rather a parable whose "irony is directed both ways."[35] In yet another substitution, Johnson's position as interpreter and critic means that her position aligns with Hurston/the daughter, yet another identification across race.

In many ways, "Thresholds of Difference," like "The Re(a)d and the Black," positions Johnson as the privileged insider, the listener in the know. Johnson, by her own account a white outsider, nonetheless understands the inside joke of the story at the end of *Mules and Men* by virtue of both her attention to Hurston's language and her own deconstructive expertise. Like the author of *Mules and Men*, Johnson engages in a "practice of... listening ethnography, a practice that itself enacts the idea of listening to someone listen."[36] Taking this line of thought further, Johnson's attempts to interpret "(clucking noise)" not only place Johnson in Hurston's position but also place her more generally in the position that—writing four years later in 1989—Mae G. Henderson reserves for Black feminist critics and authors. Henderson argues that Black women writers employ both heteroglossia (which she defines as "the ability to speak in diverse known languages")[37] and glossolalia (the ability to speak in tongues). While *glossolalia* is defined as speaking a language that cannot be translated, heteroglossia is defined by the power to hear and interpret. If, as Henderson proposes, "Black women writers speak in tongues" and Black feminist critics are "charged with the hermeneutical task of interpreting tongues," then insomuch as she attempts to interpret "(clucking noise)," Johnson possesses an intimate knowledge that allows her to write as if she is the Black feminist critic Henderson describes.[38]

Johnson's text theatrically stages her own negotiations of identity and identification in the form of an ethical dilemma about being a "white deconstructionist" speaking and writing to a specific audience or specific audiences: "In preparing to write this paper, I found myself repeatedly stopped by conflicting conceptions of the structure of address into which I was inserting myself.... It was not clear to me what I, a white deconstructionist, was doing talking about Zora Neale Hurston, a Black novelist and anthropologist, or to *whom* I was talking."[39] She begins her piece not by discussing the Hurston text with which her essay purportedly deals but with a metaquestion of the essay's address: Why, and for whom, is Johnson writing? The problem of address constitutes both Johnson's metacritical framework and her analytic for discussing Hurston's work. In fact, she ends up analyzing Hurston through the same critical framework she first applied to herself: The initial meditation on how Johnson's project complicates the insider/outsider binary smoothly segues into a discussion of the problem of address in Hurston's ethnographic studies themselves—studies that, according to Johnson, similarly complicate questions of the insider/outsider divide.

"Thresholds of Difference" garners critical response far beyond Gates's eulogistic citation. Johnson's essay is appealing bait for many of her contemporaries because, despite being a scant twelve pages long, it makes several different, and at times contradictory, moves throughout its course. One of the essay's main detractors, Elizabeth Abel, argues that "Thresholds of Difference" ultimately serves to problematically eschew important differences between Johnson and the Black authors about whom she is writing. Abel contrasts Johnson's deconstructive writing on gender with her writing on race to show how Johnson is more reluctant to erase difference across the female/male hierarchy than she is along the Black/white hierarchy: "Johnson's relentlessly deconstructive discourse on race subverts the equivalent gestures that would subject her own role as a white deconstructor to her critique of masculine deconstructions of gender. This difference within her practice of deconstruction, the undoing of a counterpart for race to the feminist resistance to deconstruction, facilitates the project of writing across race. The interlocutory situation that requires the white critic to acknowledge racial difference also requires her to dissolve the tension between literal and figurative, political and philosophical, voluntary and involuntary modes of sameness and difference."[40] This difference is occasioned by the real-world positions in which Johnson and Hurston find themselves (as white woman in the 1990s and Black woman in the 1920s, respectively). "The fluidity of [Johnson's] boundary transgression, however, conceals an important difference between Hurston crossing the boundaries between subject and object, North and South, literate and oral communities, and Johnson or her white readers crossing a racial boundary," Abel writes.[41] Arguing that Johnson plays a clever rhetorical trick that makes her "figuratively Black," Abel ultimately finds Johnson's identification far too easy, as the deconstructive analysis of "Thresholds of Difference" privileges the figurative over the literal and ends up "dislocating race from historically accreted differences in power."[42] In response to Johnson's deconstructionism, Abel calls for a materialist feminist criticism that "operate[s] from a model of difference rather than similarity."[43]

While it is true that Johnson's identifications decidedly cross race—the parallel structures of address that she lays out clearly align her with Hurston—I question whether she is passing as seamlessly as Abel would have her readers believe. Put simply, we know Johnson is white because Johnson *lets us know*. Indeed, Abel's punishing review of Johnson fails to take into account the ways in which Johnson repeatedly outs herself. When Abel argues that Johnson's "ability to fool us" rhetorically erases racial difference, she conveniently sidesteps the fact that Johnson constantly reminds her readers that she is white. Even if, by Abel's account, "in the course of Johnson's essay, a discourse on positionality comes to displace, as well as to produce, a discourse on race," the fact remains that, in contrast to her rather anonymous standpoint in "The Re(a)d and the Black," in "Thresholds of Difference" Johnson's identifications with Hurston are made explicit as well as problematized.[44]

SIGNIFYING GAPS

Indeed, whenever Johnson explicitly draws attention to her cross-racial identifications and desires, the moment catalyzes a reflection on the unknowability of self. In the first few pages of the introduction to *The Feminist Difference*, Johnson offers a parenthetical confession: "Toni Morrison's *Beloved* comes to stand as a test text for both the value and the limits of a psychoanalytic perspective, but also for the question of 'white feminist critics' obsession with African American women's texts'—an obsession which, clearly, I share."[45] The introduction's later nod to Gates's *"Race,"* *Writing, and Difference* (1986)—a volume edited by Gates in which her essay on Hurston is reprinted—adds evidence of this obsession and indicates Johnson's own affiliations with "African-American criticism," even as she sets "race" up as something "other people" are talking about. Citing not only Gates but also Hortense J. Spillers's groundbreaking work "'All the Things You Could Be by Now, If Sigmund Freud's Wife Was Your Mother': Psychoanalysis and Race," Johnson stages an imagined conversation between feminist camps and sets up yet another connection that makes clear an intellectual intimacy not only between Spillers, Gates, and Johnson but also among desire, race, reading, and writing.[46] Borrowing a page from Gates's book, there are almost always quotes around "race," linking the conspicuous punctuation to Gates's previous scholarship and to literal quoted speech.

This fleeting appearance of the first-person singular in "an obsession which, clearly, I share," relegated to the status of soliloquy by a conspiratorial em dash, constitutes a Johnsonian passing aside. Despite Johnson's wry note that her desires are already "clear," her aside is so momentary that it is easy to miss. Citing not herself but her contemporary Jane Gallop as her primary example of white feminist "anxiety" and "obsession" with both Black feminist theory and Black-authored texts, Johnson performs the very displacement she theorizes. Indeed, in a seeming mise en abyme of layered quotation, she cites others citing Gallop: "Several contributors [to *Female Subjects in Black and White*] allude to Jane Gallop's controversial formulation of her transferential relation to Black feminist critics: 'I realized that the set of feelings I used to have about French men I now have about African-American women.'"[47] Johnson, like many others, is obsessed with this quote.[48] Placed alongside the Gallop quote-within-a-quote, Johnson's own desire is displaced and then confronted in a passing afterthought, a grammatical construction that playfully mimics the same dance of disavowal and transference plaguing the white feminist scene at the time.

If intimacy engenders what Lauren Berlant calls "an aesthetics of attachment," then the obsession showcased in Johnson's parenthetical presents an attachment deeply bound up with desire.[49] In a later chapter of *The Feminist Difference* titled "The Alchemy of Style and Law," Johnson again theorizes anxiety and desire in white feminist criticism, this time situating that anxiety at an impasse she names "the lesbian gap."[50] "The Alchemy of Style and Law" is a response to the critical reception of Patricia J. Williams's *The Alchemy of Race and Rights* (1991), a postmodern work of critical legal autotheory. Diagnosing the negative feedback the work receives, Johnson argues that Williams is working between a rock and a hard place: She is criticized both because her theory-laden, postmodernist vocabulary and style purportedly address a niche, insider academic audience and because, as someone writing from the Black female subject position, any attempt to insert "the personal" into her work falls outside the acceptable bounds of legal theoretical discourse. As is typical of much of Johnson's work, she begins by writing about Blackness as a primary articulation of difference within feminist politics and theory, but she once again gets there by way of another articulation of difference: lesbian sexuality.

In this essay, as elsewhere, Johnson argues for a postmodern feminism that focuses on differences among women rather than between women and men.[51] Johnson calls the space that would address differences among women "the lesbian gap" simply because she imagines this conversation as two women facing each other. The lesbian gap stands in for the indeterminacy "produced by material difference," an indeterminacy that is important to feminist practice because "the project of

bringing about change on the basis of a category like 'woman' will eventually encounter the lack of fit between 'woman' and the heterogeneous reality of women."
The lesbian gap is thus about the rifts in feminist politics and practice that only
become visible when women face each other and about the systems of heteropatriarchy and racism that produce the gap. The gap itself, she writes, "may not have
anything erotic or sexual about it," but she nonetheless codes it as lesbian by virtue
of this imagined structure.[52] Labeling this gap "lesbian" also names sexual orientation as, like race, another possible point of practical and experiential divergence
between feminists.

Johnson introduces the gap by telling a story about the death of another critic
and colleague: Mary Joe Frug, a law professor who was murdered while Johnson
was teaching at Harvard. In this short anecdotal deviation, Johnson tells the story
of a difficult writing assignment: She must respond to an unfinished piece by Frug,
a piece commissioned by the *Harvard Law Review* and provisionally titled "A Postmodern Feminist Manifesto." The essay to which Johnson must respond is not only
unfinished; it is unexpectedly posthumous—Frug, Johnson explains, was halfway
through her *Harvard Law Review* piece when she went out on a walk and was stabbed
to death by an anonymous assailant. Johnson is faced not only with the death of a
friend and colleague but also with the daunting task of interpreting and responding to her last work—a work that is only halfway complete. Johnson describes encountering a troubling, truncated sentence:

> Not only was [Frug's] essay itself unfinished at her death; she got up to go
> out for her fatal walk in the middle of a sentence. Here is the sentence:
>
> > Women who might expect that sexual relationships with other women
> > could
>
> Then she gets up, she goes out, she dies. The sentence dangles in the
> middle of the essay, which continues for another nine pages. Now my as-
> signment is to read the text.[53]

Faced with the literal death of the author, Johnson confronts a "linguistic predica-
ment": How can she read the blank space?[54] Johnson muses on what it might mean
to try to read a structuring absence, particularly one left in the wake of Frug's murder, particularly one that has to do with the signifier "lesbian."

The trauma of this untimely murder is evident if only because its aftereffects
resonate throughout Johnson's critical oeuvre. In fact, she tells a different version
of this story in an earlier essay, "Double Mourning and the Public Sphere." Johnson's earlier essay, published in *The Wake of Deconstruction* (1994), reads at various
points as a remembrance of her former teacher Paul de Man, a eulogy for a recently

murdered feminist law professor, and a work of deconstructionist criticism. Linking the many declared "deaths" of deconstruction to the paradoxes of authorial identity after Roland Barthes's seminal essay "The Death of the Author," Johnson grapples with posthumous revelations that de Man wrote numerous antisemitic, pro-Nazi articles while he was still in living Belgium. "Should a theory be judged by the character of the theorist?" she asks. "How can such a 'character' be known? Which de Man are we judging? . . . As a literary theorist, I have come to regard 'identity' as a constantly shifting, discontinuous, ungrounded fiction."[55] In *The Feminist Difference*, Johnson tells the story of Frug not once but twice: first in the chapter following "Lesbian Spectacles" ("The Alchemy of Style and Law") and then in the chapter immediately following that one ("The Postmodern in Feminism: A Response to Mary Joe Frug," an essay, we are told, that is Johnson's initial response to Frug's unfinished text).

In trying to explain the unexplainable, Johnson, too, finds herself unable to communicate across the simple divide of author and audience. This is another gap. In every case, something is lost in translation—lost in the move between oral and written, between Black and white, between postmodernism and feminism, between lesbianism and heterosexuality, between feminism "facing out" and feminism "facing in," between "inside" the academy and "outside" it. All this depends on address across a gap of material (and, in the case of death, ontological) difference. "When it came back from its first reading, the editors had changed 'How does this gap signify' to 'What does this gap mean?'" she writes. Johnson refuses to make the edit on the grounds that is it not at all the same question: "'How does the gap signify' raises the question of what it means to mean, raises meaning as a question, implies that the gap has to be read, but that it can't be presumed to have been intended."[56] That Johnson gets to the "lesbian gap" through a discussion of Williams's style suggests that the living Black female law professor, the dead white female law professor, and the absent "lesbian" all share a postmodern academic voice that reads to both the editors of the *Harvard Law Review* and the *New York Times Book Review* like a "foreign" or "encoded" language.[57] As Johnson explains, the primary question Johnson raises—"How does this gap signify?"—fails to translate.

LOVELY COLLEGE WORDS

At other points in *The Feminist Difference*, the failure of translation paradoxically becomes the main point of identificatory connection. In a chapter titled "'Aesthetic' and 'Rapport' in Toni Morrison's *Sula*," Johnson posits that the main draw of Morrison's work (for, she notes, Black readers especially) is its ability to produce a notion of "home" that is already lost. Here, as in "Thresholds of Difference," Johnson again begins with a metaquestion regarding her audience. The chapter begins with a speculation on why *Sula* (1973) holds such importance for many Black critics: "How does *Sula*—a novel that holds up a mirror for Black men, displaced Southerners, and Black lesbians—manage to produce so strong a mechanism for recognition?"[58] After a brief survey of various critics and readers of *Sula*, Johnson goes on to argue that Morrison achieves the feeling of "lost home" by playing with the tension between two "academic and foreign" words: *aesthetic* and *rapport*.[59] Johnson pulls these words from a pivotal scene in the middle of the novel in which Nel has just walked in on her husband, Jude, having sex with her best friend Sula. The scene, which is narrated from Nel's point of view, contains the following monologue: "I just stood there seeing it and smiling, because maybe there was some explanation, something important I did not know about that would have made it all right. I waited for Sula to look up at me any minute and say one of those lovely college words like *aesthetic* or *rapport*, which I never understood but which I loved because they sounded so comfortable and firm."[60] Nel watches and waits for Sula to look up, to see her and say something, so that Nel might hear it. Nel never gets to hear the words *aesthetic* and *rapport*. Sula fails to fulfill Nel's desire to be seen and spoken to; too busy with sex, Sula fails to narrate the scene in ways that would allow for impersonal detachment, distance, or analysis. In *Sula*, Morrison frequently places Nel in the position of disinterested watcher, particularly in scenes of sex such as the above and scenes of violence such as the accidental death of Chicken Little. In this latter scene, a young Nel looks on with detached pleasure as Sula swings a toddler into the river, killing him; later, Sula will accuse Nel of "watching" while he drowned, a charge that, in making her a willing accessory to murder, strips Nel of any claim to innocence.[61]

In Johnson's essay, the guilty pleasure of watching extends to the critic/reader herself—particularly the white critic/reader. If Nel is already linked to the white critic/reader by virtue of her voyeuristic position relative to Sula and Chicken Little, she is further linked to the white critic/reader by her voyeuristic position relative to Sula and Jude. Insofar as she casts herself in the position of desiring voyeur, Johnson identifies with the protagonist Nel, who looks on in scenes of sex and violence, adultery and murder. An accidental but nonetheless "smiling" onlooker, Nel remains fixated by the scene of illicit sex playing out before her. Like Nel, the white reader takes pleasure in observing the pornographic scene of adultery playing out before her. Like Nel, they also might attempt to assuage white guilt with academic distance; by Nel's account, Sula's sexual act with Jude is the thing that the vocabulary of the academy would cover up, would make "all right." Insofar as she plays the role of literary academic, Johnson identifies with Nel's counterpart, Sula, whose college degree alienates her from Nel and the other residents of the

Bottom—*aesthetic* and *rapport* are not only "foreign" words but also "college words," employed in universities (universities, perhaps, not dissimilar to the very "French" Yale of the 1980s from which Johnson, Miller, and Gates all hail).[62] In turn, these identifications might extend to Morrison, who herself is an academic and who, Johnson observes, likely writes with the knowledge that her book will be taught to (mostly white) college students.

Ultimately, Johnson posits that the entirety of *Sula* is about the interplay between aesthetics and rapport and, by extension, about the tension between the pleasure of artistic consumption and the danger of aestheticizing death or violence. For Johnson, the strange associations of aesthetics and rapport—as seemingly arbitrary, as foreign, as denoting artistic pleasure and sincere communication, respectively—precisely constitute the key to cracking the code of Morrison's novel and, perhaps, the key to ethically reading as a white subject. "The words 'aesthetic' and 'rapport,' in addition to coming from what could be called 'another scene'—both college and foreign—also both contain silent letters, signaling their status as writing, that is, as themselves silent letters. Silent because not oral—and in writing, the sign of the oral has conventionally been the missing letter rather than the silent letter, although the missing letter is marked by a diacritical mark like an apostrophe which is all the more obviously a sign of writing in its completely unphonetic dimension," she writes.[63] The apostrophe, here a visual sign denoting an unheard phoneme, further confuses the relation between sight, hearing, reading, speaking, and writing.

As in "Thresholds of Difference," Johnson again names her whiteness. In so doing, she draws attention to an insistent cross-identification, attachment, and desire. Unlike her previously clunky introductions, this reveal remains deferred until the end of "'Aesthetic' and 'Rapport.'" Even then, Johnson's admission comes in the form of a collective pronoun, couched in an inquiry. The essay raises more questions than it answers: "And what about the white reader? Is there a greater likelihood that the white reader will merely 'watch'? Is this a form of racial voyeurism? What is the nature of our pleasure in contemplating trauma or racial injustice or the destruction of the 'home' of the other? What would be a response that would embody rapport rather than aesthetics?"[64] Breaking the fourth wall and directly hailing a group of assumed readers, Johnson's text apostrophically brings said readers into being and, in so doing, makes her white self and her white readership visible. Johnson's direct address—her "passing asides," as it were—is an example of performative intimacy with an audience; these asides are short, digressive turns away from the text and toward Johnson's readers. The *our* in "what is the nature of our pleasure" performs double duty: It outs Johnson as white by way of the personal pronoun, and it links her to other white readers by way of the plural pronoun (in other words, it is working via mechanisms of identification). The *our* in Johnson, like its first-person cousin *we*, invokes "that towering inferno of universalism" and "tantalizing hallucination" of identity-based academic discourse.[65] Johnson's prose refuses to shy away from the personal plural pronoun, but unlike a more universalizing *we*, Johnson's *our* is more specific: Here, the *we* points to her identification with a group of white readers.[66] Her *our* makes these rhetorical questions personal for white consumers of Morrison's fiction, particularly for those white readers who also write literary criticism. It also orients her question to the presumed white readership of *The Feminist Difference*; the *our* becomes a gesture that directly addresses not only white readers of *Sula* but also the imagined white readers of Johnson's critique of *Sula*, who may look to her as a critical authority or make assumptions about her identity that she seeks to undermine.

Read in the context of the 1990s, Johnson's *our* interrogates what *we* is formed and how, when white readers collectively read and witness scenes of anti-Black violence. The loaded first-person plural recalls another text published around the same time as "'Aesthetic' and 'Rapport'": Elizabeth Alexander's poignant analysis of the video footage of the beating of Rodney King published in 1994. Here, Alexander tackles the question of the *we* as it relates to shared identifications formed in the process of viewing images of anti-Black violence. In an almost direct foil to Johnson's white *our*, Alexander's *we* refers to those Black viewers who find themselves all at once the target of, witness to, and potential participant in systems of racial terror. Echoing photographer Pat Ward Williams's provocation "Can you be BLACK and look at this?" (from 1986's *Accused/Blowtorch/Padlock*), Alexander traces a history of scenes of subjection (from the whipping of Frederick Douglass's Aunt Hester/Esther, to the mutilated body of Emmett Till, to the videotaped beating of Rodney King) in order to outline how the collective memory of violence is "burned into [the] nightmares and imaginations" of Black Americans.[67] Such spectacles, she argues, ironically forge a collective Black identity even as they reinforce racist images of the Black body as something to be beaten, policed, and murdered: "The far more potent terrain is the one that allows us to explore the ways in which traumatized African American viewers have been taught a sorry lesson of their continual physical vulnerability in the United States that concurrently helps shape how to understand ourselves as a 'we,' even when that we is differentiated," she writes.[68] Alexander draws a connection between the muteness of the police brutality captured in the Rodney King video and its use as evidence against police brutality in court; this leads her to posit that the visual carries with it a unique racist power—a belief Johnson shares.

Johnson's essay, in some ways a complement to Alexander's, asks what it means "to be white and look at/listen to" Black-authored texts. Here, again, the problems presented by the (white, critical) listening ear rear their head. Autumn Womack, revisiting Alexander's analysis in the wake of George Floyd's murder in a piece titled "Can You Be Black and Listen to This?," draws attention to Alexander's optimistic faith in the aural over the visual. Reflecting on the ways in which an audio clip might participate in the same or similar systems of circulation as a video clip, Womack challenges this optimism. "Yet as these sound fragments get recomposed into political action, I am worried that the soundscape risks enacting another form of abstraction," she writes. "But when it comes to convicting offending officers in the cases of anti-Black violence, has sound delivered on its promise?"[69] On its surface, Johnson's essay grapples with the uncomfortable fact that the structure of white readers consuming Black-authored texts might all too easily replicate the scenes of subjection analyzed by Alexander, Saidiya V. Hartman, and others. To be sure, Johnson's expressed anxiety about an interested disinterest, a "racial voyeurism" that, like Nel's own watching, entails standing back in silent contemplation of the scenes of "trauma, taboo, and violation" detailed in Morrison's prose, recalls the scenes of looking described by Hartman in which the production, circulation, and consumption of scenes of Black suffering by white readers in the nineteenth century "effaces and restricts Black sentience."[70] For Hartman, white identification with scenes of suffering ends up replacing Black subjects with white subjects by way of "empathetic" relation: "Empathy fails to expand the space of the other, but merely places the self in its stead. This is not to suggest that empathy can be discarded or that . . . [the] desire to exist in the place of the other can be dismissed as a narcissistic exercise but rather to highlight the dangers of a too-easy intimacy, the consideration of the self that occurs at the expense of the slave's suffering, and the violence of identification."[71] Intimacy—because it is too easy—becomes suspicious.

But Johnson's intimacy is anything but easy. Shifting focus from the circulation of images of Black suffering to her own critical readership of mid-century Black-authored fiction, Johnson's text theatrically rehearses anxieties surrounding how to read scenes of subjection across the color line and thus undoes her own position. Johnson's focus on Nel's sin of "indifference"—a sin she extends to an imagined audience of white literary critics—leads her to depart from Hartman's analysis. While Hartman regards empathy as a mode of relation worthy of much suspicion, Johnson continues to attempt identification across race despite the attendant problematics of power entailed in such an enterprise. In so doing, her text places her definitively in the ambivalent position, famously formulated by Frederick Douglass, of being both "witness and participant" to and in systems of racial violence.[72] But as Sharpe and others point out, although Douglass describes his own experience as a Black child witnessing an act of extreme anti-Black violence, he also, in doing so, deliberately "positions his white readers to reckon with what he knows about the all-encompassing and routinized violence in slavery, positions them to see that they are a witness to and participant in brutal scenes of conception and transformation."[73] Put another way, the intimacies rehearsed in Johnson's literary criticism cleave to the monstrous intimacies named and theorized by Sharpe, albeit in a more quotidian iteration. Wary of how a desire for cross-identification or empathy across difference might result in what Hartman calls a "too-easy intimacy," Johnson performs a second intimacy with her readership, breaking the fourth wall through strategic soliloquy, various comings out, and wry allusion. In doing so, she deliberately highlights a cross-identificatory closeness that might be embarrassing, politically undesirable, or unsettling.

LOOKING LIKE A LESBIAN

Johnson's experiments with textual intimacy also complicated the autoidentificatory demands of standpoint feminist theory. Theatrically failing to identify "as" categories that otherwise obviously describe her, Johnson's *as if!* critical writing highlights the "difference within" a seemingly knowable authorial position. In "'Aesthetic' and 'Rapport,'" Johnson reads Morrison's novel "as" a white woman; shortly after this chapter, Johnson will explicitly attempt to read "as a lesbian"—one of the few times in her work where she claims to do so—in an essay titled "Lesbian Spectacles: Reading *Sula, Passing, Thelma and Louise,* and *The Accused.*" By her own account, Johnson picks *Sula* and *Passing* because they are both "crypto-lesbian" texts—that is, they both have plots structured around a homosocial bond between two women that is not explicitly sexual but, given the right reader, is interpretable as such.[74] Like her confessional in "'Aesthetic' and 'Rapport,'" Johnson's approach in "Lesbian Spectacles" explicitly foregrounds the difficulties of straightforward or obvious identification. Here, almost as if she has anticipated Miller's "Call for Papers," Johnson sarcastically details her attempts to "read explicitly as a lesbian."[75] She accomplishes this by staging her unsuccessful attempt to read two novels, Nella Larsen's *Passing* (1929) and Morrison's *Sula,* and to watch two films, *Thelma and Louise* (1991) and *The Accused* (1988). Johnson defines the project of "Lesbian Spectacles" as an attempt to "take account of my particular desire structure in reading rather than try to generalize about desire as such, even lesbian desire 'as such.'"[76]

In this way, "Lesbian Spectacles" references the spectacles of lesbian desire that Johnson sees in the fictional scenes she analyzes—the display of desire that readers and audience members need only to look for. Johnson takes inspiration from the work of Nancy K. Miller, whose essay "Untitled Work, or, Speaking as a Feminist . . ." (1991) meditates on the professional academic injunction—in women's studies departments in particular—to theorize, speak, and write from the position one finds themselves in. Similarly, Johnson defines "reading as a lesbian" as reading alongside her own desire. Such a method, she writes, "plunges the speaker into new questions of reliable representivity and identity."[77] The works that Johnson cites as critical precedents for her lesbian experiment are by Black feminist theorists: "I took my inspiration for such a textual category from two readings of literary texts: Barbara Smith's reading of Toni Morrison's *Sula* and Deborah McDowell's reading of Nella Larsen's novel *Passing*. I cite these critics not because they offer me examples of the act of 'reading as a lesbian' (Smith does; McDowell does not) but because of the nature of the texts they read."[78] The Smith essay she references is literally titled "Toward a Black Feminist Criticism," while the McDowell piece, "The 'Nameless . . . Shameful Impulse': Sexuality in Nella Larsen's *Quicksand* and *Passing*," finds its home in McDowell's *"The Changing Same": Black Women's Literature, Criticism, and Theory* (1995). As such, Johnson's tongue-in-cheek performance of "reading as a lesbian" also shows a connection between "lesbian reading" and Black feminist criticism.

In six quick pages, Johnson's essay performs the dramatic failure of autoidentification—that is, an identification that, ostensibly, squares with her own erotic desire. In doing so, her text makes painfully visible the problematics of desire and politics in feminist writing. Ultimately, Johnson ends up cutting the enterprise short: Already skeptical from the start, she finds the personal politics uncovered by this new method untenable. Johnson's initial skepticism about the difficulty of speaking and writing "as a ____" rests on the deconstructive premise that there is no stable identity, only difference, and on the psychoanalytic assumption that there is no way of "reading as a lesbian" because there is no lesbian desire "as such," no category of fully knowable, conscious, or articulated desire. In other words, because the question of "lesbian" identity or desire already proves a doozy for Johnson, the question of what constitutes "reading as a lesbian" remains unresolved throughout her essay. In a contribution to a special issue of *differences* dedicated to memorializing Johnson, Jane Gallop contends that Johnson—aware of the political paradox of identity—performs a politics of speaking "as a ____" even if she theorizes otherwise. Gallop's analysis revisits another anecdote that Johnson tells in "Double Mourning and the Public Sphere," in which a fellow critic writes her a postcard asking if the title of her essay could be construed as a reference to the figure of death in deconstructive theory. Ignoring the provided boxes for "yes" and "no," Johnson responds, "Yes and no (what else?)." Seizing on this "odd phraselet," Gallop argues that "yes and no (what else?)" accurately describes not only the typical arc of Johnson's deconstructive argument but also her relationship to identity politics. Gallop tracks instances in which Johnson purports to read or speak "as a ____," contending that Johnson is in favor of claiming and declaring one's own critical position, as when she writes "certainly, *as a lesbian*" but resists being read "as a ____" (that is, she is resistant to being interpellated as one readable identity).[79]

Some years later, Corey McEleney expands on Gallop's analysis of Johnson by way of Miller's eulogy. Taking Miller's plea for more intimate critical attention to Johnson's style as a challenge, McEleney uses Johnson's particular way of writing to issue a call for a more "astonishing," more explicitly deconstructive queer theory. At various points, by McEleney's telling, Johnson reads "with astonishment" but also with "interruption," "irony," "torsions," "gaps," and "snags"; she participates in reading "otherwise" and reading "as an 'other.'"[80] For McEleney, who draws heavily on Johnson's close association with the Yale School, reading "as a lesbian" means reading to resist identity politics—that is, reading deconstructively. "If I tried to 'speak as a lesbian,'" Johnson asks, "wouldn't I be processing my understanding of myself through media-induced images of what a lesbian is or through my own idealizations of what a lesbian *should* be?"[81] To reconcile her deconstructionist misgivings about the reliability of identity and the imperative to nonetheless read along the grain of her own erotic attachments, Johnson redefines *reading as a lesbian* to mean a kind of hermeneutics of lesbian suspicion. "I needed a way of catching myself in the act of reading as a lesbian without having intended to," she writes. "To accomplish this, I decided to look at novels or films that did *not* present themselves explicitly as 'lesbian,' but that could, through interpretation, be said to have a crypto-lesbian plot," hence *Passing, Sula, Thelma and Louise*, and *The Accused*.[82] The verbal acrobatics of this sentence—namely, Johnson's amassing of qualifiers ("could," "through interpretation," "be said to," "crypto-lesbian")—bespeaks her unease at such a reading project.

Ultimately, *Passing* "works" as a lesbian text more than Morrison's text, at least according to Johnson's "inner lesbo-meter," because of two factors: repeated negation ("It is erotic to me that Irene's 'no' constantly becomes a yes") and a description of a "long stare" between Clare and Irene.[83] Ultimately, it is not deconstructive questions of identity but the tricky politics of desire that stop her in her analytic tracks. This unease soon manifests into embarrassing and theatrical failure when Johnson realizes a shocking thing about her own disturbing attachments. Mortified, she writes that what "works" for her about the two texts she identifies as lesbian (*Passing* and *The Accused*) is in fact the erotic appeal of a power dynamic that mirrors a heteropatriarchal schema. Unable to distinguish between her own lesbian desire and her desire to own her lesbian desire (that is, unable to distinguish genuine lesbian desire from her own idea of what lesbian desire should be, especially in the context of an acceptable feminist politics), Johnson abruptly ends her essay. Having attempted her lesbian reading, Johnson concludes by admitting that the pleasures of one's criticism and desire can often clash with one's political commitments. The chapter ends just after this admission, as if criticism cannot continue in the wake of Johnson's revelation. Wary of the political implications of reading with her desire, she throws up her hands in campy resignation. As she quips in a one-sentence paragraph before concluding: "So much for reading with the unconscious."[84]

On its surface, this essay stops short because Johnson finds fault in her own motives "as" a lesbian reader. These motives are explicitly described in gendered, not racial, terms. However, tackling *Sula* and *Passing* in "Lesbian Spectacles," Johnson also obliquely explores the racial dynamics at play in her own textual object choices. Both *Sula* and *Passing* are written by Black women authors, and each novel deals specifically with a bond between two Black women who negotiate their Blackness and womanness in different ways. (Interestingly, in almost every other discussion of "Lesbian Spectacles," white critics writing about Johnson ignore these first two examples, preferring instead to skip to *Thelma and Louise* and *The Accused*. The notable exception here is Pamela L. Caughie's "The Example of Barbara Johnson," which, remarkably, ignores the lesbian discussion entirely so that she might mark Johnson's work on *Passing* as an example of Johnson's proclivity for writing about Black-authored texts.)[85] Because of her avowed method, which takes the personal as its rubric, "Lesbian Spectacles" extends this structure of desire to something that looks a lot like the structures of monstrous intimacy desire outlined by Sharpe and others—that is, an interracial interpersonal intimacy in which "'no' constantly becomes a yes."[86] If *Passing* is, as McDowell and others argue, a narrative of lesbian desire passing as a narrative of racial passing, then Johnson's analysis of *Passing* is a narrative of cross-racial desire passing as a narrative of lesbian desire. The former identified anxiety is that Johnson's desire betrays (in both senses—revelatory and traitorous) the politics of feminist criticism that works toward gender equality; the latter unnamed but still consciously performed anxiety is that Johnson's desire betrays with the politics of feminist criticism that works toward racial equality. Johnson's surprise encounter with her own white desire for Blackness, though it lurks beneath the surface, nonetheless stops her criticism in its tracks. In other words, bound up with Johnson's explicitly stated anxiety—that her personal erotic attachments to *Passing*, but not to *Sula*, reveal a personal erotic preference for the power dynamics of patriarchy—is another revelation: namely, that her critical attachments to both *Passing* and *Sula* reveal a critical and erotic preference for the asymmetrical power dynamics of white supremacy.

It is not interesting, or particularly fruitful, to chastise Johnson (the person or the critic) for these intimate critical attachments; instead, it is useful to highlight how these critical attachments are purposefully revealed and what that revelation does. In "Lesbian Spectacles," Johnson's personal positioning complicates the autoidentification that proponents of "reading as a ____" assume is simple. This disruption, once again, mirrors Robinson's "one who knows" structure: Though the text doesn't make this argument explicitly, I posit that what Johnson finds sexy about *Passing* is not merely eye contact but also the knowing look of the in-group clairvoyant—a look that is about identification in both a transitive and an intransitive sense. According to Johnson, the eye contact between the two protagonists is sexy because it conjures up the image of two women standing to face each other. For Johnson, the looks between *Passing*'s two main protagonists, Clare Kendry and Irene Redfield, become the primary site of lesbian desire. The "protracted and intense eye contact" that Johnson names as an identifying sign of lesbian structures of desire further emphasizes the visual (a theme that is indeed a trope of Larsen's text—as evidenced even on the level of the two protagonists' first names, which sonically connote "clear" and "eye").[87] But in each scene of staring that Johnson describes, the looks exchanged between Clare and Irene are much more specific. Importantly, the looks in *Passing* are looks in which each looker is cruising for information. It is the look across the gap of nonmeaning; a look that is a desiring look, engaged in the frisky business of trying to figure someone out. In looking at Clare, Irene discovers a secret about Clare: She is passing.

Despite Johnson's hesitation to read *Sula* as a lesbian text, "'Aesthetic' and 'Rapport'" and "Lesbian Spectacles" both evoke an erotics of triangulated critical voyeurism. While Johnson focuses on the looks in *Passing* in "Lesbian Spectacles," she ignores the scenes of voyeurism in *Sula*, which she analyzes at length in "'Aesthetic' and 'Rapport.'" Despite naming it as one of her four main objects of examination, Johnson reserves no more than four sentences for *Sula* in "Lesbian Spectacles." In these four sentences, Johnson concludes that the novel does not, to her, read as lesbian because the friendship between Nel and Sula is both "overinvested" and "abundantly explained" (this despite her claims, in "'Aesthetic' and 'Rapport,'" that *Sula* is a highly ambiguous text).[88] This is perhaps because eye contact, as opposed to voyeurism, assumes the (lesbian) structure of two women facing each other. In *Sula*, both scenes of watching involve a trio, either Nel/Sula/Jude or Nel/Sula/Chicken Little. Following this line of thought, *Sula*'s visual and erotic structure of triangulation would exclude it from lesbian erotics. But Johnson herself points out in her initial gloss of *Passing* and *Sula* that, in both novels, "the intensity of the relation between two women is broken by a fall into triangulation."[89] The fact that *Passing* still sets off Johnson's inner lesbo-meter suggests that a triangular structure doesn't necessarily preclude a text from lesbian erotics. If anything, this triangulation also informs Johnson's own critical desires. As Miller notes in "Call for Papers," her own literary criticism frequently constructs triangulations:

In that cognitively enviable third position, she could give the series a sense of completion, put forward a decisive-seeming last word. Johnson liked that position, and no one played it better. But this time around, more remarkably, she seems interested in provoking a series in which she would occupy not the third but the second position, after Miller's essay on Barthes, and before.... You will have grasped the open secret harbored in the essay, the wish for a *third* essay to be called—inevitably—"Bringing Out Barbara Johnson," in which Barbara would be granted, as opposed to the critical advantage of coming last, the writerly privilege of being primary.[90]

Miller, reading Johnson's text for its underlying intimacies, claims that Johnson's (alleged) desire to be brought out constitutes a perverse wish to depose the triangle in which she plays the mediating third in a conversation between two prominent critics. In disavowing the lesbian erotics of *Sula* in "Lesbian Spectacles," the text implicitly draws a distinction here between the "eye contact" in *Passing* and the voyeurism in *Sula*. If, however, we read the erotics of the watching Johnson describes in *Sula* as similar to, rather than distinct from, the erotics of the looking described in her analysis of *Passing*, we can see how Johnson's voyeuristic and/or empathetic gaze in "'Aesthetic' and 'Rapport'" is related to her performance of the desiring critical gaze in "Lesbian Spectacles."

Here, Johnson's essay flips a familiar script. She makes sexuality (usually thought of as invisible) visible and race (usually thought of as visible) invisible. As Robinson points out, "Identity politics is figured as a skill of reading by African American and/or gay and lesbian spectators of the cultural performance of passing"; or, in other words, "what the in-group recognizes in the passing subject corroborates what Marilyn Frye proposes in *The Politics of Reality*: 'What lesbians see is what makes them lesbians.'"[91] Indeed, Johnson's essay is highly concerned with sight and visibility: It is primarily interested in the seen and the unseen, in metaphors and narratives of looking and staring. The title of "Lesbian Spectacles" itself alludes to Johnson's preoccupation with sight, but it also highlights her own dual position as writer/critic and reader/spectator. *Spectacles* can mean both "visually impactful scenes or displays" and "eyeglasses," and with the double entendre Johnson-the-lesbian-critic becomes both stager of scenes and observer of them. If we interpret *spectacles* as denoting reading glasses, the emphasis shifts to the spectator without granting her omniscience—one can imagine a playful pedagogical instruction that readers "put on their lesbian spectacles" in order to see the scenes Johnson describes as scenes of lesbian desire. This first meaning of *spectacles* intimates that even a critical project that professes to read from the perspective of "the personal" requires a supplement (an aid, a tool, a lens, a corrective) and is itself not adequate to the task of reading from an authentic individual perspective. Johnson herself, without the aid of the lesbian spectacles she assumes for her project of "reading as a lesbian," might not be able to see the very structures of desire she outlines. The second meaning of *spectacle*, which connotes a perhaps embarrassingly spectacular tableau (e.g., "making a spectacle of yourself"), could refer either to the literary scenes Johnson analyses or to the spectacle of the avowedly lesbian reader—that is, the spectacular mess that Johnson makes of her analysis when she attempts to put her own desires explicitly on display.

When she writes "(Smith does; McDowell does not)," Johnson first appears to participate in the very same identity gatekeeping of which she is normally quite suspicious and that "Lesbian Spectacles" seeks to resist. According to Johnson, McDowell, even though she practices "lesbian criticism," nonetheless does not write "as a lesbian." But then again, neither does Johnson. Taking this to heart, I propose we interpret "(Smith does; McDowell does not)" as an ironic camping of the academy's policing impulse, a moment that points not to the differences between Johnson's reading method and McDowell's but rather to their similarities. Performing Johnson's earlier concept of "difference within," in which "a text's difference is not its uniqueness, its special identity," but instead "its way of differing from itself," "Lesbian Spectacles" "subverts the very idea of identity, infinitely deferring the possibility of adding up the sum of a text's parts or meanings and reaching a totalized, integrated whole."[92]

PASSING ASIDES

In Johnson's later work, we witness another intimate triangulation: that between text, critic, and reader. Never coming out outright, but instead relying on her audience's ability to read between the lines, Johnson peppers her later texts with wry parenthetical asides, breaking the fourth wall and addressing her readers directly. Johnson's asides are on full display in *Mother Tongues: Sexuality, Trials, Motherhood, Translation* (2003), a collection of essays published five years after *The Feminist Difference*. Of the relatively few critics that specifically address Johnson's writing style, almost all mention her penchant for parentheses; so frequently are they mentioned, in fact, that we might take them as a Johnsonian trademark.[93] Johnson's asides suspend the action of the sentence, acting as a soliloquist apostrophe. In *Mother Tongues*, the Johnsonian parenthetical is in full form. Breaking the fourth wall via numerous passing asides, Johnson surprises us with a low-stake jump scare (There's a person here!). This grammatical quirk illustrates Johnson's efforts to remind her audience that there is a person behind her supposedly impersonal writing style.

The first example of this type of covert outing occurs early in the introduction, in a brief riff on Sappho, literary criticism, and the obscenity trial of Charles Baudelaire's *Les fleurs du mal* (1857). Early on in the essay, Johnson writes, "(While I was working on the first version of this paper on an airplane, surrounded by two translations and two studies of Sappho, I certainly felt as if I were exposing something that I normally hide!)."[94] Enclosing this small anecdote in between parentheses, Johnson both admits to hiding something and refuses to name the something that she hides. In this way, her text plays with the ambiguous mechanisms of "bringing out" that she describes in "Bringing Out D. A. Miller": "There is thus a connection between bringing out and an artist's autobiography, but by no means a direct one." Johnson, in her analysis of Miller's book, writes that although 'the figure being brought out is present everywhere, in every representation,' it is always "supplementary and ghostly, not the painting's subject but its mourner. The lineaments of face and form are dimly recognizable in the figure, whose very superfluity in pictorial reality is a clue to its function in autobiography."[95] Outing, even outing oneself, is here staged as an ambiguous process.

Rather than simply exposing herself, Johnson instead feels "as if" she is. In this instance, Johnson imagines that her fellow plane passengers are also in the know—that is, that they are somewhat familiar with classical literature (a generous assumption). The passengers on the plane, who may or may not "know" Sappho, may or may not interpret the presence of the "two translations and two studies" as indicating anything other than an inclination for ancient poetry. But in a way, it doesn't matter. The phrase "as if" in this aside anticipates another chapter of *Mother Tongues*, in which Johnson discusses the suspension of disbelief necessary for the teaching and study of comparative literature. The "as if" in her anecdote about reading Sappho on a plane acknowledges the bad suture that occurs in any translation. In this case, in echoing the "as if" that Johnson has already theorized extensively as the main mechanism of translation, this text connects the leap of faith it takes to move across the gap created by language difference to the leap of faith it takes her to imagine herself exposing "something."[96]

Johnson's second notable parenthetical aside appears in the final chapter of *Mother Tongues*, "Animate Alphabets." In this instance, Johnson performs a subtler, though still significant, bringing out. Johnson's analysis notes the culturally imagined divide between motherhood and lesbianism, citing Ted Hughes's homophobic appeal to critic Jacqueline Rose concerning critical speculation around Sylvia Plath's sexuality: "Hughes protested, as if innocently, that his intention had been to arouse her 'common (even maternal) sensibility.'... Ted Hughes speaks to Jacqueline Rose as though she has only to imagine properly, and she will be convinced. Think like a mother, he tells her, and not like a lesbian ... or an English teacher."[97]

Hughes's plea also sets up Rose's "maternal" intuition against her literary or critical one, a point upon which Johnson harps. "Here is another example of the opposition between mothers and lesbians. As if it were impossible to be both at once," she writes.[98] Here, I read the conjunction *or* not as dividing the two subject positions *lesbian* and *English teacher* but rather as denoting their exchangeability. In both excerpts, Johnson's parentheses or ellipses bracket out near-declarations—or covert self-outings—that leave it to wise readers to articulate what Johnson herself seems hesitant to admit outright. The first passage relies on a biographical anecdote: the story of Johnson "exposing" an implied but unnamed bit of information about herself in a semipublic place. The second relies on a biographical note about Johnson that is implied but again unnamed: She is, like Rose, an English teacher. It is clear here on what side of the death-lesbian/life-mother divide "English teachers" lie.

In each passing aside, Johnson's own authorial outing relies on a metonymic relation to literary signifiers: in the first case, Sappho; in the second, English teachers. Her snarky alliance of lesbians with both English teachers and those who read ancient poetry, separated from her main argument by ellipses, is a winking nod to the antisocial thrust of writing itself. Johnson writes that Hughes's letters to Rose betray "less a form of homophobia (although it is perhaps that) than an opposition between *life* and *reading*."[99] At other places in *Mother Tongues*, Johnson traces two lines of thought: one in which "the fact that the history of lyric poetry is so bound up with the nature of elegy has created the impression that the lyric was invented to overcome death, not desire it," and another that conflates "the desire for writing with the desire for death," noting that "both are desires for something other than biological life."[100] As Johnson later puts it in her discussions of Plath, "To read is to treat as dead."[101] As she writes in "Bringing Out D. A. Miller," "It is impossible to know whether one is bringing out the person or the writings. And *that* is what Barthes means by 'the death of the author.'"[102] Johnson does not come out explicitly as a lesbian (or, we might add, as dying; by this point, Johnson had been diagnosed with a terminal illness, a biographical fact that makes her extensive discussion of postmortem criticism even more potent). The literary critic is both a writer and a reader, and their criticism may simultaneously attempt, like those writers of lyric poetry, to reanimate lost objects through apostrophe and to acknowledge the (literal or figurative) death of the author.

THE CRITICAL MIDWIFE

Miller writes, early on in his eulogy, that Johnson "had no progeny—that too was the beauty of her achievement—yet she was midwife to a multitude."[103] What is the distinction between these two metaphors—"mother" and "midwife"—for authorship and critical practice? With Johnson's own work in the background, we might take Miller's assertion that "she had no progeny—that too was the beauty of her achievement" as a testament to her queer credentials: The point of Miller's essay, after all, is to "bring out" Barbara Johnson, reading her as both a lesbian critic and a queer stylist. Johnson's lack of progeny flies in the face of a patriarchal and heterosexist order that would, as Johnson puts it, make motherhood "the standard a woman hasn't met ('She may be a CEO, but she's childless'), or lesbianism an accusation so monstrous it provokes denial if at all possible ('We know what her problem is: she doesn't like men')."[104]

Before both *The Feminist Difference* and *Mother Tongues*, Johnson's essay "Apostrophe, Animation, and Abortion" (1986) tackled the problems of motherhood, authorship, and death. Johnson's moves in "Apostrophe, Animation, and Abortion" parallel her own pivot from de Manian deconstruction to psychoanalytic feminist, Black feminist, and lesbian feminist theory—a shift cemented by the publication of *The Feminist Difference*. Her essay spans a range of cross-cultural and cross-temporal examples in the process, moving from Charles Baudelaire to Percy Bysshe Shelley to several poets of the mid-twentieth century. Shifting focus in the last half of her essay from romantic male poets to a range of abortion-related contemporary poems by female authors, Johnson notes that, in each of the poems she analyzes, the speaker's address to aborted children complicates terms of address and loss in ways that echo but do not entirely mirror the losses at stake in the poems by Baudelaire and Shelley. Beginning with Gwendolyn Brooks's poem "the mother" (1945), Johnson outlines how poetry by these authors might disrupt the usual mechanism of apostrophe and address as it appears in the poems of their romantic predecessors. Because the distinction between self and other is less clear—the speaker's self is haunted and inhabited by the ghosts of those unborn fetuses who are ambiguously subjects—it is also unclear to whom the apostrophe is really addressed. The "you" animated by the apostrophe in Brooks, Johnson explains, is all at once poet, speaker, reader, mother, and aborted child. In each of the poems Johnson analyzes, the violence is similarly ambiguous: It is often uncertain if the poem describes an abortion, a miscarriage, or simply menstruation. In other words, it is ambiguous whether the poems address aborted fetuses or merely unactualized ones.

Johnson ends her essay with an abortion poem about poetry, "To a Poet" (1974), written by the white lesbian poet Adrienne Rich. It is here that Johnson drives her point home: The lack of clarity in each poem points to the underlying cultural imperative for women to be mothers—an imperative so strong that to use the flesh other than for childbirth amounts to a kind of murder (Johnson: "The word is not made flesh; rather, flesh unmakes the mother-poet's word"[105]). In this poem, Rich figures motherhood as "the death of poetry" and, conversely, figures the prevention or refusal of motherhood as the condition for poetic creation.[106] Johnson's use of *flesh* strongly evokes Spillers's "Mama's Baby, Papa's Maybe: An American Grammar Book," published the year after "Apostrophe, Animation, and Abortion." Carefully illuminating the ways in which rhetorical structures function with political, social, historical, psychological, and economic structures at the intersection of race, gender, and sexuality, Spillers's multifaceted essay argues that the legacy of US slavery means that, for Black women, "motherhood as female blood-rite is outraged, is denied, at the *very same time* that it becomes the founding term of a human and social enactment.... In this play of paradox, only the female stands *in the flesh*, both mother and mother-dispossessed."[107]

Miller's praise of Johnson's nonmotherhood gestures toward a broader split between queerness and reproductive futurism—a split often heralded by queer theory's antisocial turn and exemplified in Lee Edelman's 1998 essay "The Future Is Kid Stuff." Edelman includes an anecdote in which, walking through Harvard Square, he sees an antiabortion sign and believes it is directed at him:

> Not long ago, on a much-traveled corner in Cambridge, Massachusetts, opponents of the legal right to abortion posted an enormous image of a full-term fetus on a rented billboard accompanied by a single and unqualified assertion: "It's not a choice; it's a child." ... As strange as it may seem for a gay man to say this, when I first encountered that billboard in Cambridge I read it as addressed to me. The sign, after all, might as well have pronounced, with the same absolute and invisible authority that testifies to the successfully accomplished work of ideological naturalization, the divine injunction: "Be fruitful and multiply."[108]

The striking scene of interpellation tackles many of the issues with which Johnson herself was concerned, among them death, reproduction, rhetoric, and address. It also constitutes a moment of cross-identification, a brief instance of *as if!* writing in which a white gay man feels himself addressed, in a way, as a failed potential mother. Indeed, Edelman's essay echoes Johnson's work not only in its overlapping subject matter but also explicitly. In his original article, Edelman notes that "many critics, Barbara Johnson among them, have detailed with powerful insight how such anti-abortion polemics simultaneously rely on and generate tropes that animate, by personifying, the fetus"; in *No Future*, he directly cites "Apostrophe, Animation, and Abortion": "Barbara Johnson, in a dazzling analysis of anti-abortion polemics like this, has demonstrated how they borrow and generate tropes that effectively animate by personifying the fetus, determining in advance the answer to the juridical question of its personhood by means of the terms through which the fetus, and therefore the question, is addressed."[109] Edelman's essay bears much in common with Johnson's: While one analysis begins, and the other ends, with a tableau of the aborted fetus, both deal with the apostrophe of the sign's direct address, and both dwell on the reproductive imperative contained within it.

As the echo in their respective titles suggest, "Animate Alphabets" and "Apostrophe, Animation, and Abortion" pair well together. As was the case with "'Aesthetic' and 'Rapport'" and "Lesbian Spectacles," reading "Animate Alphabets" and "Apostrophe, Animation, and Abortion" in conjunction reveals the unspoken racial politics at work in both articles. In her analysis of Lucille Clifton's "the lost baby poem" (1972) in "Apostrophe, Animation, and Abortion," Johnson explores how the apostrophic rhetoric of abortion may function differently within Black motherhood. Johnson infers that the speaking mother is Black via context clues that invoke *Uncle Tom's Cabin* (1852), the Vietnam War draft, and a line that addresses Black men. Johnson writes:

> The guilt and mourning occur in the form of an imperative in which the notion of "stranger" returns in the following lines:
>
> > if I am ever less than a mountain
> > for your definite brothers and sisters . . . .
> > . . . let black men call me stranger
> > always for your never named sake.
>
> The act of "calling" here coordinates a lack of name with a loss of membership. For the sake of the one that cannot be called, the speaker invites an apostrophe that would expel her into otherness. The consequences of the death of a child ramify beyond the mother-child dyad to encompass the fate of an entire community. The world that has created conditions under which the loss of a baby becomes desirable must be resisted, not joined. For a black woman, the loss of a baby can always be perceived as a complicity with genocide.[110]

Here, Johnson's unequivocal assertion that "the loss of a baby can always be perceived as a complicity with genocide" suspiciously echoes the contemporary rhetorical strategies of many antichoice activists. These rhetorical strategies capitalize on the already-extant systems that make it difficult and dangerous to mother a Black child, targeting Black women who choose to get abortions as complicit actors against the reproductive future of their race.[111] At the same time, Johnson here also alludes to the disparate ways that a white supremacist state—even one in which antichoice sentiments prevail—specifically violates the reproductive rights of Black women, often through sterilization or forced abortion.[112] Johnson ultimately reads these poets to point out the duplicitous rhetorical trick of antiabortion political rhetoric. Simply by virtue of it being rhetoric, it assumes as an axiom the very thing it is trying to prove: the subjecthood of the unborn child to which it rhetorically refers.

The systemic silences Johnson discusses so often mean literal death, for both Black women and lesbians in and outside of the academy, and this means these debates are (still) not merely rhetorical. In a work from 1994, Barbara Christian employs a potent metaphor for her own position in the academy, writing that she is "an academic mother to more children than I could have possibly imagined, and to types of children beyond my conjuring . . . at a time when my white counterparts are already academic grandmothers."[113] Grace Kyungwon Hong, writing about the untimely early deaths of nearly an entire first generation of Black feminist academics, writes that while "questions of reproduction and generality . . . might not seem to pertain to academic life, quite the opposite is true."[114] Taking these questions into account, reading Christian's metaphor about both her own relation to her white counterparts and her diverse range of students alongside Miller's portrayal of Johnson as mother to none adds another dimension to Miller's assessment. As Holland points out, the turn away from reproduction in queer theory heralded by Edelman and others "is racially marked, not because it reveals a loss of Anglo-Saxon sanguinity per se, but because it also produces reproduction as a function of white racial belonging rather than as a function of all racial belonging."[115] Miller's praise implicitly also casts Johnson as a theorist whose refusal to become a mother is tied intimately to her whiteness, as a failed white mother unable to evidence either literal or figurative white "children" in her own personal or professional lineage. As such, metaphors of motherhood or midwifery are not impertinent to Johnson's own position as a white lesbian in the humanities.

Miller's declaration that Johnson was "midwife to a multitude" at first appears to draw a simple distinction between mothers, who give birth, and midwives, who assist. But midwifery carries with it a slew of alternative associations. *Midwife* comes from an Old English word meaning "with woman," a phrase that calls to mind a practice of close reading that reads "with" a text, bringing out its stylistic idiosyncrasies and paying close attention to the author's language choice.[116] As a metaphor at the intersection of writing, birth, the legacy of transatlantic slavery, abortion, direct address, pedagogy, poetry, and death, the figure of the midwife remains an uncanny analog for Johnson's wide-ranging and identity-crossing work. As a deconstructive theorist par excellence, Johnson read both with and against the grain. Her parenthetical asides break the fourth wall of her otherwise clear or elegant (some critics might even say "detached") prose with a colloquial and teasing soliloquy; here, Johnson is perhaps most "with" us, breaking the fourth wall to bring herself out. Johnson's criticism is both "with" and "against": with it, in the sense of knowing, it seems, what is up, but also against readers' expectations and comforts, aware of the "bad suture" her critical intimacies necessitate.

The associations proliferate: Muses have been figured as midwives in romantic and lyric poetry, two of Johnson's favorite subjects. Psychoanalysts, too, are commonly analogized as midwives. Midwifery in the United States has long been racialized: Before the systematic dismantling and discrediting of midwifery as a practice began in the 1920s, most midwives working in the United States were either Black women who served as community matriarchs or newly immigrated Europeans.[117] By 1950, though midwife participation at birth had declined to less than 5 percent of all births nationwide, midwives were involved with nearly 25 percent of non-white births.[118] The figure of the midwife might also decouple reproduction from (normative) futurity. Midwives not only deliver babies at the time of birth but also often act as teachers to expectant mothers and are called on to perform or be present at abortions as well. One can also, notably, earn a certification as a "death midwife"; hospice nurses take on this extra degree to better assist those who are about to die with the dying process. In another novel by Morrison, written fourteen years after *Sula*, Amy Denver, a white indentured servant on the lam and searching for huckleberries, serves as an accidental midwife to escaped Sethe, delivering her child before abandoning them both at the Ohio River.[119]

Though Gates and Miller both imply that intimacy is bound up in structures of knowing—for Gates, Johnson's ability to know Black texts; for Miller, readers' ability to know Johnson—Johnson's cross-identifications showcase the limits of knowledge, both of self and other. In yet another tribute to Johnson, Edelman points out the irony of praising a prominent deconstructionist thinker for her comprehensible style.[120] Much like Miller, Edelman cautions against the impulse to characterize Johnson's prose as straightforward, clear, or knowable, instead arguing that the value of Johnson's work is its underlying incomprehensibility—an incomprehensibility that he links to an unknowable and untranslatable death drive as well as to the stammering foreignness of deconstruction itself: "For the otherness, the foreignness, the stammer . . . allegorize so as to make knowable, the irony we always fail to read in what we 'know' as 'Barbara.'"[121] This insight indicates a link between Johnson's deconstructive method, her passing, and how intimacy works in her critical corpus. A close look at moments where the interruptive "stammer" is most staged in her work grants us insight into the instances in Johnson that highlight how difference disrupts the otherwise easy cross-identifications she attempts; in these moments, Johnson brings out the antisocial gaps that structure our attempts at intimate relation. As such, Johnson's work performs, in Jennifer C. Nash's words, "an act of radical antiterritoriality . . . an intellectual move that eschews defensiveness and replaces it with a radical embrace of the political potentiality of intimacy."[122]

Although on its surface intimacy often involves, as Berlant puts it, "an aspiration for a narrative about something shared, a story about both oneself and others that will turn out in a particular way," intimacy might also manifest as a partial, incomplete, or failed understanding; indeed, often intimacy makes clear the impossibility of any attempt to fully know a person or text.[123] Berlant notes that "romance and friendship inevitably meet the instabilities of sexuality, money, expectation, and exhaustion, producing, at the extreme, moral dramas of estrangement and betrayal, along with terrible spectacles of neglect and violence even where desire, perhaps, endures." Critical intimacy, too, can follow this pattern: What at first seems like an easy intimacy between text and critic, or between critic and audience, might soon be derailed by the same forces of material and affective difference. This is what Candace Voglar calls "strictly self-disrupting" intimacy, one more akin to Leo Bersani's understanding of antisocial jouissance.[124] This type of self-disrupting intimacy is related to the aspect of Johnson's work concerned with, to again quote Edelman, "questions of otherness, personification, and the all-determining gap that frustrates every attempt to make acts of reading and knowing coincide."[125]

When Engell asks his audience to "imagine the impossible," he is asking his audience to think like Johnson—that is, to cross boundaries in a way that lays bare the intimate relations that structure our critical attachments and attractions. Rehearsing the gaps created by material and identarian difference, Johnson draws attention to the intimacies and routes of desire in her work. Repeatedly refusing to shy away from these difficulties born of her close encounter with texts, Johnson's *as if!* criticism showcases the gaps that remain hard to transgress, be they "(clucking noise)," the "lesbian gap," interracial intimacy, or death itself. Time and time again, Johnson's work comes up against an unknowable or unspeakable gap: among them, Hurston's untranslatable phrase, Bigger's and Miller's unheard vernacular, the silent letters of French words, or the gaps across difference that Johnson's criticism continues to attempt to bridge. In these moments of impasse, Johnson refuses the kind of distance that would resolve her implication, ultimately performing her own status as witness and participant. Does Johnson cross these gaps? Yes and no (what else?).

3

Shock Therapy

THE USES OF THE PORNOGRAPHIC

Queer literary criticism is a lot like pornography. Both flirt with truth. Both, at times, have shocked more puritanical audiences with their explicit depictions of sex, gender, or sexuality. Both could out you if you consume them at a coffee shop. Moreover, queer literary criticism and pornography are often misunderstood in the same way. While both genres traffic in claims to authenticity—through the personal or embodied anecdote, through the visual of explicit sex, etc.—in both cases the shock produced in the audience ends up troubling each genre's claim to the authentic or easily readable. In this way, both queer literary criticism and pornography carry with them an *as if!* sensibility, one in which cross-identification becomes just as much a catalyst for shock as sex itself. Nowhere is this relation clearer than in instances in which queer literary criticism and pornographic writing overlap.

Enter Robert F. Reid-Pharr.

Very early on in the introduction to his book *Black Gay Man: Essays* (2001), Reid-Pharr recounts his relationship with Rick, an "ugly, poor, white trash southerner, with a scandalously thick Kentucky accent."[1] In the middle of a discussion about identity politics and the American left, the flow of Reid-Pharr's prose is interrupted by a brief rumination on what fucking Rick is like:

> What attracts me to Rick is precisely how ugly he is—bald head, chin pointing out too far, thin body, pale skin, shocking red hair bunched around a stubby, oddly shaped, and uncut cock. . . . The image of Rick

is infinitely disruptive. He knows that he is ugly, wears his knowledge like one of the fancy-dress uniforms left over from his days in the army. He loves sex, loves men's bodies, loves the sight of my face, loves to masturbate and moon over how beautiful I am, how fucking beautiful I am. When he comes, usually standing over me, jerking hard at his dick and making those strange moon faces, the liquid spills out almost like an accident. He drawls, "Goddamn, Goddamn," as the goo hits my skin.[2]

Rick continues to pop up throughout the introduction, as scenes like this one punctuate Reid-Pharr's considerably less racy musings on the state of literary criticism in the late 1990s. The interruption quoted above is designed to shock readers. Reid-Pharr's audience might simply be confused by what seems like a logistic non sequitur, disoriented by the shift in tone, or—as the speaker seems to not-so-secretly hope—scandalized by the explicit mention of uncut cock, dick jerking, cum, etc. But this scene also anticipates other possible shocks: Rick's "shocking" red hair but also the shock of Rick's ugliness, his class position, his Southernness, or his whiteness. An avowed lover of "a certain class of ugly, southern white boy," Reid-Pharr flaunts his identifications across race, sexuality, class, or gender.[3] Here, as elsewhere in the essay collection, identity is both constructed and deconstructed in the moment of carnal pleasure, explicitly related to the reader in an interruptive change of scene.

The Rick moments in *Black Gay Man*'s introduction reflect a larger pattern. Textual interludes—typically distinguished by italics, block quotation, or both—frequently interrupt Reid-Pharr's narrative flow, disrupting the linear progress of his argument. Leaning in a little too far, these italicized moments of textual intrusion almost always depict explicit sex scenes, and feature language that Reid-Pharr himself, in his introduction and elsewhere, describes as "pornographic." In naming his own writing style "pornographic," Reid-Pharr appears to set up a dichotomy between these racy textual interruptions and his tamer academic prose.[4] I am more interested, however, in how *Black Gay Man* disrupts that clear distinction.

At another instance early on in *Black Gay Man*, in an essay simply titled "Dinge," Reid-Pharr's literary-critical analyses are once more interrupted by a personal story. Again using an italicized font, and again delving into an anecdote without warning, Reid-Pharr recounts a confrontation with a white American expat outside of a bar in Berlin. The white man, upon seeing Reid-Pharr, drunkenly relays his frustration that the German men he wants to have sex with are only interested in Black Americans. Reid-Pharr is taken aback by the man's frankness, just as his German acquaintance is surprised by the sudden visibility and undesirability of his own whiteness in the Berlin club scene. As they do in Reid-Pharr's introduction, the sex scenes in "Dinge" prompt questions about the place of embodied sex in queer criticism, a structural parallel to the substance of Reid-Pharr's argument. Though the Berlin anecdote contains relatively demure content when compared with the Rick interludes, it nonetheless does important work, linking together personal desire, academic queer theorizing, and identity politics. For Reid-Pharr, queerness engenders a certain relationship to sexual experience characterized by a hyperawareness of one's own body and the consequences of one's bodily actions. In "Dinge," Reid-Pharr unambiguously calls for a more explicit discussion of sex in the queer academic scene:

> If there is one thing that marks us as queer, a category that is some-
> how different, if not altogether distinct, from the heterosexual, then it
> is undoubtedly our relationships to the body, particularly the expansive
> ways in which we utilize and combine vaginas, penises, breasts, buttocks,
> hands, arms, feet, stomachs, mouths and tongues in our expressions of
> not only intimacy, love, and lust but also and importantly shame, con-
> tempt, despair, and hate. Because it is impossible to forget that we hold a
> tangential relationship to what Michael Warner calls heteronormativity,
> we often are forced to become relatively self-aware about what we are do-
> ing when we fuck, suck, go down, go in, get on, go under.[5]

By Reid-Pharr's estimation, "It is surprising, then, that so little within queer theory has been addressed to the question of how we inhabit our various bodies, especially how we fuck or, rather, what we think when we fuck. In the face of wildly impressive work on gay and lesbian history and historiography, gender roles and politics, queer literature and culture, we have been willing to let stand the most tired and hackneyed notions of what our sex actually means."[6] Although it stands to reason that individuals marked by the societal stigma of sexual deviance are more likely to, in Essex Hemphill's words, "think as we fuck," Reid-Pharr takes white queer critics to task for their silence regarding racial difference and, in particular, for their silence regarding white desire for nonwhite sex partners.[7]

The juxtaposition between Reid-Pharr's two major critical beefs—one, that queer critics don't talk about sex, and two, that white queer critics don't talk about race—implies an intimate link between the two. The title of "Dinge," a sophisticated pun, hints at the ways in which the sexually explicit and the racially abject might intersect: *Dinge* can all at once mean a quality that makes one dingey or dirty, a racial slur for a Black person, or, pronounced Teutonically, the German word for "thing" (a definition that foreshadows the anecdote about Berlin but that also recalls theories of the nonhuman, of sex/the Lacanian "Real," and of a history of continental philosophy beginning with Kant's "the thing in itself").[8] Sharon P. Holland theorizes this connection as symptomatic of a limit point within much of white queer theorizing—namely, the limit point of race.[9] In "Dinge" and throughout most of *Black Gay Man*, the explicitly sexual writing Reid-Pharr calls for serves as a counter to academic silence about sex acts but also to academic silence about politically problematic desire. With each interlude, his text practices what it preaches, refusing to ignore the existence of dirty, embodied sex or cross-racial, potentially fetishistic, and therefore politically problematic, sexual desire.

We might assume, at least at first, that Reid-Pharr's description of his writing as "pornographic" means that his text can be read "as" itself, a claim in direct opposition to the aim of *as if!* criticism. In her 2017 essay on gonzo porn and formalist reading, Eugenie Brinkema points out that pornography is, in many ways, a good test for the claims of surface reading.[10] Both pornography and surface reading derive from the demand for unmediated authenticity, and both purport to tell it like it is. (Or, perhaps more accurately, to show it as it is. To quote Justice Potter Stewart, one famously knows the pornographic when one sees it.)[11] Because pornography is also defined by a relative immediacy to sex, some critics and theorists still use pornography as a limit point of media, ignoring or forgetting the fact that it is still a representational genre.[12] Pornography's perceived straightforwardness, encouraged by its explicit nature, is a lot like the fantasy of textual straightforwardness fetishized by advocates of surface reading who sound the call to take "surface as literal meaning" and champion modes of criticism that reject a more "paranoid" hermeneutics of suspicion.[13] Following this logic, Reid-Pharr's insistence on including sexually explicit personal scenes in his criticism, and his repeated calls for queer criticism beyond his own that includes depictions of embodied sexual experience, might seem to align him with a belief that a writer might write authentically "as" themselves, the ultimate collapse of identification and identity.

But as Brinkema and others forcefully argue, pornography's alleged claim to and desire for immediacy, accuracy, and knowability is itself a fantasy.[14] In fact, at the time of Reid-Pharr's writing, pornography as a genre remained ill-defined and slippery. The essays in *Black Gay Man* all debut roughly three decades after *Jacobellis v. Ohio*, a landmark Supreme Court case that drastically changed obscenity law. The court's vague definition of *obscene* as self-obvious cultural production with no inherent social value precipitated what porn scholar Steven Ruszczycky calls a "new cultural ecology," one marked by a "rapid proliferation and diversification of pornographic writing."[15] Ruszczycky notes that this ruling also engenders semantic and genre-related confusion: "Instead of unrestricted speech, there is a sense of something changed by the wash of four-letter words and the clusters of smut peddlers that sprouted up across the nation's publishing landscape.... The meaning and import of all those four-letter words is far from clear."[16] According to noted porn scholar Linda Williams, it is this very ambiguity that structures legal and societal delineation and discussion of "the pornographic" in the first place. Williams helpfully coins the term *on/scenity* to highlight how pornography is, itself, a shifting and unfixed genre, arguing not only that the distinctions between the obscene and the acceptable are contextual and constructed but also that artworks or other media can be deemed obscene and not obscene at the same time.[17]

Reid-Pharr's own experimental and pornographic interludes, then, are unwelcome gatecrashers in a genre of writing well known for demarcating these distinctions in the first place: literary criticism. Distinctions between literature and pornography have historically "served the ideological ends of class differentiation."[18] Particularly in the case of experimental or modernist prose, definitions of literature have relied on distinctions between literature and pornography, in which literature "engaged the reader in the disinterested contemplation of beauty" while pornographic writing "turned one's attention toward the self-interested pleasures of the flesh."[19] Writes Ruszczycky, "The ability to produce and recognize texts with distinctly literary value was also understood to be available only to the population of White male property holders largely responsible for articulating such theories of value. In contrast, pornography increasingly described an aesthetically inferior form of writing associated with the popular entertainments of the working classes. Thus, pornography was recognizable, not only in terms of its crudeness, but also in terms of the relations of power that subordinated it to literature as the thinking man's art."[20] Debates over the distinction between pornography and art, and the stakes of this distinction, would have been front of mind in the mid- to late nineties, when the essays in *Black Gay Man* were written. *Black Gay Man* hit bookstore shelves only a decade after the so-called Helms Amendment debates, a sensationalist effort by Republican lawmakers to defund the National Endowment for the Arts by imposing strict rules against subsidizing "obscene art." Senator Jesse Helms, with the aid of other conservative senators, made it clear to the watching public that, in most cases, *obscene* meant "gay" (to take one famous example, Helms used the debates to condemn the work of photographer Robert Mapplethorpe, whom he famously described dismissively to his fellow representatives as "a known homosexual who died of AIDS, and who spent the last year of his life promoting homosexuality").[21]

Although *Black Gay Man* rarely mentions AIDS by name, it would be a mistake to divorce Reid-Pharr's "obscene" language and explicit sex scenes from the wider context of the epidemic. On the contrary, given its pornographic proclivities, we might situate his critical work more broadly within the history of gay pornographic writing, which experienced a publication and circulation boom at the time of AIDS. In ways similar to how "the attenuation of federal obscenity law established the conditions for gay pornographic writing and gay literary fiction to emerge in relation to one another," so too do the public culture wars surrounding obscenity, AIDS, and race relations in the 1990s establish the conditions for gay pornographic writing and gay literary criticism to emerge in relation to one another.[22] That is, per Ruszczycky and others, just as "any attempt to understand contemporary gay literary production must do so through an understanding of its fundamental connection to the genre of gay pornographic writing," so too must any attempt to understand contemporary queer criticism do so through an understanding of the stakes of the obscene at the time of its emergence. Just as gay activists in the early 1990s "considered how pornography itself might meet a moment when perversion, danger, and death once more were associated with homosexuality in the public imagination," so too did gay academics, Reid-Pharr among them, employ explicitly sexual language to challenge the polite identity policing of the ivory tower.[23]

Though the specific identity markers in its title might lead readers to expect otherwise, *Black Gay Man* complicates and confuses, rather than codifies, the identity categories it names on its face. Had Helms's original, much more restrictive amendment gone through, Congress would also be forbidden to fund any materials that were "indecent" or any art "which denigrated people on the basis of religious beliefs, gender, handicap or national origin."[24] Lumping denigration under the rubric of obscenity is a savvy move on Helms's part, and a telling one: Like Senator Helms (but, obviously, for different reasons), Reid-Pharr understands the obscene as a threat to both heteronormativity and identity politics. Because he is a queer theorist, and because he is an intellectual whose work remains dedicated to questioning the assumed stability or inevitability of heterosexist and racist frameworks, Reid-Pharr is trained to be wary of identity categories like "man," "gay," or "Black." His writing trucks in paradox: To disrupt the fiction of identity, he must name and employ the very categories he seeks to trouble. To drive this irony home, Reid-Pharr structures *Black Gay Man* into three parts: "Black," "Gay," and "Man," hyperbolically dissecting his intersectional identity in an act of organizational drag. The comically direct nature of both the book's title and its organization are especially droll, given that *Black Gay Man* is a work of queer criticism, a genre not particularly known for straight talk.

Importantly, almost all *Black Gay Man*'s explicit sex scenes are also moments of cross-racial, cross-class desire. Because Reid-Pharr's textual interludes also draw attention to cross-identifications across race, class, sexuality, and gender, they highlight an important aspect of critical cross-identification: It is obscene. The shock of that obscenity unmoors us and throws us into the uncomfortable space of non-meaning. I borrow *shock* from Reid-Pharr ("The Shock of Gary Fisher" in *Black Gay Man*) but also from Kobena Mercer, who connects the "shock" of Mapplethorpe to the publicly and hotly contested "obscenity" of his art.[25] Like Mercer, I define *shock* as "the state of mind resultant from a surprising or upsetting experience" or as a word denoting the surprising or upsetting experience itself.[26] Mercer, helpfully, theorizes obscenity as twofold: one, the obscenity of racial fetishism, and two, the obscenity of sadomasochistic homosexual pornography. Both obscenities produce a shock effect that Mercer links to the shock of audience participation, desire, and implication.[27] In this chapter, I outline how the shocking interludes in *Black Gay Man* constitute an *as if!* critical strategy. In *Black Gay Man*, the repeated shock of cross-identification and pornographic language serves to literally interrupt both narrative continuity and the authority of identity. *Black Gay Man*'s shocking cross-identifications, like an electric charge, power the text's identity critique.

NEVER-NEVER LANDS

In "Tearing the Goat's Flesh" (a chapter reprinted in *Black Gay Man* after its 1997 debut in Eve Kosofsky Sedgwick's edited volume *Novel Gazing: Queer Readings in Fiction*), Reid-Pharr's interruptive language productively troubles fixed categories of sexual, racial, and gender identity. "Tearing the Goat's Flesh" compares works by Eldridge Cleaver, Piri Thomas, and James Baldwin in an attempt to make sense of the virulently homophobic and misogynistic sentiment in both Cleaver's *Soul on Ice* (1968) and Thomas's *Down These Mean Streets* (1967). Reid-Pharr begins by pointing out that the explicit sexual language in *Down These Mean Streets* usually serves not to queer the narrative but rather to exonerate its protagonist from queerness. By describing the pleasure of oral sex with a man being his penis's pleasure rather than his own, for example, Thomas escapes queer stigma: "If I didn't like the scene, my pee-pee did."[28] Thomas's language is decidedly and bizarrely juvenile ("pee-pee" for penis), a move that Reid-Pharr reads as Thomas's way of escaping the condemnation of homosexuality, even when receiving a blow job from a man.[29] Read this way, it is precisely the omission of the more pornographic, sexually explicit, or "adult" words (*dick* or *cock*, say) that make Thomas straight: "By reasserting his genitalia as the privileged site of sexual pleasure, Thomas rescues himself from the never-never land of oral and anal eroticism."[30] Thomas's language rescues him from the regressive psychoanalytic oral and anal stages of sexual development—an ironic salvation, considering that it only happens because he regresses back to the vocabulary of childhood.

Significantly, *Black Gay Man* frames "Tearing the Goat's Flesh" such that Reid-Pharr's meta-analysis of his own literary-critical descriptions of sex in the essay becomes more important than his initial analysis of descriptions of sex in *Down These Mean Streets*. In a lengthy, five-page introduction to "Tearing the Goat's Flesh" titled "Prologue, or De-Queering Robert Reid-Pharr," Reid-Pharr details his experiences dealing with academic editors. In this prologue, he notes the confusion generated by his early scholarship, recalling how the seeming incongruity of his inquiry baffles his dissertation committee and, later, skeptical job interviewers who are unable to tell whether his work is "on Black American literature" or "queer theory."[31] "Tearing the Goat's Flesh," figured as the queer chapter in a dissertation primarily focused on race, confuses readers who seek to fix Reid-Pharr's critical identity within academic humanities subfields. To the academics and advisers assessing Reid-Pharr's work, the essay constitutes a queer interruption. This interruption on the level of academic genre as it is tied to identity categories thus runs parallel to the queer interruptions that happen on the language level of academic prose.

Furthermore, Reid-Pharr describes the process by which institutions (Duke University Press, Duke University, the North Carolina state legislature, etc.) censor or oppress a certain kind of sexual outspokenness. "I had used the words 'cock,' 'pussy,' and 'fuck' too often for [the editor's] tastes, and my work threatened, he argued, the relationship of the journal to the university and the state legislature," he writes.[32] Reid-Pharr eventually yields to the editor's objections, "deleting a cock here, a pussy there, and throwing up scare quotes around the odd 'motherfucker,'" but he is cognizant throughout the process of a second, less acknowledged deletion or repression. In his story about the editing and publishing process, Reid-Pharr describes how the constraints of "polite academic discourse" demand both the silencing of pornographic language and the repression of what he terms "the incredible slippage in meaning that necessarily accompanies even the most progressive articulations of modern identity."[33] In Reid-Pharr's chapter, "polite academic discourse" does not target the racism of right-wing whites—many of whom might not hesitate to use a racial slur—but rather calls out the more covert, and thus in many ways more sinister, racism of white liberal elites whose language regulation effectively represses the obscene reality of antigay, anti-Black systems of power.[34]

As is also the case with genres associated with obscenity (pornographic writing chief among them), the frame becomes an important strategy for mitigating language that might in other contexts be deemed obscene. Made nonthreatening by their inclusion within scare quotes and their place in an introductory prologue, the impolite words in Reid-Pharr's prologue thus work their way into his essay despite initial editorial censorship. These words nonetheless interrupt the otherwise domesticated mode in which Reid-Pharr writes, the unspoken rule being that it is fine to include these within a metadiscussion of language but not sincerely within the body of his actual essay. In so doing, the deleted and reinserted words draw attention to how standards of language change depending on the context in which language appears and thus draw attention to the reader's role in meaning-making.

While editing standards require that he delete and replace the *cocks, pussies,* and *motherfuckers,* Reid-Pharr also notes the ways that academically sanctioned identity descriptors affectively register as, operate near, or outright substitute for words that are labeled obscene because they are "the basest of insults." "I still have to resist the impulse to flinch when someone refers to me as a queer and to positively run for cover when someone refers to me as a black queer, as I have not yet rid myself of the suspicion, left over from childhood, that I am being politely hailed as a nigger and a faggot," he writes. "You say black gay. I hear nigger fag."[35] Reid-Pharr's recap of the academic editing process thus brings together two understandings of obscene vocabulary—the pornographic description and the racist or homophobic slur: "I also felt strongly that the editor had (dis)missed the fact that much of the essay is concerned with returning us to an understanding that black and gay identities have been creatively crafted out of the basest of insults. And, while this is indeed reason for celebration, this does not diminish the fact that a hint of that reality, our origins in the never-never world of niggers, coons, punks, faggots, and maricones is apparent in even the most positive articulations of race and sexuality."[36] The echo of "never-never world" (in the essay's prologue) and "never-never land" (in the essay's main text) draws an implicit connection between Reid-Pharr's own academic vocabulary and the pornographic language he is analyzing in Thomas.

The repetition of "never-never" alerts us once again to the connection between sexually obscene language and racially obscene language: Queerness attaches to the racial slur. Others, most notably Darieck Scott, write about this connection. In an essay titled "Porn and the N-Word" (which specifically credits Reid-Pharr as an inspiration), Scott similarly argues that the repetition of the N-word in Samuel R. Delany's *The Mad Man* (1994) "brings attention to the process of interpellation, of power-making-its-object, a recognition it helps fix on some layer of consciousness by repetition—especially, it seems to me, for readers. The naming of interpellation, calling it out, that this repetition effects, makes it, like 'nigger' itself, amenable to various uses and transformations."[37] Here, Scott explores the multiple valences of the hate speech, arguing that the repeated and repetitive verbal assaults aimed at the novel's protagonist carry both violent and sexually arousing force. In his estimation, the interruptions of racial hate speech might similarly be linked to the interruptive, unmooring, and seductive language of pornography.[38] Similarly, debates surrounding the use of *queer* in both political activism and academic criticism sometimes invoke the comparison between *queer* and other obscene slurs. Consider, for example, this striking moment in Judith Butler's *Bodies That Matter* (1993): "When and how does a term like 'queer' become subject to an affirmative resignification for some when a term like 'nigger,' despite some recent efforts at reclamation, appears capable of only reinscribing its pain? How and where does discourse reiterate injury such that the various efforts to recontextualize and resignify a given term meet their limit in this other, more brutal, and relentless form of repetition?"[39] Butler's and Scott's insistence on repetition as a possible means of resignification here predicts the violent interruptions of language throughout "Tearing the Goat's Flesh," along with other scholarship theorizing the connection between the sexually and racially obscene.

Reid-Pharr's analysis of the explicit language in *Down These Mean Streets* largely focuses on scenes of oral sex, a focus that follows a larger trend: In both queer criticism and Black studies, oral sex scenes in literature often serve as a recurring place from which to theorize the intersections of race and sex.[40] These scenes prove to be productive sites not only for thinking through ambiguity and violence but also particularly for thinking through ambiguity and violence alongside the potential perils and pleasures of cross-racial sexual encounters. Multiple critics, for example, take up the infamous "breakfast" scene from Toni Morrison's *Beloved* (1987), in which a white overseer orally rapes the character Paul D while he is imprisoned on a chain gang. Closely reading the scenes of oral rape and oral sex between men in the work of both Morrison and Baldwin, Lee Edelman examines how the twisted logics of homophobia contribute to the logics of racial oppression.[41] Some years later, Scott focuses on the ways in which Paul D grapples with the aftereffects of his oral rape and abjection, shifting focus away from the actual scene of oral rape to its implications and aftereffects on subjecthood and sexual/racial identity.[42] Scott argues that, rather than being a heterosexist foreclosure, *Beloved* constitutes a road map to alternative ways of dealing with the sexual and racial trauma of white supremacy.

The genderfuck brought on by the scene of oral rape has implications for the systems of meaning-making that rely on the clear-cut delineations of gender and genre. It makes sense, then, that queer literary criticism is often interested in these scenes. Another fictional tableau of interracial oral sex, this time from *The Mad Man*, has garnered queer literary-critical attention. Written in a very different vein than Morrison's scene of oral rape on a chain gang, Delany's multiple scenes of consensual, masochistic oral sex describe the exploits of a Black queer protagonist, John, as he sucks off a white supposedly straight man experiencing homelessness nicknamed Piece o' Shit. Writing separately and at different times, Scott and Ruszczycky both read this scene as neither transcending racial hierarchies nor enacting revenge against white supremacy; rather, their interpretations variously rest on the way in which John's deliberate pursuit of submissive, racialized BDSM encounters with white men "affords access to a power in powerlessness: John must be degraded for it to work, yet the pleasure found in such degradation marks an alternative relation to the traumas that mark him as a Black subject."[43] Notably, Delany writes the foreword to *Black Gay Man*—his intermittent presence in *Black Gay Man* not only speaks to the common threads of both pornographic explicitness and empirical description that run through much of their writing but also clues readers in to how his and Reid-Pharr's similar descriptive strategies can work against identity.[44] Heather Love, for example, makes a convincing case that the painstaking, almost anthropological descriptions of sexual commerce in a different Delany text, *Times Square Red, Times Square Blue* (1999), neither totally reinforce nor totally dissolve identity. Love's study of Delany illuminates the anti-identity thrust in his work: though Love writes that "the book is told in Delany's own voice—from a position he identifies elsewhere as *Black, gay* and *male*—and he does not mask but rather foregrounds his desire" (emphasis original, believe it or not), she ultimately concludes that, rather than solidify these three named identities, "the intense and heterogeneous 'typification' that occurs in *Times Square Red, Times Square Blue* proliferates and complicates identity markers beyond those over-determined categories of race, sexuality, or gender."[45]

Like his queer theoretical contemporaries, Reid-Pharr acknowledges the violence of oral rape scenes while still attempting to complicate already-extant, and potentially homophobic, readings that might cast oral sex between men as being solely the scene of abjection, emasculation, or domination. In his analysis, Reid-Pharr spends the most time on an extended scene in which Piri and his fellow straight-identified gang members visit a home of some male sex workers for sex and weed, and Piri has his cock sucked by a gay man nicknamed Concha (a name that, Reid-Pharr points out, means "either shell or pussy").[46] Along with the parts of the scene that feature genital/oral sex acts between men, Reid-Pharr also highlights the language that Thomas deploys when he describes smoking a joint: "No penis, vagina, breasts, or buttocks are here to alert the reader that what we are experiencing is a type of sexual intercourse. There is neither blood nor feces to act as evidence of the all-important penetration. . . . Here the erotic content is transferred from the sexual organs to the lips, a key site of homoerotic, homosexual pleasure."[47] The erotic pleasures described by Thomas expand beyond what we might call the explicitly sexual. Arguably some of the most erotically charged moments in Thomas take us not to the "vaginas, penises, breasts, buttocks, hands, arms, feet, stomachs, mouths and tongues" mentioned in the previous chapter but primarily to the lips, those secondary sexual organs so often associated with the feminine.[48]

Reid-Pharr's specific choice, in his introduction, to describe the writing in his book of literary-critical essays as "pornographic" yields further connections to the never-never land of oral eroticism. Brinkema specifically focuses on representations of oral sex to make a larger argument against "surface reading"; ultimately, her essay posits an essential link between form and how we understand "the things mouths do," insisting on the value of deep formalist critique. Drawing a helpful connection between the rhythmic violence of irrumation, the pornographic, and interrupted language, Brinkema writes that "there is a transferential contagion to the violence of forced penetration at the site of the sonant.... In sum, irrumation is a problem for representation—both in language, as groaning and weeping replace the word, and in its political-designative sense, what multiply troubles logos, disrupting oratory, discourse, argument, advocacy."[49] Brinkema's insights about the rhythmic violence of irrumation dovetail with Reid-Pharr's exploration of cross-racial violence and desire, both of which converge at the site of the oral pornographic.

Indeed, the title of Reid-Pharr's essay signals the rhythmic violence that underlies it. He takes his title from an "Abakua proverb," one that also serves as the epigraph for Reid-Pharr's essay: The proverb's meaning—"the goat who breaks the drum pays with his hide"—provides the inspiration for the essay's title, as well as the intellectual fodder for its conclusion.[50] Musing on the aphorism's brief but striking metaphor, Reid-Pharr writes:

> As Coco Fusco has suggested, even while the Abakua proverb points directly to the grave consequences of troublemaking, it demonstrates the necessity of the untamed "outsider" to the continued creativity of the rest of the community. As James Baldwin's Giovanni is slaughtered and as Thomas's effeminate gay men are fucked and beaten, a type of music is produced, a music that points the way to new modes of existence, new ways of understanding, that allow the community to escape, however briefly, the systems of logic that have proven so enervating to the black subject. The importance of the (scape)goat, then, is not so much that with its death peace returns to the village or that crisis ends. The point is not simply to expurgate all that is ambiguous and contradictory. On the contrary, as the kid is consumed and the drum is beaten, the community learns to gain pleasure from "the possibilities just beyond its grasp." It receives proof of its own authenticity and insider status while leaving open a space for change, perhaps even the possibility of new forms of joy. The boundaries are for a moment reestablished, but all are certain, even hopeful, that once again they will be erased.[51]

Reid-Pharr's explanation of his essay's epigraph thus conceives of the violent break or interruption of systems of logic as productive, even as they are also marked by a repeated and inescapable death, and his own text stylistically mirrors the substance of his argument, explicit language shockingly interrupting the flow of his polite, academic prose. The violence of these rhythmic interruptions is at once ugly, persistent, and sexy. Even though these rhythms are often literal deathblows, Reid-Pharr nonetheless maintains faith in the power of these interruptions to open into new possibilities.

THE LESBIAN-IDENTIFIED MALE-IDENTIFIED MAN

Nowhere in *Black Gay Man* is *as if!* criticism more evident than in Reid-Pharr's chapter "Living as a Lesbian," a short, intensely personal essay situated two-thirds of the way through *Black Gay Man*. Here (after the middle section, "Gay," and as the first chapter in the final section, "Man") Reid-Pharr pens a loving appreciation of the community of Black lesbian feminists he befriends while an undergraduate at the University of North Carolina at Chapel Hill in the late 1980s. The essay—first published in the anthology *Sister and Brother: Lesbians and Gay Men Write About Their Lives Together* (1994) and reprinted seven years later in *Black Gay Man*—is a constellation of vignettes mostly composed of anecdotes concerning Reid-Pharr's many close friendships with gay women, as well as tales of the myriad Black feminist mentors and theorists who have shaped him as a scholar and teacher. Several times in the eleven pages of "Living as a Lesbian," Reid-Pharr describes moments where his lesbian identification occurs simultaneously with several explicit descriptions of male-embodied sex, which obscenely interrupt the more platonic/romantic prose of the rest of the chapter.

In "Living as a Lesbian," Reid-Pharr italicizes and intersperses not only pornographic anecdotes but also block quotations by various Black lesbian feminists. Citation—the tracing of academic lineage and kinship—works similarly to pornographic interruption. A statement by the US Black lesbian feminist group the Combahee River Collective, poetry by Audre Lorde, and long excerpts from the criticism and fiction of Michelle Parkerson, Barbara Smith, and James Baldwin (as well as one poem by Reid-Pharr himself, written while he was still an undergraduate in North Carolina) interrupt his prose in long, italicized block quotes. Reid-Pharr's citation functions not only by way of his interruptive quotes but also by the repeated lists of names, which serve as a kind of bibliography or works cited within his piece: "I know all the young black female film and video makers: Cheryl, Shari, Dawn, Vejan, Yvonne, and even Michelle, not to mention Jackie W., the children's writer; Pamela, the performance artist; Cathy, the Ivy league professor and AIDS activist; bald Jackie B., the erotic poet; Jewelle who needs no introduction; and, of course, Barbara, the mother of us all."[52] The Black lesbian community Reid-Pharr describes is heterogeneous: an intersecting network of friends, mentors, ex-lovers, sperm donors and receivers, citational footnotes, radical activists, roommates, cash lenders, cash borrowers, and biological kin. Reid-Pharr's lesbian connections are political and personal, professional and pedagogical—they extend to the books on his shelf ("My files are packed with back copies of *Sinister Wisdom*, *Off Our Backs*, *On Our Backs*, and *Conditions*," he writes).[53] The essay itself borrows its title from a book of poems by Reid-Pharr's collaborator and friend Cheryl Clarke, whose influential essay "Lesbianism: An Act of Resistance" (1981) theorizes Black lesbianism as an act of political and social solidarity rather than as merely a personal identity. Beyond providing the chapter with its title and ethos, Clarke, or more often simply "Cheryl," is the primary person through whom Reid-Pharr most fully comes to intimately know his own lesbianism. Crucially, it is not only Reid-Pharr's involvement with a particular social scene but also his proximity to and expert knowledge of the Black lesbian feminist texts he cites that allow him to read, write, and live "as a lesbian."

Of all the names in "Living as a Lesbian," the one most often invoked is that of Barbara Smith, the famed critic, publisher, and activist. Reid-Pharr's essay begins with Smith: "In 1985 Barbara Smith came like a fresh wind to Chapel Hill. She brought with her a vision of home unlike anything I had imagined."[54] This sentence repeats at the end of the chapter; in fact, Reid-Pharr invokes Smith's name many times throughout his short reflection. The repeated refrain of Smith's name is not Reid-Pharr's only means of homage. His essay also takes seriously the critical call of her most famous essay, "Toward a Black Feminist Criticism," an essay that, as we have previously seen, marked a new era in Black lesbian feminist thought and practice. Like Smith, Reid-Pharr uses an expansive definition of *lesbian* that extends beyond explicit sexuality into the homosocial sphere. Such a move aligns itself not only with Smith but also with traditions within seventies lesbian feminism more generally. When Smith writes that "the very meaning of lesbianism is being expanded in literature, just as it is being redefined through politics," her words reflect a mode of analysis in the same vein as, say, that of Radicalesbians' "The Woman Identified Woman" (1970), which also expands *lesbian* far beyond its sexual signification, or Adrienne Rich's "lesbian continuum," defined broadly as the range "through each woman's life and throughout the history of woman-identified experience, not simply the fact that woman has had or consciously desired genital sexual experience with another woman."[55] In "Toward a Black Feminist Criticism," Smith expands on this idea in the name of a new critical mode, which she names "Black feminist criticism." Indeed, her analysis of Toni Morrison's *Sula* as a lesbian novel expands the definition of *lesbian* to describe something beyond sex acts, sexual desire, or sexual identity.

Reid-Pharr's citations are in many ways unsurprising, as there is little doubt that he owes much of his own criticism to the groundbreaking work done by the Black lesbian feminists of Smith's generation. "Living as a Lesbian" is an overt acknowledgment of this debt; indeed, for Reid-Pharr, a major appeal of both Black feminist theory and the Black feminist community is that they allow him to articulate his own existence without having to choose between practice and theory. Informed as it is by the Black lesbian feminist theory of the late 1970s and 1980s, we might rightly expect Reid-Pharr's scholarship to insist on the particulars of the body and its erotics. Sometimes, as in his introduction, this is indeed the case. Readers of his book, he writes, "have been surprised (pleasantly and otherwise) that I have attempted to refuse the easy distinctions between the political and the personal that continue to exist in so much of our work long after feminists presumably cleared the left intellectual environment of such odd notions."[56] As his friendships with Black lesbian feminists imbue him with a newfound "bravado" and "confidence," so too do the lessons learned from Black feminist theory embolden Reid-Pharr to write criticism that accounts for sex, race, and embodiment.[57]

But Reid-Pharr's invocation of seventies lesbian thinkers in "Living as a Lesbian" in a text rife with penetrative gay male sex adds another, thornier layer to the work of the other anecdotal interludes that punctuate *Black Gay Man*. It is significant that the moments where Reid-Pharr most doubts his lesbian identifications are the most explicit parts of his essay; they, again, occur at interruptive, italicized sex scenes that seem far removed from the mostly platonic descriptions of the society of lesbian poets, academics, artists, and activists with whom he is most comfortable. In the gay male space of the bathhouse, Reid-Pharr finds his lesbian identifications problematized by his access to male homosexual/homosocial space, by the physical act of fucking, and by the larger social privilege of relative safety afforded by his masculinity. "Now I find myself asking whether in the bathhouse, the most sacred of male enclaves, where my masculine body and affected macho style increase my worth in the sexual economy, I am still lesbian," he writes. "Is it lesbianism that spills out of the end of my cock as bald-headed men with grizzled beards and homemade tattoos slap my buttocks and laugh triumphantly? Is it lesbianism that allows me to walk these difficult streets alone, afraid only that I will *not* be seen, accosted, 'forced' into sexual adventure?"[58] Reid-Pharr's lexicon makes stark the embodied difference between the cisgender lesbians with whom he feels kinship and the cisgender gay men of the bathhouse. Throughout "Living as a Lesbian," encounters with his body startlingly return Reid-Pharr back to Black gay manhood. Even as he aspires toward romanticized lesbianism, Reid-Pharr remains attentive to the moments in which his attempts at homosociality within his community of Black lesbians come up against seemingly unbreachable rifts of physical difference.

Stopped short in his female identification by an encounter with his penis and the penises of the bathhouse men, Reid-Pharr appears to suture gender identity to the shape of one's genitalia. These moments, to be sure, indicate limit points in Reid-Pharr's thinking—limit points that betray a particular type of binary thinking in certain strands of early queer theory. Reading Reid-Pharr's bodily interruptions as moments of gender limitation or gender policing reproduces what Grace Lavery terms "egg theory," a critical mindset that is, in her words, "about a transsexual desire that [queer theorists] kept at arm's length."[59] Coming against the perceived limit point of gender essentialism, egg theory views gender transition as conservative, "gauche," and generally opposed to queer theory's more liberatory view of gender as fluid, playful, and dynamic.[60] Ironically, as Lavery aptly demonstrates, such a position ends up reinforcing the very gender essentialism against which queer theory purports to fight.

As such, these passages might be misread as shocking Reid-Pharr out of the supposed fantasy of living as if a lesbian and back to the purported reality of living as a gay man. Reid-Pharr's textual-sexual interludes, read this way, also risk reinforcing a theoretically constructed divide between lesbians and gay men—one that would associate a desexualized "erotic" with the former and a hypersexualized "pornographic" with the latter. Reid-Pharr's specific term *pornography*, as well as his authorial choice to include explicit scenes of sex, further invokes the specter of gender essentialism. The term *pornography* particularly complicates Reid-Pharr's repeated citation of Audre Lorde, whom he cites six times in *Black Gay Man* (once in the chapter "Dinge," four times in "Living as a Lesbian," and once in "It's Raining Men," a chapter reflecting on the Million Man March). Like Reid-Pharr, Lorde advocates for a mode of politics that is informed by the personal erotic rather than by patriarchal methods that are ostensibly divorced from the experience of feeling.[61] This is, undoubtedly, in line with the political project of *Black Gay Man*. However, in "The Uses of the Erotic" Lorde perhaps most forcefully draws a distinction between the pornographic and the erotic, a distinction Reid-Pharr seems to elide.[62] Sticking with the term *pornographic*, Reid-Pharr sits squarely against the antiporn feminists, of which Lorde was one. Implicitly invoking the antiporn debates of the so-called feminist sex wars of the late 1970s and early 1980s, Reid-Pharr raises the specter of gender.[63] Williams, for example, writes about "related debates about pornography within feminism, in which a 'bad,' androcentric pornography is often opposed to a 'good,' gynocentric eroticism."[64] Reid-Pharr, though, reverses this feminist reading. In the introduction to *Black Gay Man*, he writes that "it has been the case that the individuals who have responded to previous versions of these essays remark the odd slippage in my writing between the academic and the pornographic, the rigorous and the soft."[65] The binarism Reid-Pharr sets up here is hyperbolically gendered—the academic is rigorous and political while the pornographic is soft and personal.

But while gender fixity is undoubtedly one possible reading of Reid-Pharr's vocabulary, I am more interested in how his pornographic interludes work similarly to and in conjunction with his continual citation of Black lesbian feminists. In another such interlude, Reid-Pharr describes the difficulty of holding on to both a gay male and a lesbian identity while looking in the mirror: "Even as I stand before the bathroom mirror, my dick tucked between my legs so that only the bushy triangle of pubic hair is showing, I continue to smell my own heavy man's smell."[66] When he presents his desire for and identification with men/masculinity as inimical to lesbian identity, Reid-Pharr rebuffs his faith in Rich's "lesbian continuum." In this mirror scene, Reid-Pharr takes a familiar Lacanian stage and introduces a new element: smell. In so doing, he takes a relatively abstract moment that is well known in the critical theory canon and interrupts its predictable telos—a.k.a. ego formation—by way of an embodied experience. Smell, far less theorized than sight or even sound, nonetheless has disciplinary power. Lucas Crawford, for example, points out that because it is attached to the shaky science of male and female pheromones, smell is sometimes figured as "the sense that cannot be 'fooled.' . . . The resultant binary economy of smell implies that heterosexuality is hardwired."[67] Encountering an impasse when he smells his "man's smell," Reid-Pharr performs the pervasiveness of the binary gender system, extending gender's stronghold to the tertiary senses. At the same time, perhaps because of smell's often overdetermined correlation to a gender binary, it is a sensory realm ripe for campy subversion or, in Crawford's terms, a sense susceptible to "transing potential."[68] An unexpected, interruptive smell such as the one Reid-Pharr encounters "disrupts our sense that we live only in the present; it uses the body as an archive that moves people; it clouds our separations; it communicates to those who would never think of talking to us; it is gender in motion, midair and inhaled."[69]

The mirror scene in "Living as a Lesbian" also presents a narrative that complements another, fictional, mirror scene frequently taken up by queer and transgender literary critics: namely, the scene in Radclyffe Hall's *The Well of Loneliness* (1928) in which the protagonist Stephen laments her masculine body while standing in front of a bedroom mirror.[70] Just as others read Stephen's anguish as the result of an ambivalent or melancholic relationship to available fixed gender categories, so too do I read Reid-Pharr's mirror scene as a staged negotiation of identity meant to call into question identification's physical and social arbiters. While Reid-Pharr delights at the transgender potential of his "fleshy thighs," Stephen is miserable at the sight of "slender flanks"; while Reid-Pharr's essay appears in a book titled *Black Gay Man*, Hall describes Stephen's body in this scene, Love cogently notes, as "so white."[71] Despite these notable differences, in both scenes, Reid-Pharr and Stephen arrive at a kind of autoerotic melancholy, an ambivalence about their own bodies brought on by stroking, smelling, and seeing. Expanding on preheld notions of gender as primarily seen, Reid-Pharr's emphasis on smell introduces the messiness of existence back into an old critical trope. His sensory experience, here in the form of an interruptive smell, conflicts with, but does not necessarily contradict, the theoretical and social connections he has forged in other aspects of his existence.

Rather than enforce a gender binary, the ruptures in "Living as a Lesbian"—and elsewhere in *Black Gay Man*—throw readers into disarray. Reid-Pharr's identifications quickly become quite complicated, especially at the scene of gay male sex. Recounting one such scene, he writes:

> Of late I have taken to rubbing my face along the cocks and balls and inside the buttocks of my lovers, hoping that in their scent I might find something of my own, or my father's, or his own unknown father's. I lick the sweat off bellies spilling over too-tight jeans, suck gobs of chest hair, and underarm hair, and scrotum hair into my mouth, gorging on the rough texture, begging to be pinned down to the bed, to be penetrated by a vigorous and vibrant masculinity. My lovers whisper, "Whose pussy is this?" as they struggle to slip their cocks into my ass. I haven't the heart to answer simply that it is my own.[72]

When Reid-Pharr admits that he lacks the heart to leap from metaphor to literalism, he nonetheless acknowledges a possibility (perhaps, if we take this as paralepsis, even a longing) that he might "simply" be a woman. Just because gender and sex present a difficulty in these scenes does not mean that the physical or embodied experiences that Reid-Pharr describes (sucking scrotum hair, rubbing cocks and balls, etc.) are always or even primarily incompatible with a lesbian or female identity. Here, the physical experience of penile ejaculation does not preclude one from being a lesbian or from being a woman. In these moments, the text's self-described "pornographic" interruptions interrogate the difficulty of navigating the (ever-shifting) embodied prerequisites of gender identification within a rigid system of gender policing.

Crucially, anatomy does not preclude Reid-Pharr from being a lesbian; rather, his own attachment to Black gay masculinity does. It seems Reid-Pharr merely doesn't have the heart to fully surrender the power that results from calling oneself a man and being read in the world as such. At the same time, this power is complicated by other intersections of Reid-Pharr's identity. The irony of this interruptive moment and the moments like it appears to trade on a rigid understanding of gender in which man=cock, a formula that betrays a deeply transphobic logic. But Reid-Pharr's identification is not just, or even primarily, a body problem in this passage. Rather, it is Reid-Pharr's desire for and identification with the macho style of the bathhouse men that makes him both more and less a lesbian. He attributes his ability to enter, exist in, and survive all-male homosocial and homosexual spaces to a learned lesbian "bravado," but ironically, it is in these all-male spaces that Reid-Pharr's lesbian identifications are most challenged.[73] In a striking moment, Reid-Pharr admits that he feels anxious about the prospect of not being sexually hailed or accosted on the street (an anxiety, I would wager, few of his female-identifying compatriots share). In so doing, Reid-Pharr alludes to a problematic sexual desire that looks very much like Leo Bersani's early theorizations of gay machismo, in which sincere sexual desire for and aspirational identification with masculinity butt heads with the political desire to do away with heterosexism and misogyny.[74] But it also looks very much like even earlier lesbian feminist debates about butch gender presentation and sexuality, in which the stakes are quite similar: Again, desire, identification, and the allure of masculinity or its subversion are all at play. On the one hand, Reid-Pharr is unwilling to surrender the joke of a gay man calling his male partner's asshole a pussy (in twenty-first-century parlance, we might say "bussy" instead, to similar effect), a move that could be read as an attempt to retain masculine privilege. On the other, this scene winkingly acknowledges the ways in which Blackness, gayness, and bottomness are, like womanness, mutually and differently oppressed under patriarchal and white supremacist systems.[75]

Viewed this way, the multiple, overlapping, or seemingly conflicting identifications in "Living as a Lesbian" might constitute, in the words of Rinaldo Walcott, "modes of self-fashioning that allow for a reconstruction of Black manhood from the place of incoherence and femininity which might be best exemplified, or at the least typified, in recent representations of and by Black trans-cultures, but not exclusive to them."[76] These conflicting identifications allow Reid-Pharr to reach toward his own moments of what he calls lesbian "transcendence," a word whose polysemous prefix predicts later transgender studies work that theorizes *trans* as a type of transitivity, translation, or transfiguration.[77] Feminist theory in the vein of Smith and Lorde and contemporary transgender studies are both "theories in the flesh"; both think through the ways embodiment relates to gender and race.[78]

At the end of "Living as a Lesbian," Reid-Pharr concludes, "I began to understand lesbianism as a state of being that few of us ever achieve. To become lesbian one has to first be committed to the process of constantly becoming, of creatively refashioning one's humanity as a matter of course."[79] Reid-Pharr regards gendered subjecthood with productive and provocative ambiguity, one that anticipates more recent articulations of embodiment and identity in transgender theory: To borrow C. Riley Snorton's term, Reid-Pharr's identifications transfigure Black women's studies, expanding and complicating ideas of who is recognizable "as" a Black lesbian feminist.[80] Lesbianism in *Black Gay Man* is at various points theoretical, citational, platonic, sexual, embodied, and aspirational—where Sedgwick might use *queer* or where more recent scholars might use *trans*, Reid-Pharr, like his Black feminist forebear Smith, uses *lesbian*. Reid-Pharr's tale of cross-identification in "Living as a Lesbian," repeatedly frustrated by his own pornographic interruptions, is a tale of neither foreclosure nor achievement. Neither fully accepting nor fully rejecting the possibility of his own lesbianism, Reid-Pharr insists on cross-identifications that fuck us up.

THE LIVING END

The cross-identifications showcased in "Living as a Lesbian" complement the troubled identifications at work in one of the essays in Reid-Pharr's collection, "The Shock of Gary Fisher." Here, Reid-Pharr examines Gary Fisher's scandalous and pornographic posthumous collective works, *Gary in Your Pocket* (1996). Once again, Reid-Pharr argues that there is little difference between the accepted academic discourse of identity categories and the obscene discourse of the racial slur. For Reid-Pharr, the barrage of graphic language in Fisher speaks to the inescapable enmeshment of the history of slavery and racial violence with Americans' most personal and individual desires and actions. Instead of reading Fisher's relentlessly repeating graphic language as jarring, Reid-Pharr argues that this obscene repetition might also have the opposite effect: As scenes of abject racial and sexual violence repeat throughout *Gary in Your Pocket*, readers might become inured to their initial shock. In "The Shock of Gary Fisher," Reid-Pharr once again employs interruption. Stylistically mirroring and literally copying Fisher, Reid-Pharr peppers his own text with shocking quotations from *Gary in Your Pocket*. Several times throughout "The Shock of Gary Fisher," Fisher's prose interrupts Reid-Pharr's literary analysis, each time again offset in quoted italics.

"Living as a Lesbian" and "The Shock of Gary Fisher" share attributes beyond their mutual penchant for textual and sexual interruption. Most obviously, these two essays share a setting: Most of Fisher's anecdotes take place while he is in graduate school in Chapel Hill; in "Living as a Lesbian," Reid-Pharr also focuses primarily on his experiences while he is working and living at the University of North Carolina at Chapel Hill. Both essays refuse to separate the sexual from the academic and the personal from the professional. Both essays, notably, also are concerned with the creation of a citational and literary canon. For Reid-Pharr, something about Fisher's explicit and inappropriate desire makes him difficult to include in a canon of Black male writers. The shock of Fisher's work is not just the shock of the obscene lurking underneath the everyday (though that is undoubtedly part of the experience of reading *Gary in Your Pocket*) but also the shock of the obscene as a necessary mechanism of the everyday. In other words, the shock of Fisher is the shock of realizing that the obscene is on/scene, bound up with the way identity, identification, and desire function. Rejecting the mode of criticism that would unambiguously label Fisher's work "Black gay male literature," Reid-Pharr writes: "Is this black gay male literature? Yes, if the quality of one's literature is simply a favor of phenotype and the reports of one's sexual practice. If, however, we mean to ask whether Fisher participates fully in the established idioms of Black (gay) American literary and cultural production, then I must express at least some doubt."[81] The "(gay)" qualifying parenthetical here signals a moment of outreach to Reid-Pharr's readership, a break in the fourth wall that signals an uncertain relationship between sexuality and the established idioms of Black cultural production.

Here, Reid-Pharr's text links its argument about Fisher back to its author by way of Reid-Pharr's own biographic proximity to his subject. Reid-Pharr, whom we might in some ways also count as one of the "self-identified Black gay authors" he references, has much in common with Fisher. Moreover, unlike the other authors with whom he contrasts Fisher (Baldwin, Richard Wright, etc.), Reid-Pharr closely matches Fisher in both "phenotype and the reports of one's sexual practice" and "idioms of . . . literary and cultural production."[82] Like Fisher, he lived for a while in Chapel Hill, North Carolina; like Fisher, he has professional and personal connections to Sedgwick; like Fisher, he has an affinity for Southern white men; like Fisher, he is positioned in the academic fields of literary queer criticism and critical race theory. At first, then, it would seem that "The Shock of Gary Fisher"—in contrast to "Living as a Lesbian"—is an essay about a critic's relatively straightforward identification with his subject.

But the interruptive Fisher quotes in "The Shock of Gary Fisher," like the formal textual breaks in "Living as a Lesbian" and other places throughout *Black Gay Man*, also produce a shock effect that signposts moments of authorial identification across gender. Consider, again, Reid-Pharr's claim, late in his essay on Fisher, that "what is more stunning, what shocks is that Fisher says, without flinching, that the black is not inculpable, that she is as much perpetrator as victim. As we will see, Fisher's constant return to the erotics of slavery and his insistence that the black is always an active and potent agent within these erotics not only places him among the most perverse of Black American authors but suggests a model of black subjectivity and black expression that at once masters and deforms some of the most cherished idioms of Black American vernacular tradition."[83] Reid-Pharr here makes the case that the shock generated by Fisher's obscene and often limit-pushing poems, daily records, and essay drafts is the shock of mutual implication—that is, the shock of realizing the dependence of Black identity on white supremacy. Notably, unlike in the rest of this chapter, Reid-Pharr uses the feminine pronoun *she* as a general or universalizing pronoun ("she is as much perpetrator as victim"). This choice may seem strange, given that the reading subject of his essay is hitherto identified as male. The appearance of *she* could indicate a desire to continue the work of much Black feminist thought to theorize through and with the perspective and experience of Black women—indeed, to posit Black womanhood as an alternative center from which to theorize in the face of a white androcentric universal. It could also indicate a desire to, as Snorton writes, "practice black (male) feminism in the space of transition," a practice that "calls for feminist scholars to exert theoretical pressures on the category of maleness, itself—to allow it to destroy itself—and in so doing to allow black feminisms radical inclusivities to reemerge."[84] Perhaps the brief shift in gender pronouns is more akin to the campy and familiar *she* frequently used to address drag queens or femme gay men.[85] In either case, the appearance of *she* indicates a connection between the obscene shock of Fisher and movement across gender. In this curious moment in the text, the specific individual author "Gary Fisher" expands into the capacious figure of, in Reid-Pharr's words, "the black" and, in so doing, becomes female. The shock of Fisher's prose and Reid-Pharr's argument is enough, it appears, to briefly destabilize the identity categories of gender.

This trend—in which Reid-Pharr's attempts to complicate racial identity carry with them a parallel attempt to complicate gender identity—continues in the paragraphs to follow. Arguing for a more ambiguous, complicated authorial relationship to identity, Reid-Pharr writes: "The question that this leaves us with is, 'How can we read Gary Fisher as a black man?' Given my argument that Fisher repeatedly takes up the particularly shocking notion of a Negro racial identity not only produced in direct relation to white hostility but produced in a manner that takes sublime pleasure in the white's domination, it taxes the imagination to place him neatly alongside Toni Morrison, John Edgar Wideman, James Baldwin, or even the growing number of self-identified black gay writers."[86] It is slightly unclear, here, whether "as a black man" refers to "Gary Fisher" or "we," and the telling ambiguity of "as" in "How can we read Gary Fisher as a black man?" further indicates the slippage between identity and identification.

For Reid-Pharr, the very prospect of Fisher's inclusion seems to expand and explode the canon at the very moment at which Reid-Pharr invokes it. His move betrays his suspicion of any canon-forming process, a suspicion that Fisher's work shares. Both Fisher and Reid-Pharr, notably, refuse to separate the sexual from the academic and the personal from the professional. Again employing the pronoun *she*, Reid-Pharr writes:

> For Fisher the individual who would know is never innocent, never wholly separate from even the most ugly truths that she uncovers. In order to master fully the intricacies of Western modernity, one must expose oneself to degradation and disease, even though the likely consequence of such exposure is death. My thinking in this matter has been strongly influenced by the fact that Fisher believed he contracted H.I.V. as a student at the University of North Carolina during one of his many study sessions in the Wilson Library, that the mastery of his subjects was coterminous with the disease's mastery of his flesh. . . . The piling on of forms of mastery—literary, scientific, sexual—is so very overdetermined as to seem obscene.[87]

In Fisher's journals, cultural knowledge in a white supremacist society is itself both a means of survival and a fatal disease; his time spent in the library of a historically and predominantly white institution literally kills him. How does one read this alongside the deadly literary dalliances of Gary Fisher, contracting HIV in a University of North Carolina library? With the above scene of lethal literary reference in the back of our minds, how are we to read the citational celebration of the tight-knit academic-activist community in "Living as a Lesbian," which also takes place in Chapel Hill? On the one hand, it seems that Reid-Pharr sets up his liberating Black lesbian bibliography as an alternative to Fisher's deadly critical canon: library as agent of death. On the other hand, Reid-Pharr's citational practices in his "Living as a Lesbian" essay lead us back to the repetitious violence theorized and rhetorically performed (via the stylistic trope of interruption) in both "Tearing the Goat's Flesh" and "The Shock of Gary Fisher."

Though "Living as a Lesbian" has *living* in its title, it too ends on the sobering note of death. Reid-Pharr concludes his ode to Black feminist theorists with a necrology, reflecting on the isolation he experiences in the wake of the rapidly increasing death toll wrought by continued state violence against the Black communities he has become a part of. The inescapable specters of illness and death precipitate his disenchantment with the utopian promise of Black lesbianism. "It would be years before I would look up to find that as I searched for home I continued in my isolation," he writes. "It was the death of Pat Parker that first alerted me to the fragility of both our dreams and our community. First her then Joe Beam then Donald Woods then David Frechette then Rory Buchanan then James Baldwin and Roy Gonsalves then Audre Lorde herself."[88] The litany of names at the end of Reid-Pharr's essay heeds Baldwin's call—made sixteen years earlier—to "bring out your dead."[89] Echoing Baldwin's own list of Black children murdered in Atlanta between 1979 and 1980, Reid-Pharr presents his readers with a list of names whose sobering rhythm mirrors the beat of the repetitious rhetorical shocks found elsewhere in *Black Gay Man*. In Reid-Pharr's list of the dead, all the women he lists died of breast cancer and all of the men died of AIDS-related complications (with the exception of Baldwin, who died of stomach cancer in 1987).

Reid-Pharr's list of names also reminds readers of the ways in which the labor of criticism affects those who practice it on a material level. This list of names also echoes more recent meditations on the dangers of being a Black feminist in what Jennifer C. Nash calls the "killing engine of the university."[90] Reflecting on Barbara Christian's 1994 remarks about the paucity of Black women in the academy—and more specifically within Black feminist criticism itself—Grace Kyungwon Hong writes:

> I cannot suppress my suspicion that we are indeed facing a moment when this "distinct irony," this "tremendous loss," is occurring, but in a way Christian never might have imagined. I am forced to consider that this bleak future may have come to pass, not only, as Christian so presciently foretold, through the dismantling of redistributive mechanisms that might have enabled current and future generations of Black feminists to enter the academy but also because so many of the Black feminists of Christian's and later generations have died prematurely—struck down by cancer and other diseases—including Christian herself in 2000.[91]

Reid-Pharr's exploration of Fisher's remarkable hypothesis that he contracted HIV in the library stacks, read alongside the citations in "Living as a Lesbian," reveals another important connection between both chapters: namely, that they both take seriously the life-and-death stakes of identification in academic criticism, particularly for Black feminist and queer scholars.

At the end of "Dinge," Reid-Pharr reminds his readers that the call to "think as we fuck" is also a call to openly acknowledge that the circumstances of identity and embodiment influence desire: "We must insist on a queer theory that takes the queer body and what we do with it as a primary focus, lest we allow for the articulation of a queer subjectivity that never recognizes the differences we create and carry in our bodies, including not only race but gender, health, and age, to name only the most obvious categories."[92] The inclusion of "health" as an identity category in the catalog of "differences" Reid-Pharr lists suggests that there is more at stake than just literary-critical codes of conduct. Although *health* could undoubtedly mean many things, health as an identity category gestures to the ways in which the AIDS crisis makes serostatus yet another means of classifying persons—that is, an identity category of its own.⁹³ That the chapter pivots to discuss a particular type of white silence—white gay silence about interracial sex—implies a link between AIDS discourse and the discourse around cross-racial desire, though the specific effects of AIDS on cross-racial sexual encounter remain undertheorized in his piece.

For the most part, though, Reid-Pharr does not take this tack; rather, the threat of AIDS lurks just below the surface of this entire chapter, and he only mentions the disease once by name. In this singular instance, Reid-Pharr names the epidemic via the "community" it engenders: "The H.I.V./A.I.D.S. community helped focus our thinking about issues of risk, disease, and decay."⁹⁴ In the years directly following the apex of AIDS-related deaths in the United States, this would have been a more obvious connection. Indeed, such an invocation recasts Reid-Pharr's initial use of *silence*: The word recalls ACT UP's famous slogan, "SILENCE=DEATH"—a phrase that would still be freshly ringing in the ears of queer critics writing at the time "Dinge" was first published. Reid-Pharr suggests, by way of "the H.I.V./A.I.D.S. community," that marginal queer populations might move us away from the fantasy that all queer sex is liberatory. What Reid-Pharr does not state outright is that the increased dangers of acquiring HIV might also increase the self-awareness or self-reflection he posits as distinctly "queer" at the start of his essay. If this hypercognizance is already extant before AIDS, the new threat of HIV transmission within the gay male community that surfaces by the time "Dinge" is published heightens both the stakes of sex and the awareness of these stakes.

In 2014, twenty years after "Living as a Lesbian" was first published, Reid-Pharr pens a blog post for the *Feminist Wire* titled "This Useful Death." Halfway through the short, polemical essay, Reid-Pharr reminds his audience of the precarity of the past, by way of a cliché of the present: "Gay men of my generation, particularly black gay men, are continually reminded of how lucky we are to be alive."⁹⁵ Castigating those for whom politics begins and ends at this trite injunction, Reid-Pharr laments that modern queer activism, lulled into "a vehicle of capitalist hegemony" and "freighted with narrow self-interest and cynicism," has abandoned its radically disruptive potential. As a remedy for this normative malaise, Reid-Pharr conjures a familiar figure: Audre Lorde. Championing Lorde's later work on "health, desire, embodiment, and dying"—work that takes seriously both "the erotic" and the realities of dying of terminal cancer—Reid-Pharr again waxes universal, even as he invokes the specific. A mutual claim to death, bound up in a mutual claim to embodied erotics, produces, for Reid-Pharr, both radical disruption and profound solidarity:

> If we are to take seriously Lorde's call for women, people of color, and so-called sexual minorities to engage and celebrate the power of the erotic

then we must attend to the fact that to be human is first and foremost to be animal. We eat, drink, laugh, cry, fight, fuck, give birth, suffer, and die.... The gay man, vulgar and feral, skin against skin, locked in sweaty embrace with a partner not yet become a lover is a being in struggle against its own domestication, a citizen with his eyes cast beyond the state. The same man, standing wounded and alert by the side of his dying mother feels within himself a force, an erotics of living *and* dying that has the potential to disrupt both self and society.[96]

In the deaths of his mother, his Black gay compatriots, and Lorde, Reid-Pharr finds a point of connection, a "frailty and funkiness" that "forces recognition of our profound connection to the rest of existence." In his list of names, Reid-Pharr attests to the divide most impossible to cross—the divide that Sedgwick calls "the ontological crack between the living and the dead."[97] In doing so, he performs what Hong describes as "two contradictory political imperatives: that of mourning death and understanding death as proliferative."[98] A Black gay man in America, Reid-Pharr is already part of a population targeted for extermination from multiple angles.

The threat of annihilation threatens different people differently. But there is also something shared in feeling the threat. The cross-identification that Reid-Pharr performs cannot be fully understood without the historical context in which it occurs and without a wider understanding of the state racism and misogynoir that put both Black gay men and Black lesbians at high risk. During an epidemic, that already-extant danger increases exponentially. It is precisely at this moment of mourning that the paradox of queer identificatory politics at the peak of the AIDS crisis emerges. For it is in the mutually shared vulnerability to terminal illness, directly brought on by state-sanctioned denial of care, that we find a common point of solidarity between Black lesbians and Black gay men.

Taken together, the intertextual citation and the intratextual interruption in "Living as a Lesbian" and "The Shock of Gary Fisher" reproduce the rhythmic shocks theorized in Reid-Pharr's other work. There are several ways to read these recurrent interruptions. They may be the rhythmic blows of gay bashing, akin to the steady death drive of homophobic violence described in Edelman's *No Future* (2004)—a "rhythm" that "beats out, with every blow of the beating delivered to Matthew Shepard's skull, a counterpoint to the melody's sacred hymn to the meaning of life."[99] They may be the sonic, ambiguous blows of the whip that echo in the background of Isaac Julien's *The Attendant* (1993) or the recurrent and repetitive rhythms of anti-Black violence in the wake of slavery.[100] At the same time as they conjure the specter of death, such rhythms and breaks may be the scansion of a line of poetry by Reid-Pharr, Clarke, Hemphill, Lorde, or others. They may also be the repeatedly sought-out violence of staged domination ever present in the memoirs of Fisher, an erotic of power, pain, and pleasure that Fisher himself called "obsessive."[101] Shocks are also, of course, electric; a shock is a zap of energy that might turn on a light bulb, power an engine, violently condition a desired sexual response, or, as Mary Shelley might have us imagine, wake a dead body. The interruptive rhetorical shocks in Reid-Pharr's prose also recall the violent openings of possibility that emerge at the end of "Tearing the Goat's Flesh": Here, rupture and death become, impossibly, a way of forging the radical new. Read another way, Reid-Pharr's interruptions mirror the violence that, in the era of AIDS, constitutes a point of fleeting but nonetheless extant identification across gender and race. The formal breaks in Reid-Pharr's work signal an interruptive and repetitive violence, the shared experience of which links the Black gay man to the Black lesbian feminists with which he identifies.

These options are not mutually exclusive but rather paradoxical: They abruptly undercut Reid-Pharr's cross-identifications while simultaneously providing the tenuous link that allows for Reid-Pharr's ability to write (and live) across difference. In fact, ironically, it is their very nature as shock—be it the shock of interruption, obscenity, or violence—that allow these textual moments to facilitate Reid-Pharr's identification across difference. Such interruptions trouble the distinction between practice and theory, between academic and obscene.

4

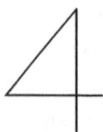

Gay-Male-Oriented and Now

TENDENCIES' TENDENCIES

Like many Duke University Press books, Eve Kosofsky Sedgwick's *Tendencies* (1993) boasts a captivating cover. A photograph takes up most of the book's front cover. In it, we see a closed ticket booth fashioned out of chicken wire and unfinished wood. The setting of the photo is ambiguous, though it appears to be a rural fairground; there are pink and white trailers in the background, and a hand-painted sign announces admission prices for adults, children, and children under six. These details fade into the background in the presence of the photo's remarkable focal point: a large, flat piece of plywood propped up on the wall of the ticket booth. The painted image on the plywood is arresting. Four people, absent any context, lean sharply slantwise; from left to right, a man leans in a severe diagonal line toward a child, a woman, and a man, who recoil backward at an angle complementary to their aggressor. Their mutually slanting bodies, which defy both the laws of physics and the conventions of realist painting, underscore the strange comedy of the image, and the man's and the family's exaggerated tilt contributes to the painting's absurdist, folk art charm. At the same time, that exaggeration is uncanny, even slightly unsettling. The title formatting of the book on which this photograph appears reinforces both the man's aggressive forward slant and the family's hyperbolic withdrawal—above the image, the word TENDENCIES appears in all caps, harshly italicized, in slender sans serif. Crack the spine, and this pattern repeats: On the title page, a gigantic slanting *T* towers over the rest of the title, its stem a bold black slash mark. Just in case readers did not quite pick up on the motif, on the first page of each chapter, Sedgwick's block paragraphs are justified obliquely, so that their edge forms yet another slant.

Were readers of *Tendencies* to eventually shift their focus from the book's aesthetic style to its argumentative substance, they would find that these proliferating diagonal lines hint at the collection's main thematic motif: crossing, or moving from one point to a different point. *Tendencies* is a text that enacts multiple crossings (of academic taboos, of genres, of schools of thought, etc.), but its most obvious and prevalent crossings are its author's multiple identifications across difference. Consider this opening scene from the foreword of *Tendencies*:

> At the 1992 gay pride parade in New York City, there was a handsome, intensely muscular man in full leather regalia, sporting on his distended chest a T-shirt that read, KEEP YOUR LAWS OFF MY UTERUS. The two popular READ MY LIPS T-shirts marketed by ACT UP were also in evidence, and by the thousands. But for the first time it was largely gay men who were wearing the version of the shirt that features two turn-of-the-century women in a passionate clinch. Most of the people wearing the version with the osculating male sailors, on the other hand, were lesbians. FAGGOT and BIG FAG were the T-shirt legends self-applied by many, many women; DYKE and the more topical LICK BUSH by many, many men.... And everywhere at the march, on women and on men, there were T-shirts that said, simply: QUEER.[1]

Throwing her audience directly into a bustling and angry crowd, Sedgwick both underscores the violent immediacy of the moment and describes a coalitional politic engendered by crisis. As Sedgwick goes on to explain, the cross-gender, cross-sexuality identification that she observes at the 1992 gay Pride parade epitomizes *Tendencies'* idiosyncratic understanding of *queer*. "Titles and subtitles that at various times I've attached to the essays in *Tendencies* tend toward 'across' formulations: *across genders, across sexualities, across genres, across 'perversions,'*" she writes. "The word 'queer' itself," she observes at one point in her foreword, "means *across*."[2] Questionable etymologies aside, the point remains: Cross-identification drives Sedgwick's early critical endeavor.

Those familiar with Sedgwick's writing know that identification across difference is both a widespread theme and a recurrent method throughout her oeuvre—so much so that it has become, as Ramzi Fawaz recently puts it, "nearly a cliché" to discuss cross-identification in Sedgwick.[3] Most often, critical commentary on this aspect of Sedgwick's work focuses on her overt and generative identifications with gay men, but a few others note Sedgwick's tendency to identify across multiple lines of difference, including "genders, sexualities, classes, ethnoracial formations, temperaments, abilities, nationalities, and family ties."[4] Usually, these critical commenters praise this identificatory impulse, arguing that the recurring moments of unexpected identification in Sedgwick's work challenge the reifications of identity to which queer theory is so opposed. While much ink has been spilled on Sedgwick's lifelong and effusive identification with gay men and as a gay man (both by herself and by critics who read her), scholarship on this Sedgwickian idiosyncrasy tends toward full praise or indignant condemnation. While Sedgwick's identifications across gender and sexuality are well known and often celebrated, her identifications across race are typically either elided or condemned. Nonetheless, her uncanny ability to forge modes of connection across these all-too-rigid categories has variously been described as a reparative practice of loving relationality, experimental permeability, solidarity across stigma, and communism, to name but a few.[5] Sometimes, but much less often, Sedgwick's promiscuous identifications are met with more suspicion: For a few more ornery critics, Sedgwick's compulsion to identify with a myriad of subjects who are interpellated differently than she is and who experience life differently than she does is at best an attempt at coalition that ends up willfully ignoring material difference (i.e., a well-meaning but ultimately harmful fantasy) and at worst an appropriative and domineering gesture (i.e., an aggressive and totalizing will to "know" the other).

In either case, with all but a few exceptions, not enough attention is paid to the moments in which Sedgwick meets this identificatory crossing with difficulty rather than ease. The diagonal lines on the front page of *Tendencies* gesture toward impasse and interruption as much as they gesture toward chiasmus and coalition. Like the slash mark that both divides and sutures the Frankensteinian conjunctive *and/or*, these diagonal lines at various points connote rupture, barrier, and movement across. Notoriously, Sedgwick's texts are, by and large, not interested in identity formation via direct identification; instead, these early writings more often explore complex and messy identifications across identities. By her own admission, Sedgwick becomes a critic via "tortuous," "alienating" cross-identifications.[6] From the first page of *Tendencies* onward, Sedgwick's early writing stages scenes of alloidentification that repeatedly, and often spectacularly, break down. As such, *Tendencies* provides an example par excellence of the type of performative bad passing I have been exploring thus far.

Regardless of where readers stand vis-à-vis the political and theoretical ethics of Sedgwick's identificatory writing, little attention has been paid to the thing that most interests me about these much-discussed moments of identification across difference: the fact that, quite simply, they are usually clumsy. At times, these leaps of recognition seem easy, but often, Sedgwick comes up against what she calls the "aching gap in the real."[7] It would be a mistake, however, to read Sedgwick's multiple encounters with this aching gap as failures of identification or as testaments to the impossibility of writing and reading across identities. In examining these moments, my aim is not to expose the identifications Sedgwick stages as fraudulent, fantastical, or failed. While these moments certainly clue readers in to the incommensurate ways in which race, gender, sexuality, and other identity categories are structured, experienced, and theorized, *failure* is not the right word for the phenomenon I trace here, because it is these moments of spectacular difficulty that drive and, indeed, sustain her inquiry.[8] Rather, focusing on moments of negative relation or breakdown in Sedgwick's work might more effectively illuminate how her spectacularly bad passing leads us toward an understanding of identity in which disconnect is not the saboteur of identification but rather part and parcel of it.

Often, these texts arrive at Sedgwick's avowed identifications through scenes of embarrassment. The anecdotes that populate her pages overshare information, revel in humiliation, and often recount an awkward malfunction. That's not to say that the author herself is embarrassed by the stories that she tells—in fact, the perverse charm of her work is that she revels in the revelation. I use *embarrassment* here to name a particular type of staged shame. Unlike more straightforward feminist anecdotes whose primary purpose is to open theory to the "real" world of lived experience, Sedgwick's embarrassing tableaux are first and foremost staged. Strategically revealing her own embarrassing stories, Sedgwick makes a scene, in more ways than one. Writing that "fortunately, the visibly chastised is by now my favorite style," Sedgwick creates a theater of embarrassment that makes her at once deliciously vulnerable (exposed) and impressively nervy (brave enough to showcase her identifications).[9] Shame is not the only affect in the background here: Indeed, the temper-tantrum implications of the phrase "making a scene" additionally serve as a reminder that the original motivation for Sedgwick's piece was a call for papers for a conference at Columbia University whose theme was the "Poetics of Anger."[10] Motivated by both a masochistic and a sadistic pleasure, Sedgwick's embarrassing anecdotes do something more than simply open the real world up to her readers. Joseph Litvak calls this tendency to be "self-critical but not exactly self-deprecating" Sedgwick's nerve, an apt term because it both takes guts and evinces nervousness.[11] It's a strategy equal parts risky and pushy; the effect is both disarming and charming.

The theatricality of embarrassment challenges the authenticity typically tied to theory done in an anecdotal vein. In *Tendencies*, embarrassing anecdotes are a useful signpost for these moments of disruption that propel *as if!* criticism: The moment of embarrassment, calculated to both humiliate the author and surprise the reader, acts as a punctum that disrupts the otherwise untroubled identificatory paths in Sedgwick's writing. Reading these anecdotes as staged scenes of embarrassment, readers are not really catching Sedgwick doing anything but, perhaps, acting; she is caught in the act of acting ashamed or angry. Personal anecdotes reveal both how Sedgwick comes to recognize herself in text via (embarrassingly) circuitous routes and how others (to her embarrassment) neglect to recognize her the same way. By looking at places where Sedgwick performs her own personal embarrassment, we can start to glean how these performances display the negative relation at the heart of all of Sedgwick's identifications.

THE WOMAN-IDENTIFIED MALE-IDENTIFIED WOMAN

An early instance of critical identification across difference, "A Poem Is Being Written" is an exemplary model of the kind of cross-identification that runs throughout *Tendencies*. In this highly personal, theoretically ambitious article first published in 1987—and later reprinted as the eleventh chapter of *Tendencies*—Sedgwick analyzes several poems she wrote as a child to tell the story of her own development as, in her words, a "homosexual" reader.[12] As "A Poem Is Being Written" progresses, it shifts its narrative focus from Sedgwick's early poetry to her childhood experiences with disciplinary spanking, theorizing a link between her young fondness for enjambed poetic verse and her experiences of being spanked. In a final, spectacular pivot, Sedgwick confesses the essay's greatest scandal: By Sedgwick's own psychoanalytic self-diagnosis, her memories of corporal punishment and poetic enjambment later manifest in her own unnamable (because gravely undertheorized) anal eroticism and penchant for queer reading.

Even as it purportedly adopts the anecdotal method associated with feminist identitarian knowledge production (consciousness raising, standpoint theory, etc.), "A Poem Is Being Written" complicates the idea that one could write from a stable perspective at all. Indeed, many of the stories she tells already explicitly tell us this. By her own account, Sedgwick's exposed poetry parallels the exposed ass of a beaten child, and both exposures provide the background for Sedgwick's explorations of her own current poetic and critical proclivities. The scene of spanking—a scene saturated with the excruciating libidinal excitations of humiliation, exhibitionism, pain, and pleasure—serves all at once as a site of embarrassment, vulnerability, and aggression writing (indeed, we might associate the phrase "making a scene" more with a child's temper tantrum than with a piece of literary criticism). Sedgwick does this in a characteristically provocative way, baring her ass for her audience. Is she preparing to bottom? Is she expecting a spank? Or is this more of a roguish moon? While the essay's subject matter threatens its author's position as an expert, the move still feels aggressive: She's either topping from the bottom or playfully flashing us without our consent.[13]

"A Poem Is Being Written" is the story of how Sedgwick becomes a critic, but more specifically, it is the story of how she becomes a male homosexual reader. Noting poetry's and spanking's shared rhythmic and theatrical qualities, she links her anal erotic attachments to both a cross-gender affinity with gay men and a penchant for what she calls "homosexual reading." The primal scenes described in "A Poem Is Being Written" sow the seeds for Sedgwick's later adult symptoms, sexualities, and critical methods and styles. Sedgwick devotes as much time to detailed description of her personal erotics of the ass (spanking, anal sex) as she does to describing her personal erotics of writing and reading (enjambment, criticism), refusing to take the parallel development of these two erotic sensibilities as pure serendipity. The result of this confluence is that "A Poem Is Being Written" does not separate the corporeal/corporal and the textual. As "A Poem Is Being Written" makes abundantly clear, Sedgwick first comes to her own queer consciousness at the scene of reading and acts on this consciousness through published critical writing: "Along with, at any rate, my practice of homosexual reading—a well-taught skepticism about the representative adequacy of language, consorting perhaps not oddly with a pressing sense that there was something somewhere else for it to be adequate to, and with a (to me now) most imposing deferral of the question what any of this had to do with *me*—there was developing something else too, which I did not at the time think of as a practice of homosexual writing."[14]

Insofar as Sedgwick's homosexual reading consists of rooting out hidden gay male subtext (the unmentioned act of sodomy in Oscar Wilde's *Britannica* entry, for example), it constitutes a specific practice of paranoid criticism and of cross-identificatory alliance: Her own homosexual feeling stems from her recognition of a shared suspicion. "A Poem Is Being Written" narrates a process of self-discovery that begins with a sneaking suspicion, felt at age twelve, that both childhood authorities and the authors of texts she was reading as a child were purposefully omitting things:

> Nothing—no form of contact with people of any gender or sexuality—
> makes me feel so, simply, *homosexual* as the evocation of library after-
> noons of dead-ended searches, "wild" guesses that, as I got more ex-
> perienced, turned out to be almost always right. Why, when I ask the
> *Britannica* about the crime of Oscar Wilde, does it tell me about "offenses
> under the Criminal Law Amendment Act," nowhere summarized? If in-
> formation is being withheld (and to recognize even that is a skill that it-
> self requires, and gets, development), must it not be this information? I
> don't know whether there can be said to be for our culture a distinctive

practice of "homosexual reading," but if so, it must surely bear the fossil-marks of the whole array of evasive techniques by which the *Britannica*, the *Reader's Guide*, the wooden subject, author, and title catalogues frustrate and educate the young idea.[15]

It is possible to view this impulse as a symptom of a more suspect objective, an obsessive need to get it all down, to categorize, to classify; here, Sedgwick's is the reading that controls, that polices identities via an ever-more-vigilant taxonomy. The results of such an accounting run counter to the very anti-identitarian politics with which Sedgwick seems to align.

But knowing is never easy, nor is it simple.[16] The multiple comings-out in "A Poem Is Being Written" proliferate a myriad of sometimes conflicting, sometimes shifting identities. Unlike many conventional coming out stories, Sedgwick's confessional, psychoanalytic mode allows her to come out as multiple identities to her readers, each time using a "[verb] as a [noun]" formula that again recalls Jane Gallop's formula "reading as a ____." She reads "as a poet," needs and loves "as a woman," and enjoys a sex act—anal penetration—that, she points out, is commonly referred to as "being used as a man."[17] Even Sedgwick's self-identification as a critic is twisted and tricky. Only once in "A Poem Is Being Written" does Sedgwick identify as a writer of criticism, and she does so by way of fiction; in a quoted excerpt from her poem "The Warm Decembers" (1994), the self-referential character E is described as both a critic and a poet, but only in the wake of a telling typo: E is "'an important writer of fiction and poetry,' / of criticism and poetry, of course it is meant to say."[18] By specifically naming her paranoid impulse to read between the lines "homosexual reading," and subsequently labeling her own forays into both poetry and criticism "homosexual writing," this work sets the stage for her own queer literary-critical practice, rooted in a strong identification with gay men.

In a climactic coming out moment, the "as a" trope proliferates, and these different ways of being, recognizing, reading, writing, and desiring become increasingly difficult to distinguish: "In among the many ways I do identify as a woman, the identification as a gay person is a firmly male one, identification 'as' a gay man; and in among its tortuous and alienating paths are knit the relations, for me, of telling and of knowing."[19] The word *tortuous*, which also appears in her parenthetical explanations of her male identification—"(Femaleness is always (though always differently) to be looked for *in* the tortuousness, in the strangeness of the figure made between the flatly gendered definition from an outside view and the always more or less crooked stiles to be surveyed from an inner)"—makes its second debut in this coming out scene.[20] The extra emphasis afforded by the echo of *tortuous/tortuousness* drives home the twisted, sometimes painful relationship to identification elucidated in Sedgwick's work. It is on this tortuous moment that I want to linger—and not only because my students, without fail, read *tortuous* as *torturous*, a telling mistake. *Tortuous*, like *queer*, also comes from an etymological root meeting "twist" (*tortuous* from the Latin *torque*, to twist; *queer*, again, from the Proto-Indo-European root **terkw-*, to twist).[21] Here, the deferral of the question of identity is not unlike the suspension of belief crucial to Johnson's "as if" reading, in which readers must suspend their own disbelief in the validity of their (actually imperfect) translation. This essay outs Sedgwick. But outs her as what? A woman? A gay person? A homosexual? A gay man? A feminist with an "intensively loaded male identification"?[22] The question, not unanswered so much as answered too much, interrupts the easy flow of her prose, drawing her readers' attention to the impasses produced by her circuitous routes of recognition, to the anxiety, embarrassment, and pleasure produced by those proliferating routes, and to the repeated failure of her audience to recognize those routes as valid.

Sedgwick's use of *homosexual* carbon dates her essay. The word *queer* doesn't appear in her first two widely celebrated works, *Between Men* (1985) and *Epistemology of the Closet* (1990). This aspect of the story of queer theory's early days is well known and often repeated in its origin stories. The word *queer* doesn't show up really at all in these early works; it is only later, as queer theory develops into a legible field, that Sedgwick fully embraces the term. Replacing the earlier formulas *gay-male-oriented analysis, antihomophobic reading,* and *homosexual reading* with *queer theory,* the genesis story that queer theory tells itself runs the risk of erasing the specificities of the field's arrival. The turn from *gay male* and *male homosexual* to *queer* in Sedgwick's work had consequences for both queer theory and Sedgwick's reception within the academy. As Lee Edelman argues, one effect of this switch from *gay-male-oriented analysis* in *Epistemology* to *queer theory* in Sedgwick's later work has been the elision of specific differences of gender and sexuality, and in particular it erases the historical friction between some strands of feminist theory and gay and lesbian theory.[23] In this genealogy, the substitution of *queer theory* in place of the earlier and more specific formula *gay-male-oriented analysis* allows feminism and queer theory to exist in a more peaceable relation: "There are reasons, of course, why feminism can couple more comfortably with queer theory than with a 'gay male-oriented' analysis. The latter would foreground divisions (between male and female, between gender and sexuality) while the former suggests more pacific or even reparative encounter."[24] Read this way, Sedgwick's continued attention to, theorization of, and orientation toward gay men and gay male structures of desire is a substitution: Her theoretical focus replaces her own desire, figure, and name with the desires, figures, and names of gay men. This substitution allows her to become a knowing and powerful subject, despite her claim to a methodology that resists the mastery of knowing. Edelman's valuable take illuminates a troubling tendency of queer theory to mythologize its inception, and I agree that Sedgwick's older phrase, *gay-male-oriented analysis*, does more to heighten divisions that the new and more forgiving formula, *queer* theory, sometimes elides.

But Sedgwick's essay does not mask these moments of disconnect; rather, it brings them to light. Examining the cross-identification in Sedgwick's work, Robyn Wiegman argues that Sedgwick's invocation of *queer* signals a "confrontation with convergences," a move that, in a climate quite suspicious of Sedgwick's nonlesbian identity, functions "*as a defense* against the charge of appropriation, inauthenticity, and heterosexual complicity."[25] The term *queer* thus takes on an anti-identitarian charge. Rosy interpretations of Sedgwick's writing have focused on convergence rather than confrontation. But the frequent occurrence of disconnect or bad passing in *Tendencies* and elsewhere in Sedgwick's work constitutes a pattern that, when tracked, reveals a strategy of performed, calculated self-exposure that highlights the difficulty of difference. This chapter first examines these more explicit scenes of disconnect before marking the same patterns in Sedgwick's easier, more infamous, and much more discussed identification with (usually white) gay men. Focusing on moments of spectacular cross-identification in Sedgwick teases out a pattern of staged embarrassment that is integral to her writing across difference.

Although it is explicitly about her identification with gay men, "A Poem Is Being Written" covertly nods to Sedgwick's identification with lesbian womanhood, as well as with Black womanhood. These second, subtler moments of embarrassingly difficult cross-identifications constitute Sedgwick's first attempts at the radical cross-identification that will manifest fully in her later work. With the exception, perhaps, of the aforementioned embarrassment of failing to identify with her younger self, Sedgwick's first declared major identificatory embarrassment in "A Poem Is Being Written" is her failure to identify as a woman-identified woman. I deliberately maintain the redundancy of "identify . . . identified" here to draw a distinction between two different but related identificatory problems in Sedgwick: the first, her difficulties identifying as a "woman," and second, her difficulties identifying as a "woman-identified woman." The latter difficulty admits embarrassment about not reading, writing, or fucking "as a lesbian"—an embarrassment that Sedgwick alludes to at several points in "A Poem Is Being Written." Though her text performs the shame of not quite identifying as a lesbian (precisely what that would entail, she does not entirely say) in the body of her essay, Sedgwick mostly chooses to stage this embarrassment discreetly, in parenthetical asides, discursive footnotes, and sly paraleipses.

This embarrassment first sneaks its way into a paragraph explaining why Sedgwick has chosen to read anality as male, despite the somewhat inconvenient fact that assholes do not exclusively belong to men. In this remarkable passage, Sedgwick insists that reading the eroticized asshole as male, and then almost always male homosexual, is both in accordance with the popular imagination and crucial to the project of her essay. Furthermore, Sedgwick notes, female anality does not carry with it associations with lesbianism in nearly the same way that male anality carries associations with male homosexuality: "Aside from the well-rehearsed though controversial asymmetries between the cultural importance of (the regulation of) male homosexuality and that of lesbianism, there is the further obvious asymmetry, more important here, that female anality hasn't, to put it mildly, the representative relation to lesbianism that male anality has to male homosexuality. In fact, one of the few topoi in which the female anus ever becomes sexually visible is that of a woman's 'being used as a man,' as a receptive homosexual man or a man who is being raped."[26] Fascinatingly, "A Poem Is Being Written" does bring up the ever-present possibility of a lesbian anal erotic, if only through a kind of paraleipsis, by telling her readers that a lesbian anal erotic is not what she is going to tell them about. At first glance, "A Poem Is Being Written" only conveniently sidesteps the objection that people of multiple genders and sexes have assholes but also dismisses the possibility, for example, of cultural imaginings of the female anus as a second vagina rather than simply as a substitute of a gay man's anus.[27] A female erotic of the asshole—lesbian or otherwise—is, at this point in the essay, unimaginable. Like the exposed ass, Sedgwick's possible but unfulfilled identifications themselves seem to be a site of shame or embarrassment, visible only in the endnotes or in parenthetical asides. True to this pattern, Sedgwick follows the above paragraph with a telling and rather teasing extratextual annotation, wedged in the endnotes: "Though interestingly, it is almost only in contemporary lesbian writing (of a particular, 'politically incorrect' libertarian stamp) that there is anything informative or engaging at all about women's anuses and their pleasures."[28] Here, the text still leaves open alternate interpretations of her own sexual proclivities, even if she relegates these possibilities to her essay's formal discursive marginalia.

A few pages after Sedgwick's assertion that lesbian sexuality is not going to be what her essay is about, "A Poem Is Being Written" again opens the possibility of a lived lesbian sexuality. Following the confession of her absent survival drive, Sedgwick writes, "The depression of these teen years, at any rate, I survived through passionate and loving relationships with—have I mentioned this?—women."[29] Sedgwick immediately couches her potential lesbianism as a missed opportunity, even, in her words, "failure": "I have spent—wasted—a long time gazing in renewed stupefaction at the stupidity and psychic expense of my failure, during that time, to make the obvious swerve that would have connected my homosexual desire and identification with my need and love, as a woman, of women."[30] Here, shame is a psychic expense: Sedgwick recounts her stupefied embarrassment at failing to notice the obvious.

Embarrassment, here, is about Sedgwick's own delay in realizing something in herself. Melissa Solomon, writing on Sedgwick's vicarious lesbian imaginary, smartly describes the impasse that this delay can create, noting that, in *Tendencies* and elsewhere, "two different but uniquely powerful routes ... begin moving toward a common destination precisely at the point where the transitivities of affect and knowledge cross, in this order: (positive) affect to 'gender' and (negative) knowledge to 'sexualities.' When this transitivity is missing, the tautology Sedgwick describes in 'A Poem Is Being Written' freezes the possibility of lesbian realization, which is still 'stupefied' and 'stupid' in the face of even certain knowledge that hasn't any transitive potential."[31] At other points, Solomon names the space created by this impasse as a space of yearning and transition, a "lesbian bardo" to spend time in. Solomon explains this realization as "coming to" rather than "coming out," noting that realization has, in this case, a different relation to knowledge.[32] Once again, the gap or impasse produces desire and pleasure, in addition to embarrassment and anxiety.

Staging spaces of yearning and of embarrassment draws attention not only to Sedgwick's own personal feelings and thoughts about the missed lesbian connection but also cleverly to the demands of the academic authorities to which she directs her prose. In another enclosed parenthetical only a few paragraphs after her coy admission-cum-dismissal of lesbian longing, Sedgwick not only outs herself as a male-identified feminist woman writer but also as someone who took embarrassingly long to come to that conclusion:

> (Perhaps I should say that it is not to me as a feminist that this intensively loaded male identification is most an embarrassment; no woman becomes less a woman through any amount of "male identification," to the extent that femaleness is always (though always differently) to be looked for *in* the tortuousness, in the strangeness of the figure made between the flatly gendered definition from an outside view and the always more or less crooked stiles to be surveyed from an inner. A male-identified woman, even if there could thoroughly be such a thing, would still be a real kind of woman just as (though far more inalterably than) an assimilated Jew is a real kind of Jew: more protected in some ways, more vulnerable in others, than those whose paths of identification have been different, but as fully of the essence of the thing.)[33]

Though the paragraph reports a lack of embarrassment on Sedgwick's part, the double couching of her assertion in a nested parenthetical aside tells a different story. The punctuation bespeaks the same hesitation performed in her previous qualifying notes and stages her anxiety regarding her own misaligned critical loyalties. The entire explanation is, in typical Sedgwickian fashion, verbose, and her sentence structure quite complex; there are two sets of parentheses nestled inside a third set of parentheses. In this convoluted parenthetical, Sedgwick defensively negotiates between two contradictory demands on her knowledge production: a patriarchal and reactionary academy, on the one hand, and a newly carved-out feminist academic space, on the other.

The fact that Sedgwick was largely recognized as a married heterosexual woman, and not as a lesbian, made her work particularly susceptible to a certain stripe of lesbian feminist critique. Sedgwick is performing for those second-wave feminists whom she knows will police her. The political struggles of the sixties and seventies no doubt ushered in the new trend of personal reading and writing that Sedgwick's essay, at surface, appears to exemplify. In her 2008 preface to *Epistemology of the Closet*, for example, she goes so far as to acknowledge that her own so-called textual preference for personal, first-person writing stems from her feminist training: "Another aspect of *Epistemology of the Closet* that stands out on rereading is its insistent perspectivism. Along with the ready use of the first person, this may have been something learned from 1970s feminist writing."[34] To be sure, the phrase "male-identified woman" is meant to remind readers of the title of the famous Radicalesbians polemic "The Woman Identified Woman" (1970) that had rocked the second Congress to Unite Women just seventeen years prior. In this inflammatory declaration, lesbian members of the Congress to Unite Women blatantly assert not only that the question of sexual relations between women is central to the project of female liberation but that women who remain "male-identified in [their] heads . . . cannot realize [their] autonomy as human beings."[35] In the Radicalesbians' manifesto, *woman-identified woman* becomes nearly synonymous with *lesbian*, defined capaciously as "the range of all women condensed to the point of explosion."[36] As "The Woman Identified Woman" makes abundantly clear, a particular brand of seventies feminism, on which many academics of Sedgwick's generation cut their teeth, remained quite invested in an author's avowed sexual preference as a determinant of their feminist legitimacy—a litmus test that Sedgwick, by her own admission, would perhaps not pass. Musing on Nancy K. Miller's charge to "write 'as a feminist,'" Gallop writes that "the temptation to identify . . . textual preference as feminist recalls the urge to identify a feminist sexual preference. That tendency was all the rage in the seventies feminism. . . . Many feminists (both lesbian and heterosexual) now feel that it was a mistake to attempt to label as feminist what anyone did 'in the flesh of practice.'"[37] Gallop's observation hints at how Sedgwick's embarrassing admissions of male identification confound the idea that reading is as straightforward as many second-wave feminists would have it.

Rather than hide Sedgwick's politically problematic identifications, "A Poem Is Being Written" uses the personal—the very mode of writing that many feminist circles demanded at the time—to fight these policing logics. Sedgwick's open admission—at conferences, in her writing, and elsewhere—that she was not a lesbian already put her at odds with many leading feminist academics at the time. Heather Love, for example, notes that "the vision of a queer community of outsiders is driven by Sedgwick's complex identification with gayness, and as a gay man. This act of cross-identification was unsettling for many gay, lesbian, and feminist scholars, who articulated fears of appropriation and also anger and disbelief that queer studies would be the province of straight academics."[38] Though Love writes that "debates surrounding Sedgwick's identification across gender and sexuality, explosive at the time, seem almost quaint in the context of more thoroughgoing critiques of queer imperialism," she is also quick to point out that the initial spirit of these debates is far from over: "The scandal of queer's reach across difference has only grown since Sedgwick was attacked at conferences and in print."[39] Wiegman, recalling a lesbian studies conference at Yale, observes that "Eve's triangulated identification as a married woman who loved and studied gay male life in the context of Western cultural organization was taken as a political as well as professional threat to feminist and lesbian feminist audiences. . . . In the early days of institutionalizing identity-oriented knowledges, when discerning an identity object of study from the vantage point of 'being it' was what identity studies meant, Sedgwick understood well the dicey terrain in which her first book, *Between Men*, maneuvered."[40] Drawing attention to the complicated modes of alloidentification at work in Sedgwick's criticism, she recollects how identity-conscious lesbian feminists repeatedly lobbed the refrain "Are you a lesbian?" at Sedgwick during gay and lesbian studies conferences. Sedgwick's vocal academic and social interest in gay men at times exacerbated this friction, especially because she was working in a moment where lesbian feminists increasingly had to grapple with the presence of gay men in their social and intellectual milieu. What she confesses in "A Poem Is Being Written" does not bolster her credibility with other feminists; if anything, it places that credibility in jeopardy.

WHITE ASSES

Another qualifying amendment in her story of anal affinities, again nestled quietly in an endnote, brings Sedgwick's otherwise muted musings on racial difference into sharper relief. In an endnote to "A Poem Is Being Written," Sedgwick comments on the (possible) difference race makes:

I understand that there are strong cultural differences in these percep-
tions: for instance that Afro-American eyes find it easier to see women's
bodies—and through them, women's character, their sway, their sexuality, these not being figured either as minimalness or as tight muscular
control—as being strengthened, not discredited by their substance. (Still,
"the sexual politics of the ass are not identical to the sexual politics of the
asshole" . . . : I am told, though I can't make a generalization of my own
about this, that a high valuation in Afro-American culture of women's
substance including the rear end coexists with an attitude toward anal
eroticism that is as severe as the Euro-American. "You've got the right
church," Bessie Smith sings, "but the wrong pew.")⁴¹

At first glance, it would seem that Sedgwick includes this endnote largely to cover
her own ass; the qualification is meant to avoid the trap of painting all backsides
with the same race-ignorant brush. Her discomfort manifests, again, in stylistic
couching. Sedgwick can only come to this information secondhand ("I am told"),
having no way of making "a generalization of [her] own" (though, of course, one
could argue that she goes on to do just that). She also falls back on passive voice
and oblique acting subjects, she participates in verbal acrobatics that make "Afro-
American eyes," and not acting Black subjects, the subject of her sentence, so that
there appear to be no agential actors with which to identify at all. If we were to read
this moment ungenerously, we could say that Sedgwick's text here participates in
what Sharon Patricia Holland calls "a certain mode of queer theorizing that cannot account for itself without the body's erasure—even in its precise moment of
absolutely recognizing and inscribing it."⁴² Sedgwick sidesteps the body by citing
"strong cultural differences," a curious move that allows her to also ignore a long
and racist history—one spanning from Saartjie (Sarah) Baartman to "The Champagne Incident" and beyond—in which the ass becomes the overdetermined site
of Black female sexuality.⁴³ Here, Sedgwick seems unwilling to insert herself into
this history, even as she duplicates racist assumptions in her broad descriptions of
cultural divide.

Nonetheless, in this lengthy endnote, Sedgwick's text gestures toward different possible interpretations of her case study. The result of this addendum is a
small, whiplash-producing sortie into the possibility of identification across race,
a dip into an imagined alternative alliance—not with gay men but with the bisex-
ual, double-entendre-wielding blues woman to whom this endnote refers in its final sentence. Though brief and sequestered, Sedgwick's ruminations on the "high
valuation in Afro-American culture of women's substance including the rear end"
point at fruitful points of cross-racial connection at the intersection of "fat" and

"woman."[44] As is the case with the possibility of a lesbian anal erotic, this identification remains largely unspoken, at least when compared with her later identification with male homosexuality. Though Sedgwick is quick to dismiss the possibility of Black female anal pleasure, holding that the "sexual politics of the asshole" is likely largely the same across race, the pleasures of spanking, after all, are not primarily rectal but gluteal. Given Sedgwick's hunch that the "sexual politics of the ass" might be different across race, we might infer that Sedgwick's own experiences with the pleasures of the ass lead her to identify with the imaginary Black subjects she conjures. Already, in titling her work "A Poem Is Being Written," Sedgwick alludes to Sigmund Freud's "A Child Is Being Beaten," a case study that not only interlaces reading and masochistic sexual fantasy but also does so—importantly—by naming an erotic identification with subjugated Black characters: Freud diagnoses his white patients' fantasies of beaten children as the result of, among other things, reading the whipping scenes in *Uncle Tom's Cabin*.[45]

We also learn from this endnote that it is more embarrassing for Sedgwick to identify with Bessie Smith than it is for her to identify with Oscar Wilde (read: harder for her to publicly identify with Black women than it is to publicly identify with gay men). This, again, is a testament to the different ways in which race, gender, and sexuality are conceived within the identity knowledge fields in which Sedgwick is writing. This is evident in the ways in which Blackness attaches itself to "cultural" difference differently than other types of difference, including gender, sexuality, and ethnicity. Consider again the text's assertion that "a male-identified woman, even if there could thoroughly be such a thing, would still be a real kind of woman just as (though far more inalterably than) an assimilated Jew is a real kind of Jew."[46] Sedgwick alludes to her own Jewish identity twice in her essay. In both instances, Jewishness is something that has been only recently assimilated. The first mention appears in a description of childhood spanking; the second, in a description of the first time she learns about gayness, when her elementary school French teacher is arrested for soliciting sex from men at a local YMCA. In this later passage, especially, Sedgwick's assimilation into urbanity is, in part, brought about by both her language education and her education in matters of sexuality: "In fact, 'urbanity' itself must have been, for reasons you can already gather (secular Jewishness, the Cold War era siting, the premium on the rendering unrecognizable of violence) a potent though not uncontested value in this family—and a badge of it, of course, the learning of French."[47] Here we see a confluence of knowledge, language, urbanity, secularity, and legitimacy that informs the analogy (male-identified : feminist :: assimilated : Jew). In antisemitic Cold War suburbia, Sedgwick is urbane only insofar as she can assimilate her Jewishness into American whiteness; in a sexist academy, she is only a credible academic insofar as she can assimilate her femaleness into maleness.

Beyond serving as a comparison for Sedgwick's male identification, the figure of the assimilated Jew in "A Poem Is Being Written" foreshadows her later discussion of Esther in *Epistemology of the Closet*, in which she offers an extended meditation on the similarities and differences between how the gay closet functions and the function of other "ethno/cultural/religious oppressions."[48] By her explanation, "Racism, for instance, is based on a stigma that is visible in all but exceptional cases (cases that are neither rare nor irrelevant, but that delineate the outlines rather than coloring the center of racial experience); so are the oppressions based on gender, age, size, physical handicap."[49] That Sedgwick employs this comparison to explicate the closet provides clues about how identity knowledges' understandings of racial identity delimit her capacity for cross-identification across racial difference differently than, say, her identification across sexuality or gender.

Many theorists have by now lingered on this remarkable passage in which, as Siobhan B. Somerville puts it, "Sedgwick seems to accept rather than to question the overarching cultural assumption that certain categories, especially race, are legible in a way that gay identity is not." Somerville describes this move as one of ascribing greater "legibility" to racial difference, noting that Sedgwick argues that antisemitism is more analogous to homophobia because "the stigmatized individual has at least notionally some discretion . . . over other people's knowledge."[50] Visibility is important because of its privileged relationship to representation, a concept that will later prove crucial to Sedgwick's complicated queer politics and critical writing strategy. Because Sedgwick's understanding of racial identity is less capacious and more bound to the visual than her understanding of things like sexuality, ethnicity, or, to a slightly lesser extent, gender, moments of cross-racial identification—more specifically, moments of identification that cross the Black–white color line—often become the staged site of Sedgwick's most spectacular and exhibitionist identificatory attempts. These attempts, because they are so potent, become some of her most generative sites of critique and inquiry.

SMUGGLING, STRUGGLING

While each of the moments in "A Poem Is Being Written" discussed above contains aspects of *as if!* writing, it emerges more completely in her later work. To understand how Sedgwick's other early texts stage the difficulties of identification in a more explicit vein, it is helpful to take a brief detour away from *Tendencies* to an essay published in a multiauthored collection the same year and later republished in part in *Touching Feeling: Affect, Pedagogy, Performativity* (2003). The essay, titled "Socratic Raptures, Socratic Ruptures: Notes Toward Queer Performativity" (retitled simply "Interlude, Pedagogic" ten years later), recalls a rally Sedgwick attended during her tenure at Duke University. Once more employing embarrassing anecdotes, Sedgwick recollects how she and some of her colleagues gathered alongside members of a local Ad Hoc Coalition of Black Lesbians and Gays, along with allies from the ACT UP-Triangle chapter, to demonstrate against a local PBS news station for censoring a scheduled airing of Marlon Riggs's *Tongues Untied* (1989). The protest aimed to address the urgent need for Black queer representation in the media in the moment of AIDS and, more specifically, in a moment where willful ignorance of already hypervulnerable populations amounted to the state-sanctioned murder of Black gay men at an unprecedented rate.

As Sedgwick notes, the strategy of the protest was twofold: first, to "shame" University of North Carolina PBS into airing the documentary, and second, to "smuggle" Black queer bodies into the daily news cycle by virtue of the media spectacle of the protesters themselves. She writes, "With the force of our bodies, however, and in that sense performatively, our object was not merely to demand representation, representation elsewhere, but ourselves to give, to *be* representation: somehow to smuggle into the prohibitive airwaves some version of the apparently unrepresentably dangerous and endangered conjunction, queer and Black. . . . Smuggling, performatively: 'Present! *Ecce homo*'—a self-validating, hence self-referential form of meaning guaranteed by its relation to embodiment."[51] For Sedgwick smuggling, like shame, is performative. This is not the first time Sedgwick has used the verb *smuggling* in reference to representation: It also appears in "Queer and Now," the first chapter of *Tendencies*. Drawing on J. L. Austen, as well as on other queer theorists such as Judith Butler, Sedgwick writes that language, particularly the language of coming out, "can be said to produce . . . effects of identity, enforcement, seduction, [and] challenge." Sedgwick writes, "I'm the more eager to think about performativity, too, because it may offer some ways of what *critical* writing can affect (promising? smuggling?)."[52] The appearance of *smuggling* in both essays highlights how the political strategy that Sedgwick and her compatriots attempt to enact at the protest is tied to the specific idea of performativity elaborated in "Queer and Now." In both cases, Sedgwick's strategy of smuggling holds the potential for queer resistance to the censoring and genocidal regimes of governmentality that seek to erase not only representations of certain identities but the people to whom those identities attach.

Despite what Sedgwick may argue on the surface, her text is not invested primarily in a politics of representation. Far from describing a politics of individual or liberalist self-determination, Sedgwick's performativity is more complicated. Simply put, for Sedgwick, to say, "I am queer," is to become queer. About halfway through the meandering and polemic "Queer and Now," Sedgwick bombards her readers with a nonexhaustive, though quite extensive, list of categories that may or may not fall under the heading "queer." *Queer*, she writes, means "the experimental linguistic, epistemological, representational, political adventures attaching to the very many of us who may at times be moved to describe ourselves as (among many other possibilities) pushy femmes, radical faeries, fantasists, drags, clones, leather-folk, ladies in tuxedos, feminist women or feminist men, masturbators, bulldaggers, divas, Snap! queens, butch bottoms, storytellers, transsexuals, aunties, wannabes, lesbian-identified men or lesbians who sleep with men, or . . . people able to relish, learn from, or identify with such."[53] The long list of names that might mean "queer" all at once signal Sedgwick's infectious deconstructive enthusiasm, her childlike eagerness, and her paranoid impulse to uncover and name—critical affects quite familiar to those who have read "A Poem Is Being Written." This Pride parade of disparate and deviant identities performs a similar deviant pleasure to the one that "A Poem Is Being Written" narrates: homosexual reading, the critical pleasure of naming, rooting out, or guessing at gayness. Significantly, by also naming "people able to relish, learn from, or identify with such" as also queer, Sedgwick makes readerly identification not a precursor to but the main aspect of queer experience.

In contrast to the utopian flexibility of *queer*, the different but mutually informed visual coding systems used to enforce race and gender in the United States at the time of Sedgwick's writing make her cross-identifications difficult. Indeed, they render the jump between identifying with the Black gay men for which she advocates and being recognized as one of them difficult, if not impossible. In "Socratic Raptures, Socratic Ruptures" she and her fellow white protesters learn this the hard way: "At the same time, our 'smuggling' activity of embodiment, however self-referential, could boast of no autonomy from the oblique circuits of representation. At least because the majority of our smuggling-intent bodies were not themselves Black, many of us who had so much need to make a new space for Black queer representation were haplessly embroiled in the process of reference: reference to other bodies standing beside our own, to the words on our placards, to what we could only hope would be the sufficiently substantial sense—if, indeed, even we understood it rightly—of our own intent."[54] The haplessness of identity's reliance on reference becomes abundantly clear when, after standing for some time in Durham's stifling summer heat, Sedgwick faints and creates a separate spectacle of her own. The scene, and the confusion of those responding to it, condenses the complications and confusions that trouble both identity and identification. Sedgwick's anecdote illustrates a problem: namely, that, in the words of Holland, "race and racist practice mire an unfettered feminism in the materiality of the body and the idea of the limit."[55]

Sedgwick's white, female-presenting body—on exhibit to the reporters and the public—throws a wrench in her plan to smuggle images of Black queer bodies, and with them the positive representations of Black gay male desire, onto the airwaves. In yet another self-deprecating anecdote, Sedgwick's text confronts the fact that its author is not able to performatively represent the group with which she is trying to identify. In an extended parenthetical, Sedgwick goes so far as to list the many ways her identifications produce "an aching gap in the real":

> (Displacements: the white skin of someone to whom Black queer invisibility had come to feel—partly through representational work like *Tongues Untied*, partly in the brutalities of every day's paper, partly through transferentially charged interactions with students—like an aching gap in the real; the legible bodily stigma not of AIDS but of a "female" cancer whose lessons for living powerfully with I found myself, at the time, learning largely from men with AIDS; the defamiliarization and indeed the gaps of de-recognition toward my "own" "female" "white" body, experienced under the pressure of amputation and prosthesis, of drugs, of the gender-imploding experience of female baldness; the way in which, whatever one's privilege, a person living with a grave disease in this particular culture is inducted ever more consciously, ever more needily, yet with ever more profound and transformative revulsion into the manglingly differential world of health care under American capitalism.)[56]

Reflecting on the event, Sedgwick imagines the reporters and medical responders trying to understand the sight of a white, fat, "weirdly bald" female cancer patient lying unconscious in the middle of the rally with an angry sign, an "African hat," and a black "SILENCE=DEATH" T-shirt.[57] The result is a spectacular instance of bad passing: Sedgwick's purported identifications fail to align with the systems of representation and visuality that she comes up against in the material world.

And yet, "Socratic Raptures, Socratic Ruptures" has the nerve to continue showcasing her identification with/as Black, gay men living with HIV, despite the risks that go with admitting to these cross-identifications. Telling a story in which these cross-identifications go spectacularly unrecognized not only risks casting any attempt at identification across race as doomed to fail; it also carries significant risks to the reputation of the storyteller herself: She might well be condemned for the attempt, accused of taking up space in a way that further erases the visibility of the people she is attempting to support. But "displacement" (as opposed to Edelman's "substitution") suggests deferral rather than substitution. Defined as "removal of a thing from its place; putting out of place; shifting, dislocation," *displacement* suggests a relational approach to representation, one not reliant on fixed identity categories.[58] Labeling her identificatory obstacles "displacements" rather than "substitutions," Sedgwick's text theatrically grapples with the gap between identification and representation/perception. She can thus theorize material condition while still having the nerve to insist on her own desire to represent and identify.

"FRACTURED AND THEREFORE MILITANT"

Cross-identification is on full display in the last chapter of *Tendencies*, an essay-eulogy that preemptively memorializes Sedgwick's then-dying friend Michael Lynch. The piece, titled "White Glasses," also lays out a theory of the coalitional politics that the AIDS crisis engenders. In it, Sedgwick ruminates on the white glasses she and Lynch both wear and explores the "uncanny effects" of their shared fashion choice.[59] Whereas previously Sedgwick had written of her identification, in "White Glasses," she writes about her identity: "The stubborn magical defiance I have learned (I *sometimes* feel I have succeeded in learning) in forging a habitable identity as a fat woman is also what has enabled the series of uncanny effects around these white glasses; uncanny effects that have been so formative of my—shall I call it my identification? Dare I, after this half-decade, call it with all of a fat *woman*'s defiance, my identity?—as a gay man."[60] This important move, made early in the essay, makes an identificatory claim to an identity—gay man—that disrupts the identity category that she is most likely to represent—fat woman.

At the same time, and despite the faith she has previously put in the power of the queer performative to manifest identity, her transformation is not easy, nor is it ever presented as complete. Just as "Socratic Raptures, Socratic Ruptures" highlights how the politics of racial identity formation get in the way of her cross-racial identification, Sedgwick's repeated failures and hesitations in "White Glasses" hyperbolically highlight (and call out) the systems of representation, visuality, and external perception that fail to recognize her transgender identification. Even in this paragraph, Sedgwick's identity as a fat woman is just "*sometimes*" successful; perhaps it is even more constructed, forged, than her identity as a gay man. The hesitation with which Sedgwick posits her "identity?," the insistent and defensive italics of "*woman*," the parentheticals and em dashes, all indicate a tenuousness and hesitation that throws the legitimacy of each identification into question. In fact, "White Glasses" is rife with examples of Sedgwick attempting to identify with/as something but not completely. Not just here but throughout this text, it seems we witness scenes of the displacement identification at every turn—a strange pattern, considering that this text often serves as the foremost example of Sedgwick's critical cross-identifications.

Key to understanding these connections are the iconic glasses to which the title of Sedgwick's piece refers. While at first the glasses constitute a shared point of identificatory connection between her and Lynch—to the point where, in her words, "it sometimes amazes me that anyone can tell us apart"—this identification can only go so far before it is rendered invisible and impotent by the constraints of social context, connotation, and visibility.[61] Shortly after her initial identification with Lynch, Sedgwick notes that "white the pastel sinks banally and invisibly into the camouflage of femininity, on a woman, a white woman," while "in a place where it doesn't belong, on Michael, that same pastel remains a flaming signifier."[62] For Sedgwick, the fact that "white glasses" can signify both flaming radicality and complicit normality is testament to the fact that position, identity, material condition, history, embodiment, and social interpellation complicate and at times undermine the easy identificatory politics most celebrated by Sedgwick's brand of queer theory and queer activism.

Sedgwick similarly theorizes the ways in which race thwarts her easy identifications: Crucially, it is not just on a woman but on a *white* woman that Sedgwick's fashionable specs lose their intended effect. Though she refers to Lynch simply as "a man," the text twice describes Sedgwick as "a white woman." The first instance is quoted above. The second, from the following paragraph, elaborates her frustration with the way her whiteness erases the subversive power she wants to grant her fashion choice: "A white woman wearing white: the ruly ordinariness of this sight makes invisible the corrosive aggression that white also is: as the blaze of mourning, the opacity of loss, the opacity loss installs within ourselves and our vision, the unreconciled and irreconcilably incendiary energies streaming through that subtractive gap, that ragged scar of meaning, regard, address." White, Sedgwick explains, is also "the zero-degree no-color of (not the skin of Europeans themselves but) the abstractive ideology of European domination."[63] The "white" of "White Glasses" thus takes on a secondary racial definition: not just the pastel pigmentation of Lynch's frames but the violence of white power. Somewhere between these definitions of *white*—one a flashy fashion choice, the other a perniciously invisible racist system—is Sedgwick's understanding of racial difference as a difference strongly demarcated by systems of visual representation. David L. Eng, remarking on this same asymmetry, argues that Lynch's gayness complicates his whiteness, rendering it visible and uncomfortable: "If, as Eve Sedgwick says of her friend Michael Lynch—a gay, white male—whiteness somehow 'doesn't belong' on him, remaining a 'flaming signifier,' it is because the crucial and mandatory combination of heterosexuality and whiteness has been violated and transgressed. In his 'flaming' queerness, the whiteness of Michael Lynch is suddenly brought into relief, rendered visible and disconcerting."[64] Eng's take adds another interesting layer to the cross-identification taking place in "White Glasses": Read with this in mind, Sedgwick's cross-identification with Lynch marks a desire for her own whiteness to be rendered both "visible and disconcerting" in ways that might disrupt or transgress structures of white supremacy. As she is in the fainting scene of "Socratic Raptures, Socratic Ruptures," Sedgwick is here once again stopped short by both her own gendered female body and her racialized white skin, as well as by the histories of subordination and domination they both cite.

It is possible to read Sedgwick's nearly-there-ness, her coming out and going back in again, as born of the same hesitations that nefariously raise their ugly heads at any effort at gender self-determination. Grace Lavery, for example, reads Sedgwick's early work as an early example of "egg theory"—that is, "the type of reasoning that trans people use, prior to transition, to prove transition's impossibility or fruit-lessness." Of Sedgwick's many instances of transgender identification with gay men, Lavery reads "White Glasses" as "a text whose egg theory seems designed to provoke trans readers to bifurcated rage and sympathy."[65] Focusing on the moments in "White Glasses" when Sedgwick's cross-identifications, however defiant, remain inhibited or shut down, she argues that the voices against which Sedgwick is most defensive are not the imagined voices of heteropatriarchy and homophobia but rather the imagined voices of those who have, in fact, taken the material steps of gender transition:

> Where, after all, does the sudden surge of defensiveness come from? Has someone been telling Sedgwick that she shouldn't identify as a gay man? If so—and here is where the ironic bifurcation of interest in "White Glasses" reveals itself as egg theory—then the dominating voice against whom Sedgwick articulates her defiance is not the voice of (let us risk being embarrassed and call it) the patriarchy; rather, the voice that must be forced back is the voice of the tranny herself, for whom only an elect cadre can be allowed to make such identifications. Sedgwick's rage is not directed at anyone who might, indeed, impede the expression of gay male identity, but at those who are perceived as already having made the crossing.[66]

In other words, even as Sedgwick might claim her identity as a gay man in text with a kind of "stubborn magical defiance," repeatedly staging the impossibility of full transition might well be read as defeatist, at best, and, at its worst, blatantly transphobic. Lavery argues that if we extrapolate egg theory to its logical conclusion "in a context in which the same genocidal animus Sedgwick correctly attributed to 1980s America is now being directed against trans people—by a political and cultural establishment that threatens, routinely, to prevent us from accessing medicine, restrooms, rape crisis centers, and so forth," then its "practical manifestation . . . would be the removal of health care provision for trans children."[67] The stakes of Sedgwick's performance of egg theory are high, and taken straight, such a performance has catastrophic material implications.

Though they may be strange bedfellows, Edelman and Lavery both have a problem with Sedgwick's identification with gay men, albeit from very different angles. Lavery's critique of Sedgwick is complementary to Edelman's earlier take: For Edelman, Sedgwick's stubborn identification with gay men is too easy—or, at least, it is too easily subsumed under the capacious header of "queer" by those who wish to gloss over "divisions (between male and female, between gender and sexuality)." For Lavery, Sedgwick's identification is too difficult. That is, it is too difficult for Sedgwick to imagine the possibility of more fully crossing those divisions between male and female in the name of gender self-determination. For Lavery, Sedgwick's refusal to go all the way is symptomatic of a much larger and troubling trend within queer theory as a whole—namely, that most queer theory follows a transphobic logic that sides with abstraction over embodiment. In tracing a strain of egg theory throughout early queer criticism, she cogently notes that "several figures within queer theory either wrote, at the time, about a transsexual desire that they kept at arm's length (most famously Eve Kosofsky Sedgwick), or made late-career pitches to trans identity claims."[68] Sedgwick's defensiveness and vacillation vis-à-vis her own gay male identity/identification foreshadows a split between queer and trans theory in which certain queer theorists laud queerness as "revolutionary" while denouncing embodied transness as "accommodationist."[69] In any case, Edelman's and Lavery's two incisive arguments similarly paint Sedgwick's identifications across gender as appropriative, transphobic, and born of a tyrannical will toward mastery.

Contrary to Edelman and Lavery, I read Sedgwick's exhibitionist failures of identification as also moments of perverse, paradoxical, insistent connection. Moreover, Wiegman's detailed analysis of feminist scholarly resistance to Sedgwick recasts her defensiveness as also motivated by feminist gatekeeping around her identificatory claims to womanhood. In other words, we need not, nor should we ever, take Sedgwick straight. Leaning into both the implications of the genealogy that Edelman lays bare and the identificatory impasses Lavery so expertly highlights, I want to take seriously a genealogy that names the phrase *queer theory* as not the salve for but the inheritor of reading strategies that bring difference and division to the fore. Refusing to gloss over the impasses presented by its author's white, female body, "White Glasses" lays bare the transphobic and racist structures that produce and regulate identity, and it continues in spite of them—often via creative routes that take into account other possible alloidentifications. Consider, for example, Sedgwick's discussion of the mutual ways she and Lynch connected:

Our most durable points of reference were lesbian. My favorite picture of Michael was taken in Willa Cather's bed. We are both obsessed with Emily Dickinson. Tokens, readings, pilgrimages, impersonations around Cather, Dickinson, and our other lesbian ego ideals shape and punctuate our history. The first thing Michael did after my diagnosis in February was to bundle into the mail to me a blanket that has often comforted me at his house—a blanket whose meaning to him is its association with the schoolteacher aunt whose bed he used to lie in in childhood, sandwiched in the crack between her and her lifelong companion, wondering whether (after all, he was adopted) it might not be this Boston marriage whose offspring he somehow really, naturally was. If what is at work here is an identification that falls across gender, it falls no less around sexualities, across "perversions." And across the ontological crack between the living and the dead.[70]

The proliferation of possible opportunities for recognition in Sedgwick parallels the proliferation of sexual identities and ways of thinking sexuality beyond object-choice that can be found throughout her work and, in turn, lead to partnerships that cross "perversions," that cross states of health, and even that cross states of being (as Grace Kyungwon Hong says, "The theoretical and political practice of 'difference' holds in suspension the ostensibly mutually exclusive states of life and death").[71] In a curious moment in "Queer and Now," Sedgwick declares that "among the striking aspects of considering closeted-ness in this framework, for instance, is that the speech act in question is a series of silences!"[72] While in this passage *silence* is taken to mean "the closet," Sedgwick's strange postulation that silence can itself be a speech act echoes ACT UP's famous formulation "SI-LENCE=DEATH," an equation that, transitively, complicates the place of death in "Queer and Now." By implicitly giving death/silence/the closet the power of a speech act, particularly alongside discussions of speech acts that declare and create one's own queerness, Sedgwick performatively identifies with the dead, even as she explicitly and politically offers strategies to prevent queer death. Such moments betray the links between death, close reading, and Sedgwick's *as if!* critical strategies.

Nowhere is Sedgwick's nerve clearer than in her most ambitious identity crossing: that across states of being. "White Glasses" is but one example in a myriad of Sedgwickian memorials; here, Sedgwick's cross-identifications are tellingly predicated on a relationship to precarious mortality. As Ellis Hanson recently points out, "For a literary critic publishing with university presses, [Sedgwick] has offered us a surprising number of academic yet very personal elegies, and queer ones at that, for men who had little or no future: for Divine, Michael Lynch, Craig Owens, and Gary

Fisher." So prevalent is this pattern that, Hanson later quips, "most of *Tendencies* could easily have been published under the title *Let Us Now Praise Dead Gay Men*."[73]

Most infamous of such cross-identifications is Sedgwick's mentorship and patronage of Gary Fisher, a Black, gay graduate student living with HIV whose stories, journals, notebooks, and poems she later published in the posthumous collection *Gary in Your Pocket* (1996). A controversial publication, *Gary in Your Pocket* is, in large part, a chronicle of Fisher's erotic negotiations of white supremacy: Several of the documents contained within it record, in vivid detail, Fisher's self-described "obsessive" pursuit of submissive sex with white men and chronicle Fisher's own participation in staged scenes of intense racial and sexual debasement—rough oral, piss play, slave play, etc.[74] The parallels between the racial power dynamics of Fisher's sex life and the racial power dynamics of Fisher's scholarly life make Sedgwick's patronage especially unseemly to queer and feminist scholars invested in an antiracist project; as Hanson starkly puts it, the circumstance of *Gary in Your Pocket*'s publication "celebrates the connection between not only a gay Black man and a married white woman but also a submissive Black man and the white men who agreed to dominate him."[75] The parallel structure of this sentence draws a connection between the racialized power dynamics of Eve and Fisher and the racialized power dynamics Fisher sought out in his sex life. It is hard not to draw a parallel, as Hanson does, between the power dynamics Fisher sought out in his sex life and the power dynamics between a white editor and her Black pupil.

Lurking behind these critiques, though, is another possibility: a white critic identifying not with Fisher's white doms but with Fisher himself. Musing on her conflicted feelings about the project in *A Dialogue on Love* (1999), Sedgwick reiterates her interest in what she calls this "border-crossing position," understanding her relationship to Fisher not only as an identification across race, age, gender, and sexuality but also, ultimately, as an identification across the divide between the dead and the living.[76] In the afterword to *Gary in Your Pocket*, Sedgwick goes so far as to confess that she dreamed "as" Fisher during the editing process, "clothed in the restless, elastic skin of his beautiful idiom."[77] Certainly, Sedgwick's use of *skin* recalls the ways in which Black skin comes to substitute for an entire racial schema, a pattern that makes Sedgwick's own conscious or unconscious racial fetishism hard to deny. But Sedgwick's own intimate cross-identification—as well as Fisher's identifications with her—complicates this simple read. José Esteban Muñoz, writing on Fisher and Sedgwick's "strange and compelling" relationship, takes care to note that there is nothing inherently equalizing in Sedgwick's border crossing; their friendship and collaboration does not erase position, power, or material condition. Rather, for Muñoz, Sedgwick's and Fisher's identifications with each other constitute a "queer politics of the incommensurable" in which relationships are forged "both despite and because of a difference that marks the (im)possibility of politics."[78] Teagan Bradway sees the Sedgwick–Fisher collaboration as a potentially utopian political project, one that "affirms the unruly circuits of identification as a potential source for relationality, and possibly political solidarity, across the boundaries of social difference."[79] Not substitution but displacement: Sedgwick's identifications persist not despite but because of the seemingly unbreachable gaps that propel and entice her.

When Sedgwick was diagnosed with breast cancer in 1991, she found herself part of another stigmatized, precarious identity set: She, suddenly, is unwell and dying. When Sedgwick identifies with AIDS victims while she herself is in ill health, her identification exemplifies what Sara Ahmed calls Sedgwick's "sensitivity to stigma"—that is, Sedgwick's tendency to attempt solidarity across difference via a shared assumption of stigma or harm, guided by the belief that "an experience of a proximity to one kind of stigma can create a sensitivity to other kinds."[80] Ahmed bases "sensitivity to stigma" on Sedgwick's own definition of queer politics as "voluntary stigma" in "Interlude, Pedagogic" (notably, the 2003 rewrite of "Socratic Raptures, Socratic Ruptures").[81] Musing on the difference between stigma voluntarily assumed and stigma involuntarily acquired, Ahmed points out that sensitivity to stigma—particularly when wielded by well-meaning white people— is a double-edged sword, one that often signals "whiteness that wants proximity to the very scenes of its undoing, where the un-doing is at once a re-doing."[82] Even so, Ahmed writes, Sedgwick's political strategy of sensitivity to stigma might still be strategically mobilized toward a politics of shared burden-holding across difference.[83]

In drawing implicit and explicit connections between herself and Lynch, Sedgwick also enacts what Ramzi Fawaz elsewhere calls "ill liberalism," a political positionality—informed by the experience of being unwell, precarious, or otherwise "sick"—that retains the liberal commitment to democratic freedom and political recognition while rejecting humanist notions of progress.[84] This ill liberal ethic catalyzes her most remarkable moments of cross-identification, including this passage, which appears three-quarters of the way through "White Glasses":

> It's as though there were transformative political work to be done just by being available to be identified with in the very grain of one's illness (which is to say, the grain of one's own intellectual, emotional, bodily self as refracted through illness and as resistant to it)—being available for identification to friends, but as well to people who don't love one; even to people who may not like one at all nor even wish one well. All of these may nonetheless be brought consciously, even if hatingly, into the

world of people living with this disease—just as, whatever one's privilege, a person living with fatal disease in this particular culture is inducted ever more consciously, ever more needily, yet with ever more profound and transformative revulsion into the manglingly differential world of health care under American capitalism.[85]

In *Tendencies* and elsewhere, Sedgwick's recognition of mutual suffering at the hands of the state recalls the politics of solidarity-via-impending-death that became the rallying cry of Queer Nation and other AIDS activist groups.[86] Musing on the confluence of her emergent breast cancer and the moment of Lynch's death, Sedgwick finds that identification is made easier, more possible, by the shared precarity of long-term fatal illness.

If the extended ending clause of the long sentence quoted above seems familiar, that is because it has already made an appearance here, in a different context: the last forty words of the above block quote appear, nearly word for word, in the section of "Socratic Raptures, Socratic Ruptures" quoted earlier in this chapter:

(Displacements: the white skin of someone to whom Black queer invisibility had come to feel—partly through representational work like *Tongues Untied*, partly in the brutalities of every day's paper, partly through transferentially charged interactions with students—like an aching gap in the real; the legible bodily stigma not of AIDS but of a "female" cancer whose lessons for living powerfully with I found myself, at the time, learning largely from men with AIDS; the defamiliarization and indeed the gaps of de-recognition toward my "own" "female" "white" body, experienced under the pressure of amputation and prosthesis, of drugs, of the gender-imploding experience of female baldness; the way in which, *whatever one's privilege, a person living with a grave disease in this particular culture is inducted ever more consciously, ever more needily, yet with ever more profound and transformative revulsion into the manglingly differential world of health care under American capitalism.*)[87]

This self-plagiarizing echo, besides providing an uncanny sense of déjà vu, corroborates the connection between the "displacements" theorized in "Socratic Raptures, Socratic Ruptures" and the misrecognitions staged in "White Glasses." These displacements, experienced in the space of the gap between racial and gender identification and racial and gender identity, refuse to gloss over the differences that identity discourse produces. In this way, Sedgwick's embarrassing anecdotes constitute moments of, in Holland's words, "reimagining the erotic life of racism," wherein "the focus on quotidian racist practice and its manifestation in the sphere of the erotic (who we love and how we reproduce) might disrupt our rather static notions of the Black body and its historical repertoire (or the potentiality of its repertoire?) and the white critical body as it seeks to politely trespass upon it."[88] This is, somewhat counterintuitively, Sedgwick's coalitional strategy: The very differences she highlights reveal violent systems whose effects, though felt differently, are felt by everyone.

The repeated staging of failed identification across difference, so prominent in *Tendencies*, revitalizes a mode of critical thought that does, in fact, privilege division. In so doing, it invokes a cross-identificatory, coalitional politics that, quite paradoxically, takes as its point of solidarity the very divisions of difference that seek to upend it. Switching the focus not toward Sedgwick's ease at identification but toward her performatively embarrassing struggle to cross-identify reveals a slightly different, though related, axis of her politics. At the end of her meditation on Sedgwick's sensitivity to stigma, Ahmed reminds her audiences that "the sorrow of the stranger is pedagogic not because it teaches us what it is like or must be like to be a stranger, but because it can estrange us from the familiar. The familiar is revealed when we cannot pass into it."[89] Focusing not on "sensitivity to stigma" alone but on the staged failures of that sensitivity illuminates an alternative politics of solidarity. Such a politics, paradoxically, relies on the embarrassing failure of white sensitivity to adequately breach the chasms of difference brought on by incommensurate systems of oppression. It is precisely when this strategy falls short that we see Sedgwick's queer solidarity in action. In these moments, Sedgwick's failure brings to light the oppressive systems that violently create and maintain difference.

Sedgwick ends "White Glasses" with a meditation not on Lynch's fashionable frames, a symbol both intimate and personal, but on the AIDS quilt, a symbol both gut-wrenchingly colossal and explicitly political. A quilt, itself a patchwork of different squares, is an easy metaphor for coalition. The individual memorials on each square of the quilt, rather than representing specific identities, instead represent a myriad of shifting occupations of identity and voice ("in the panels of the quilt, I see that anyone, living or dead, may occupy the position of the speaker, the spoken to, the spoken about").[90] The personal ability of "anyone" to occupy the position of speaker translates to a political ability to militarize across difference: "Churned out of this mill of identities crossed by desires crossed by identifications is, it seems—it certainly seemed in October 1987—a fractured and therefore militant body of queer rebellion."[91] On the one hand, the "fracture" that Sedgwick names draws her readers' attention to the impasses produced by her twisting routes of identification and the repeated failure of her intended audience to recognize those routes as extant. On the other hand, Sedgwick's staged, clumsy, embarrassing cross-identifications repurpose the very division caused by systems of stigmatization into a means of identifying across difference.

Hand-stitched and meant to "conform to the unique shape of a body," a quilt is, in addition to being a potent political symbol, an intimate object.[92] Shifting from a rubric of "coalition" to a rubric of "intimacy," as Jennifer C. Nash suggests, might "blur the boundaries of who these analytics 'belong' to, who they can—or should—describe." Intimacy, Nash proposes, "suggests the permeability between concepts and their imagined 'origins.' And between bodies. . . . Including the possibility of being done and undone through relationality."[93] *Tendencies* is interested in the *queer* that means "to cross." *Queer*, in *Tendencies*, does not replace, cover up, or substitute Sedgwick's orientations; rather, it precisely names the discomfort—or, to use Sedgwick's word, the displacement—felt in the act of crossing.

Conclusion
On Recognition

When I encountered queer theory in the mid-aughts, it hit me with the force of an exclamation point. At that point I was a glass-closeted freshman, a Californian adrift in the alien space of the Northeast liberal arts university. Inspired and electrified by the new consciousness-raising demands of an actively political student body, but still unable to quite name the positions and desires from which I spoke, I found in queer literary criticism a blueprint for being in the world. I fell in love with most of the theorists I encountered. I identified—in a way that felt, to me, relatively uncomplicated—with all of them.

Among those early pieces of queer literary criticism to which I cathected, hard, was Eve Kosofsky Sedgwick's "A Poem Is Being Written" (1987). Here was an essay describing, with what felt at the time like bizarre accuracy, my own familiar tendencies: a geeky adolescence spent composing poems, a repressed and as of then unacted-upon love of women, an enduring (and maddeningly inarticulable) identification with gay men, a perverse affinity for both long sentences and anality, and a reflexive narcissism that I hoped others found charming. Here was close reading, threateningly close, world-shakingly close in a way I could not articulate for many years, after more reading, more queer theory, more copies of articles and more borrowed books, and, eventually, more sex.

What strikes me now is the irony of this primal scene. "A Poem Is Being Written" narrates a process of queer critical identification that is far less straightforward than the identification I experienced upon first reading it. The irony of my early attachment to and identification with Sedgwick is, in fact, its ease. For the thing that is precisely queer about Sedgwick's criticism is her own counterintuitive, tortuous relationship to identity, identification, and critical object-choice. Because it foregrounds transgressions of identification across identities, Sedgwick's early work is a superlative example of *as if!* criticism.

Some might call Sedgwick's mode of cross-identificatory reading an exercise in empathy. It is an age-old cliché to assert that reading, in general, fosters empathy, defined as the ability to understand and share the feelings of another—sympathy's more sensitive, emotional cousin. Victorian novelist George Eliot, in 1859, writes that "the only effect I ardently long to produce by my writings, is that those who read them should be better able to imagine and to feel the pains and the joys of those who differ from them in everything but the broad fact of being struggling, erring human creatures."[1] Contemporary YA science fiction author Malorie Blackman, in a 2014 interview with the *Guardian*, declares that "books allow you to see the world through the eyes of others. Reading is an exercise in empathy; an exercise in walking in someone else's shoes for a while."[2] Even science agrees: A psychological study by David Comer Kidd and Emanuele Castano, published in *Science* in October 2013, concludes that reading literary fiction "does indeed enhance" the "human capacity to comprehend that other people hold beliefs and desires and that these may differ from one's own beliefs and desires."[3] Within a liberal sensibility in which the capacity to comprehend difference is valued, empathy is usually considered a societal good, something to be cultivated and encouraged.

Our current political moment has recast even this milquetoast empathy as sinister. Indeed, recent right-wing attempts to ban "social-emotional learning" in public education only enforce empathy's liberal credentials, casting empathy as, in the words of one progressive political commentator, "a Trojan Horse for left-wing ideologies of race, gender and sexuality."[4]

Were that the case! More often, the liberal ethic of empathetic reading is, in the words of author and essayist Elaine Castillo, an "incomplete politics": a simplistic formula that "makes a kind of superficial sense—and produces a superficial effect." Castillo cautions against such well-intentioned declarations: "The problem with [empathy-oriented] reading is that in its practical application, usually readers are encouraged—by well-meaning teachers and lazy publishing copy—to read writers of a demographic minority in order to learn things; which is to say, as a supplement for their empathy muscles, a metabolic exchange that turns writers of color into little more than ethnographers—personal trainers, to continue the metaphor. The result is that we largely end up going to writers of color to learn the specific—and go to white writers to feel the universal."[5] In other words, rather than producing solidarity, the characterization of reading as inherently empathic reproduces the very power dynamics that it claims to challenge. Reading with empathy, at its worst, can be extractive, one-sided, or ineffectual. Is there, then, a way of reading and writing across difference that is neither invested in liberal ideas of empathy nor dismissive of oppression?

I am drawn to *as if!* criticism because the promiscuous, gleeful cross-identifications it showcases make it harder for conservatives to cast queer critics in the role of killjoy or identity police and because this mode of critical writing is less easily co-opted by right-wing rhetoric. On March 22, 2022, Texas Senator Ted Cruz made headlines for a bizarre line of questioning during the Ketanji Brown Jackson Supreme Court confirmation hearings. His verbal barrage aimed to expose Jackson's liberal agenda. What began as a tirade against transgender rights protection ended with Cruz asking Jackson if she believed that he could "decide to be an Asian man": "Under the modern leftist sensibilities, if I decide right now that I'm a woman and apparently I'm a woman, does that mean that I would have Article 3 standing to challenge a gender-based restriction? . . . Tell me whether that same law applies to other protected characteristics? . . . For example, I'm a Hispanic man, could I decide if I was an Asian man? Would I have the ability to be an Asian man and challenge Harvard's discrimination because I made that decision?"[6] There is much to say about Cruz's diatribe. His main point of comparison, curiously, involves affirmative action, an education policy to which Republicans have historically been opposed. His use of *leftist* (as opposed to, say, *liberal*) ham-fistedly remixes Joseph McCarthy. He chooses to be "Asian" in his hypothetical passing narrative, sidestepping questions of whether or not it would be possible for him to "decide" to be Black, and shrewdly employing a long-standing strategy of trying to divide minority populations around the affirmative action question.[7] He invokes Harvard, an institution that both he and Jackson attended and a university whose cultural prestige makes it at once exceptional and a stand-in for higher education more broadly. Ultimately, Cruz's rhetorical question, to which the implied answer is "no," plays gender and race against each other to bolster a transphobic agenda. Drawing the analogy between gender and race, in this case, leads to the conclusion that a free-for-all on gender is a slippery slope to a free-for-all on race—an outcome that, Cruz implies, is at best absurd and at worst very dangerous. After all, if a society built on the oppression of nonwhite people and women relies on hierarchies of power that are bolstered by the dual myths of race and gender essentialism, a more fluid understanding of these categories would register, for conservative politicians, as a threat to the very fabric of society itself.

The rhetorical strategy exemplified in Cruz's SCOTUS confirmation hearing cross-examination is, for all its buffoonery, quite savvy: Such a strategy notices and co-opts a (relatively new) progressive tendency to regulate who can speak for or identify with certain groups. Transphobic politicians like Cruz cleverly mimic this tendency when talking about race to delegitimize progressive projects of gender and sexual autonomy. Capitalizing on and repurposing the language of identity policing around race, reactionary politicians such as Cruz attempt to showcase the hypocrisy of progressives who reify racial categories while seeing categories of gender and sexuality as mutable. Indeed, the politicians behind the current deluge of reactionary legislation are quite fond of pointing out the contrast between the so-called politically correct regulating of racial identity categories and the politically correct liberation of gender and sexual identity categories. Cruz and his allies do this in order not to question and destabilize the categories of race but to further demarcate and control the categories of gender.

I'm wary that my plea for more leniency when it comes to critical cross-identification will unintentionally position liberal academic orthodoxy as the ultimate police presence on campus. This claim rings especially ironic at a time when literal police presence on campuses across the nation has reached its fever pitch. Even though I am annoyed at certain self-policing tendencies within liberal academic identity knowledge fields, I also have no interest in unwittingly conjuring up the Right's popular boogeyman (the killjoy feminist academic) as *as if!*'s foil. To be sure, Sara Ahmed's valuable work on the figure of the "feminist killjoy" illuminates how the accusation "killjoy" slyly recasts the pointing out of violence as the violent act itself: The killjoy is the killer rather than the structures she names, illuminates, and critiques.[8] As such, "free speech" and "academic freedom" now more often enable false claims of right-wing victimhood—claims all the more ironic considering that universities across the United States are currently mobilizing riot cops against protesting leftist students.

Even still, injunctions within knowledge identity fields that take a hard line on who can speak "as ____" often unintentionally align with a conservative—and often downright reactionary—project: Both arguments rest on a relatively straightforward relation between identity, identification, and knowledge. Given the strategic co-option of identity politics by people like Senator Cruz, one might expect those on the left to reach for a different tactic. But although most left-leaning academics argue that race, like gender, is not rooted in essential biology, race and gender nonetheless get treated differently when it comes to self-determination and the right to speak and write "as" a particular subject. K. Marshall Green, for example, points out that in the face of spectacular and inflammatory instances of academic cross-racial passing and identification, race is again often placed in opposition to gender, and as such treated as essential. This move not only calcifies racial categories; it also ignores the ways gender and race are historically and presently concomitant.[9]

Beyond its concerning tendency to shut down conversations and complex analysis, a narrow view of the possibilities of cross-identification also robs us of the pleasures of counterintuitive or surprising identification. Indeed, the appeal of the *as if!* criticism I discover in early queer theory is, in large part, the transgressive joy each author takes in the project of cross-identificatory critique. Not only do Deborah E. McDowell, Barbara Johnson, Robert Reid-Pharr, and Sedgwick appear to operate with more abandon than that which is afforded to those working in feminist and queer theory today; the fact that their texts revel in this recklessness also does valuable work pointing out the ludicrous project of identification more generally. In our current moment, the appeal of *as if!* criticism is that it does not foreclose the possibility of coalition simply because trying to understand means engaging in the (impossible) project of breaching difference. *As if!* criticism engages this project through shocking moments of interruption, doubling back, intimacy, and embarrassment. In so doing, it reveals a critical impulse to identify across the explicit gaps of material difference and lived experience. Reading, at least in part, is about the repeated attempt to cross those gaps, despite knowing the gap between self and other is unbreachable.

It is one thing to claim that reading begets empathy; it is slightly different to claim that reading, rather than fostering empathy, instead fosters an intoxicating, possibly dangerous or destabilizing overidentification, an *unheimlich* closeness that is often too close for comfort. D. A. Miller has a name for this phenomenon. Miller, yet another scholar writing queer literary criticism in the 1990s, makes frequent cameos throughout this book, though he never receives top billing—strange, considering that his book *Jane Austen, or The Secret of Style* (2003) explores the use of voice and address in *Emma* (1815), a novel whose plot is famously reimagined in *Clueless* (1995), the very film that inspired the exclamation point in *as if!* For Miller, overidentificatory reading such as this might well be called "Too Close." "The practitioner of Too Close Reading is never as lonesome as he might appear, nor his findings as singular; he is always partnered with an author-text to which he can't help getting, in this relational sense as well, inordinately close," Miller writes. "It is through consenting to this undue intimacy, with its blurred boundaries and invaded spaces, that Too Close Reading acquires its weird psychic density."[10] This is reading beyond empathy—the real threat that book banners imagine.

By my calculation, Miller was the first queer theorist I ever wrote about, for an undergraduate midterm assignment. The assignment was an analytic essay about a piece of literary criticism, written in the voice and style of the piece of criticism it analyzed. Our task was to hyperbolically mimic, even mock, the authors we were studying. In practice, this meant mirroring their tone, imitating their language quirks, and adopting their punctuation habits—a weird mix of RuPaul's "Snatch Game" and "Lip Sync for Your Life." Much as language learners first exaggerate an accent so that they might master pronunciation, so we were instructed to hone our readerly ears, paying attention to voice so that we might develop tastes that would later inform our own stylistic choices. When I got this assignment, I chose to mimic Miller. The class had read *Place for Us: Essay on the Broadway Musical* (1998) a few weeks before, and I recognized in Miller a skillful stylist whose markedly flamboyant, effortlessly exacting prose I found equal parts seductive and enviable. I peppered my paper with covert references to golden age musicals, as he had done; I delivered an essay written in the most showstopping style I could muster. The license to campily ventriloquize was thrilling. *Anything you can do, I can do better.*

Miller does this, too, in his extended essay *Bringing Out Roland Barthes*. As Johnson notes, Miller campily ventriloquizes Barthes's French mannerisms in the first sentence of his book ("long before I, how you say, knew myself").[11] In mimicking Barthes, Miller stylistically alludes to other similarities between himself and the famous French poststructuralist: That is, Miller recognizes in Barthes's writing an unnamed gay sensibility—a sensibility with which Miller, as a gay writer himself, identifies.[12] This is, of course, Johnson's snide point in "Bringing Out D. A. Miller": Miller's essay about Barthes is just a thinly disguised essay about himself.

If this accusation sounds familiar, that might be because Sedgwick, in her well-known introduction to *Novel Gazing: Queer Readings in Fiction* (1997), "Paranoid Reading and Reparative Reading; or, You're So Paranoid, You Probably Think This Introduction Is About You," lobs a similar charge at queer literary criticism. In "Paranoid Reading and Reparative Reading," Sedgwick names Miller's New Historicist work *The Novel and the Police* (1988) as the example par excellence of paranoid criticism, a critical method roughly equivalent to Paul Ricoeur's hermeneutics of suspicion. Whereas Johnson's book review of *Bringing Out Roland Barthes* is, if a little teasing, ultimately appreciative of her friend Miller's need to root out or uncover hidden subtext, Sedgwick's essay constitutes a multipronged breakdown of the limitations of such a strategy. The essay, now infamous, precipitates a schism in queer literary criticism and in literary criticism more broadly. The split between paranoid and reparative influences the split between the antisocial and the utopian (in queer theory) and the split between belief in depth and faith in surface (in literary theory).[13]

Nearly thirty years after Sedgwick's essay, an increasingly fascist Right has realized the political potential of equating reading not just with empathy but with conversion. Under this logic, representing queer identities in literature and curricula turns straight children gay. Similar suppression efforts argue that representing nonwhite racial identities in literature and curricula turns white children into self-hating white people. Book bans, syllabus challenges, school board outcry, and campus panic are prongs in this familiar, but this time particularly virulent, attack. These attacks are fueled by the fear that the encounter with difference, and potential identification across difference, will change people. It will change the way they think, or the way they identify, or who they fuck.

Don't tell Moms for Liberty I said this, but it's true. Identification and conversion are hard to separate, harder than it is politically wise to admit. Sometimes—often, in the case of queer reading or queer desire—they are the same.[14]

Another word for these transformative routes of queer identification and conversion is *recognition*. Late in the introduction to *Novel Gazing*, Sedgwick notes that many of the essays collected in the volume both model and analyze "queer *recognition*," a phenomenon she variously describes as a "model of . . . reading" that is "a much more speculative, superstitious, and methodologically adventurous state where recognitions, pleasures, and discoveries seep in only from the most stretched and ragged edges of one's competence," "the moment of a younger reader's queer recognition," and the "recognitions implicit in queer pedagogy."[15] There is also "the shock of queer recognition," a shock that Sedgwick describes as only one step to the side of "the uncanny shock of strangeness."[16] And then there are recognitions that produce a poststructuralist conundrum ("the brush of recognitions that both strain toward language and systematically elude it") and those "slantwise" recognitions that happen across identities ("the slantwise recognitions that pass between women and gay men").[17]

Of the many aspects of "Paranoid Reading and Reparative Reading; or, You're So Paranoid, You Probably Think This Introduction Is About You," I find its snarky subtitle hardest to swallow. My own readerly and writerly queer recognitions and cross-identifications have been the catalysts of intense change. Of course, "You're So Paranoid, You Probably Think This Introduction Is About You" irks me because I feel particularly called out by its accusation (proving the point, I know). But more importantly, it baffles me, if only because thinking an essay is about you seems to me precisely in line with the modes of reading most celebrated in Sedgwick's bold treatise. This is the irony encapsulated in the Carly Simon song that Sedgwick's title tropes: Queer recognition is motivated by the suspicion, both paranoid and reparative, that you are not the only one. This suspicion might be overly identificatory or dangerously transformative, but that isn't cause for dismissal. On the contrary—that's the whole point.

Notes

INTRODUCTION

1. Harris quoted in Browne et al., "Watching White People."
2. Sedgwick, *Epistemology of the Closet*, 5.
3. Sedgwick, *Epistemology of the Closet*, 81.
4. Murray-García and Tervalon, "The Concept of Cultural Humility."
5. Hong, *Death Beyond Disavowal*, 141.
6. For a comprehensive list of these fields, see Wiegman, *Object Lessons*, 2n2.
7. Queer studies, queer theory, and queer literary criticism are three separate but related ideas. In this book, *queer studies* refers to an academic field of study focusing on gender, sexuality, sexual orientation, and sexual stigma. *Queer theory* refers to an analytic within queer studies that approaches sexuality and gender as socially constructed—with the understanding that there are many queer theories, all of which approach, describe, and critique the social construction of gender and sexuality differently. *Queer literary criticism*, as I employ it, refers to academic writing on works of literature that uses queer theory as its primary analytic.
8. Butler, "Imitation and Gender Insubordination," 18.
9. Butler, "Imitation and Gender Insubordination," 13.
10. As Wiegman and Elizabeth A. Wilson point out, defining *queer* as purely and simply oppositional robs it of its initial deconstructive potential and, as such, of its ability to theorize identity as complicated, socially contextual, or changing. Wiegman and Wilson attribute this tendency among queer theorists in large part to queer studies' historical pattern of defining itself against "normativity": "While 'queer' has etymological connections to movements that transverse and twist . . . its most frequent deployment has been in the service of defiance and reprimand. The allure of moving *against* appears to have had greater critical currency" than the more intimate and complicit gesture of moving *athwart*" (Wiegman and Wilson, "Introduction," 11). Kadji Amin, in his recent piece "We Are All Nonbinary: A Brief History of Accidents," tells a similar story from a slightly different angle, one that traces a similar pattern within transgender studies. Amin notes a recent trend among thinkers in "minoritarian fields" toward insistence on the one-to-one, unproblematic relation between identification, identity, and identity categories, such that "nonbinary" itself, for example, becomes a fixed identity category, ironically diametrically opposed to "binary" (Amin, "We Are All Nonbinary," 106).

11. Roderick A. Ferguson, for example, has done work to uncover queer theory's intellectual debts to the Black feminist thinkers of the 1970s, while Heather Love further credits mid-century, state-sanctioned sociological studies of deviance with making significant contributions to current understandings of queerness. Ferguson, *Aberrations in Black*; Love, *Underdogs*.

12. Eng et al., "Introduction," 7.

13. Washington, "The AIDS Epidemic."

14. Crimp, "Right On, Girlfriend!," 15.

15. Jagose, *Queer Theory*; Rand, *Reclaiming Queer*; Wiegman, "Heteronormativity."

16. Crimp, "Right On, Girlfriend!," 15.

17. Mercer, "Skin Head Sex Thing," 22.

18. Dreisinger, *Near Black*, 24.

19. In English, this argument works on a grammatical level. The syntactical work of *as* in the construction "to read as X" is already ambiguous: *As* is both a preposition used in reference to a thing's function or character ("I was working as a waitress in a cocktail bar") and an adverb used to compare two different but similar things in a simile ("Hop in my Chrysler, it's as big as a whale").

20. Johnson, *A World of Difference*, 38.

21. To be sure, it is possible to imagine and name authors who implement these tactics in genres beyond literary criticism, particularly in memoir and paraliterary fiction. In *As If: Modern Enchantment and the Literary Prehistory of Virtual Reality*, for example, literary critic Michael Saler uses *as if* to describe a specific readerly mindset, what Saler terms the "ironic imagination" (22). Beginning with New Romance, detective, science fiction, and fantasy novels of the late nineteenth century and ending with a gesture toward the virtual realities of the present day, Saler argues that these self-reflexive texts train their readers to hold two worlds in their heads at once (this world and the world of the text) and thus lend themselves particularly well to social projects that extend beyond their pages: online communities, fan clubs, cosplay conventions, and so on. For Saler, the double consciousness required to deeply engage with these alternate realities means that consuming fiction is not merely a matter of escapism but rather one of worldmaking; "ironic imagination" allows modern readers to approach fictional worlds as if they were real while still maintaining critical distance.

22. Reid-Pharr, *Black Gay Man*, 153.

23. Fuss, *Identification Papers*, 2.

24. Sedgwick, *Epistemology of the Closet*, 61.

25. Butler and Martin, "Cross-Identifications," 3.

26. Fuss, *Identification Papers*, 2.

27. Amin, "We Are All Nonbinary," 117.

28. Amin, "We Are All Nonbinary," 115.

29. Muñoz, *Disidentifications*, 5.

30. Muñoz, *Disidentifications*, 8.

31. Muñoz, *Disidentifications*, 6.

32. N. K. Miller, *Getting Personal*, 34.

33. Miller cites both Johnson and Sedgwick as examples of "reading as." She also lists Barbara

Christian and Barbara Smith, authors who both serve as important critical interlocutors in my own project. Though she groups these critics and others together as examples of "personal criticism," Miller also takes care to note the differences in their approaches: Johnson's "Gender Theory and the Yale School" includes a "third-person cameo" (Miller, *Getting Personal*, 2); Sedgwick's "A Poem Is Being Written" constitutes "an academic (degree-zero) anecdote from the authorizing groves of campus life" (1); Christian's "Black Feminist Process: In the Midst of . . ." demonstrates how Christian "thinks aloud, so to speak" (10); Smith's "Toward a Black Feminist Criticism" involves "self-representation as political representivity" and constitutes a plea for more representation of "women . . . like herself" (2). Unlike Miller, I am interested in the ways in which these authors undermine the assumption that they are writing "as" themselves.

34. Fournier, *Autotheory as Feminist Practice*, 3.
35. Fuss, *Identification Papers*, 2.
36. Caughie, *Passing and Pedagogy*, 3.
37. Caughie, *Passing and Pedagogy*, 25.
38. Caughie, *Passing and Pedagogy*, 47; Mercer, "Skin Head Sex Thing," 19.
39. Halperin, *How to Be Gay*, 259.
40. Mercer, "Skin Head Sex Thing," 22.
41. Mercer, "Skin Head Sex Thing," 21–22.
42. Berlant and Edelman, *Sex, or the Unbearable*; Weiner and Young, "Queer Bonds," 224.
43. It is instructive, for example, that the history of blackface minstrelsy and the history of US camp practice are inseparable histories: Their overlap reveals the ways in which vectors of identity such as race, gender, and sexuality are at the same time incommensurate and mutually constitutive of one another. The connection is not only historical but formal—so much so that some theorists of camp argue that camp, far from having a "consistently progressive politics," might instead "be, after all, a kind of blackface." Robertson, "Mae West's Maids," 394.
44. Berlant and Edelman, *Sex, or the Unbearable*, 5.
45. Sedgwick, "Paranoid Reading and Reparative Reading," 28.
46. See Wiegman, *Object Lessons*, 328: "The status of class as an object of academic inquiry is an interesting one, as it has never accrued institutional attention as an identity knowledge. In fact . . . identity knowledges were crafted in the divergence of race and gender from class analysis, primarily through the critical figure of Marx, giving rise to a split within left political theory that remains animated, if not at times quite toxic for understanding how structural inequalities and identities are formed today."
47. Brim, *Poor Queer Studies*, 10.
48. It is instructive, for example, to consider Yale's place in Butler's anecdote. While they may be making a point about the university system more broadly, the significance of "Yale" in Butler's "I was off to Yale to be a lesbian" cannot be overlooked. Not only does Yale serve as the primary site of American deconstruction (so much so that "The Yale School" has come to synecdochally stand in for US deconstruction as a whole [Redfield, *Theory at Yale*]); it is also, as Butler's anecdote reveals, a site of emergent identity-based student activism, colloquially known as "the gay Ivy" long before queer theory arrived on campus (Lassila, "Why They Call Yale the 'Gay Ivy'"). New ways of thinking and theorizing were

catalyzed in the clash of these two ideologies of identity. As Corey McEleney notes, 1980s Yale serves as a crucible for the type of queer criticism this book interrogates; indeed, several of the theorists who populate this book overlapped at Yale graduate school at its most Paul de Man–ian moment (McEleney, "Queer Theory and the Yale School"). Several former Elis play an important role in this book: Johnson, Sedgwick, and Reid-Pharr, but also Butler, Lee Edelman, Henry Louis Gates Jr., Joseph Litvak, D. A. Miller, and all attended Yale graduate school during its deconstructionist heyday. See also Wiegman's quip in the introduction to *Object Lessons*:

> While we can't fix our desire (and who would want to), we can follow its effects on the disciplinary apparatus, which means considering how...the political imaginary generated by queer critique becomes a disciplinizing apparatus, not simply because the critical authority we have amassed to proclaim in not-identity arises from our institutional location as experts in identity knowledges, but because the claim for being political in the process that everywhere underwrites left identity critique is the most heavily invested sign of our professionalization in identity domains. *You can't get to Yale without it*, which means, Dorothy, we are really not in Kansas anymore. (125, emphasis added)

49. Litvak, *Strange Gourmets*, 29.
50. Ferguson, *Aberrations in Black*, 128.
51. Spillers, "'All the Things,'" 77.
52. At once humiliating and delightful, this shock is, in the words of camp theorist J. Bryan Lowder, "not unlike the shock of unexpectedly encountering your best friend on a crowded street in a foreign county.... The rush is recognition before cognition, affiliation without identification, id exploding from your psyche like the little mouth in *Alien*" (Lowder, "Joan Crawford's Cream Pantsuit"). See also a quote often (mis)attributed to either F. Scott Fitzgerald or Mark Twain: "An exclamation point is like laughing at your own joke."
53. McEleny, "Queer Theory and the Yale School," 144.
54. Stockton, "Rhythm," 346.
55. Johnson, *A World of Difference*, 16.
56. Sharpe, *Monstrous Intimacies*.
57. Hartman, *Scenes of Subjection*, 20.
58. Edelman, "Learning Nothing," 125.
59. Cohen, "The Radical Potential of Queer?," 143.
60. Sedgwick, *Tendencies*, 129.
61. Gomez, "Repeat After Me," 935.
62. Centers for Disease Control and Prevention, "HIV and AIDS."
63. Similar political and rhetorical strategies are in full force today. Spurred by white nationalism, it is advantageous to the new right to argue that race is a fixed identity category, knowable and policeable. Fueled by antitrans vitriol, it is advantageous to politicians to argue that gender is immutable, biological, and unchanging. Emboldened by US backing, it is advantageous to those invested in Gaza's destruction to argue that Jewish Americanness is a fixed, one-note identity.
64. Hong, *Death Beyond Disavowal*, 7.

65. Hong, *Death Beyond Disavowal*, 15.
66. Berlant and Edelman, *Sex, or the Unbearable*, 50.

ONE. MISCARRYING ON

1.   McDowell, *"The Changing Same,"* xi.
2.   McDowell, *"The Changing Same,"* xviii.
3.   McDowell, *"The Changing Same,"* xxii.
4.   *Oxford English Dictionary*, s.v. "qualification (n.)," March 2024, https://doi.org/10.1093/OED
     /6607729647.
5.   McDowell, *"The Changing Same,"* xiv.
6.   McDowell, *"The Changing Same,"* xviii.
7.   Clarke et al., "Conversations and Questions," 107.
8.   Clarke et al., "Conversations and Questions," 108.
9.   Clarke et al., "Conversations and Questions," 108–9.
10. Smith, "Toward a Black Feminist Criticism," 137.
11. McDowell, *"The Changing Same,"* 9, 23.
12. McDowell, *"The Changing Same,"* 9.
13. Clarke et al., "Conversations and Questions," 123.
14. It can only be left to speculation whether Walker's later love affair with singer-songwriter
     Tracy Chapman would have changed Clarke's opinion on this. Walker, *Gathering Blossoms
     Under Fire*, 367–90.
15. Jones et al., *Ain't Gonna Let Nobody Turn Me Around*, 130.
16. Smith, "Toward a Black Feminist Criticism," 142.
17. Clarke, *"But Some of Us Are Brave,"* 784.
18. Butler, *Bodies That Matter*, 174.
19. Butler, *Bodies that Matter*, 173.
20. Ferguson, *Aberrations in Black*, 130.
21. Ferguson, *Aberrations in Black*, 126.
22. Awkward, "Response," 74.
23. Clarke et al., "Conversations and Questions," 107.
24. McDowell, *"The Changing Same,"* iii.
25. McDowell, *"The Changing Same,"* 104.
26. McDowell, *"The Changing Same,"* 101.
27. McDowell, *"The Changing Same,"* 105.
28. McDowell, *"The Changing Same,"* 102.
29. Awkward, "Response."
30. McDowell, *"The Changing Same,"* xvi.
31. McDowell, *"The Changing Same,"* xvi.
32. McDowell, *"The Changing Same,"* 108.
33. Gallop et al., "Criticizing Feminist Criticism," 364.
34. Gallop et al., "Criticizing Feminist Criticism," 394. Gallop's infamous quote reappears
     in Barbara Johnson's *The Feminist Difference* (11), Elizabeth Abel's "Black Writing, White
     Reading" (470), Bette London's *Writing Double* (87), Pamela L. Caughie's *Passing and Ped-*

agogy (91), Kathleen Daly's "Different Ways of Conceptualizing Sex/Gender in Feminist Theory and Their Implications for Criminology" (44), Jeffrey Gray's "Identity Cards" (24), and chapter 2 of the current volume.

35. Gallop et al., "Criticizing Feminist Criticism," 353.

36. McDowell, *"The Changing Same,"* 175.

37. Stowe, "Sojourner Truth, the Libyan Sibyl," 473.

38. Hartman, *Scenes of Subjection. Uncle Tom's Cabin* appears, for example, in case fifty of Richard von Krafft-Ebing's *Psychopathia Sexualis* and Sigmund Freud's "A Child Is Being Beaten," a case study that will briefly raise its head again in chapter 4.

39. Morrison, *Beloved*, 324, quoted in McDowell, *"The Changing Same,"* 172.

40. Morrison, *Beloved*, 43, 222, 189, 226.

41. McDowell, "The Changing Same," 156.

42. *Oxford English Dictionary*, s.v. "read (v.)," September 2024, https://doi.org/10.1093/OED /7142905628.

43. McDowell, *"The Changing Same,"* 160.

44. McDowell, introduction to *Passing*.

45. McDowell, "'It's Not Safe. Not Safe at All'"; McDowell, *"The Changing Same."*

46. This citation appears in Butler's *Bodies That Matter*, Johnson's *The Feminist Difference*, Katie Ryan's "Falling in Public," Laura Doyle's "Transnational History at Our Backs," Keguro Macharia's "Queering Helga Crane," and Rafael Walker's "Nella Larsen Reconsidered," to name a few.

47. Clarke, *"But Some of Us Are Brave,"* 785.

48. McDowell, *"The Changing Same,"* 79.

49. McDowell, *"The Changing Same,"* 79.

50. McDowell, *"The Changing Same,"* 79.

51. McDowell, *"The Changing Same,"* 79.

52. McDowell, *"The Changing Same,"* 80.

53. McDowell, *"The Changing Same,"* 81.

54. McDowell, introduction to *Passing*, xvi; McDowell, "It's Not Safe. Not Safe at All," 619; McDowell, *"The Changing Same,"* 80.

55. Baz Dreisinger, for example, argues that one indication of "moments of unease about racial categories" in US history is a resurgence of interest in the phenomenon of racial passing. Dreisinger, *Near Black*, 124.

56. McDowell, introduction to *Passing*, x.

57. McDowell, introduction to *Passing*, x.

58. McDowell, *"The Changing Same,"* 80, 83.

59. McDowell, *"The Changing Same,"* 79.

60. McDowell, *"The Changing Same,"* 88, 95.

61. McDowell, *"The Changing Same,"* 91.

62. McDowell, *"The Changing Same,"* 88.

63. Johnson, *The Feminist Difference*, 158.

64. Johnson, *The Feminist Difference*, 158.

65. McDowell, *"The Changing Same,"* xi.

66. McDowell, *"The Changing Same,"* xviii.

67. McDowell, *"The Changing Same,"* xvi.

68. McDowell, *"The Changing Same,"* xviii.

69. Christian, *New Black Feminist Criticism,* 209.

70. Hong, *Death Beyond Disavowal,* 127.

71. Nash, *Black Feminism Reimagined,* 3.

72. Nash, *Black Feminism Reimagined,* 35.

73. Nash, *Black Feminism Reimagined,* 3.

74. Nash, *Black Feminism Reimagined,* 5.

75. Nash, *Black Feminism Reimagined,* 58.

76. None of the top ten syllabi resulting from a quick Google search for "queer theory syl-labus," for example, mention McDowell. A similar search for "queer theory reading list" yields the same result. Even though these conceptual and historical links exist between McDowell and her queer theoretical contemporaries, current queer critical boundaries as delineated in queer theory syllabi or in suggested reading lists leave McDowell for the most part conspicuously absent.

77. Notably, Butler is also writing about *Passing* around the same time as McDowell, publish-ing "Passing, Queering: Nella Larsen's Psychoanalytic Challenge" in their second book, *Bodies That Matter.* Unlike "The 'Nameless . . . Shameful Impulse,'" Butler's piece primar-ily uses a queer framework—the term *queer* appears twenty-nine times in their essay while *lesbian* occurs only twice. This difference betrays a terminological shift. In the seven years that pass between the first iteration of McDowell's *Passing* essay (the introduction pub-lished in 1986) and *Bodies That Matter* (published in 1993), *queer* became more legible as a concept that, in the eyes of theorists like Butler, encompasses the complicated psychic and libidinal intertwining of gender, race, and sexuality. In other words, at least by 1993, there is something about the descriptor *lesbian* that precludes it from the heavy intersec-tional lifting that theories of Larsen's novel require. Both word choice and authorial po-sitionality thus might be contributing factors to McDowell's relative exclusion from the queer theoretical canon.

78. Johnson, *Mother Tongues,* 60.

79. Berlant and Warner, "What Does Queer Theory Teach Us," 345, 348.

80. Huffer, *Mad for Foucault,* 34.

81. Holland, *The Erotic Life of Racism.*

82. Nash, *Black Feminism Reimagined,* 4.

83. Nash, *Black Feminism Reimagined,* 13.

84. Holland, *Erotic Life of Racism,* 27.

TWO. BARBARA JOHNSON'S PASSING

1. Gates and Engell, "Barbara Johnson Memorial Service."

2. Gates and Engell, "Barbara Johnson Memorial Service."

3. Abel, "Black Writing, White Reading," 483.

4. M. H. Washington, "Barbara Johnson, African Americanist," 168.

5. Ronell, "Surrender and the Ethically Binding Signature," 143.

6. D. A. Miller, "Call for Papers," 368.

7. D. A. Miller, "Call for Papers," 370.
8. D. A. Miller, "Call for Papers," 368.
9. D. A. Miller, *Bringing Out Roland Barthes*, 18.
10. D. A. Miller, "Call for Papers," 368.
11. Sharpe, *Monstrous Intimacies*, 190.
12. Sharpe, *Monstrous Intimacies*, 190, quoting Stoler, *Race and the Education of Desire*, 164. I am grateful to Julien Fischer for the observation that this quote itself, as a quote that itself is citing a quote, performs a citational ventriloquism that could well relate to the modes of cross-racial identification in which my analysis is interested.
13. Holland, *Erotic Life of Racism*, 3, 7.
14. D. A. Miller, "Call for Papers," 368.
15. D. A. Miller, *Bringing Out Roland Barthes*, 3.
16. Johnson, "Bringing Out D. A. Miller," 5.
17. Johnson, "Bringing Out D. A. Miller," 7.
18. Johnson, "Bringing Out D. A. Miller," 5.
19. Johnson, *The Feminist Difference*, 65.
20. Johnson, *The Feminist Difference*, 67.
21. Johnson, *The Feminist Difference*, 65.
22. Washington, "Barbara Johnson, African Americanist," 167.
23. Goffman, *Stigma*, 63.
24. Robinson, "It Takes One to Know One," 719.
25. Robinson, "It Takes One to Know One," 721.
26. Robinson, "It Takes One to Know One," 723.
27. Sedgwick, *Epistemology of the Closet*, 80.
28. Sedgwick, *Epistemology of the Closet*, 80.
29. Stoever, *The Sonic Color Line*, 7.
30. Stoever, *The Sonic Color Line*, 5.
31. Furlonge, *Race Sounds*, 5, 9.
32. Robinson, "It Takes One to Know One," 724.
33. Moten, *In the Break*, 42.
34. Moten, *In the Break*, 42.
35. Johnson, "Thresholds of Difference," 288.
36. Furlonge, *Race Sounds*, 21.
37. Henderson, "Speaking in Tongues," 22.
38. Henderson, "Speaking in Tongues," 37.
39. Johnson, "Thresholds of Difference," 278.
40. Abel, "Black Writing, White Reading," 484.
41. Abel, "Black Writing, White Reading," 482.
42. Abel, "Black Writing, White Reading," 483.
43. Abel, "Black Writing, White Reading," 485.
44. Abel, "Black Writing, White Reading," 482.
45. Johnson, *The Feminist Difference*, 12.
46. Spillers's piece already anticipates many of the issues raised in *The Feminist Difference*, including questions of speech as a matter of power, "speaking for," ownership, and intra-

gender critical conversation: "*Within* genders, the Black intellectual class is establishing few models of conduct and social responsibility, but perhaps change is in the making. Relatedly, we appear to be at a crossroads in trying to determine who 'owns' African-American cultural production as an 'intellectual property,' who may 'speak' for it, and whether or not 'possession' itself is the always-exploitative end of kinds of access, even when the investigator looks like me" (Spillers, "'All the Things,'" 77). This emphasis on quoted speech later leads Johnson to similarly articulate racial identity in terms of what is spoken or heard rather than what is seen (as is the case with her writing on Wright).

47. Johnson, *The Feminist Difference*, 12; Abel et al., *Female Subjects in Black and White*.

48. An obsession that, clearly, I share (see chapter 1).

49. Berlant, "Intimacy," 285.

50. Johnson, *The Feminist Difference*, 191.

51. In her introduction, in a humorous rumination on the many possible ways feminists can differ, Johnson lists "feminists for and against the anti-pornography ordinance, the difference-versus-equality debates, the essentialism-versus-postmodernism debates, the Black feminist critiques of white feminism, the Marxist feminist critiques of bourgeois feminism, the international feminist critiques of first-world feminism." Johnson, *The Feminist Difference*, 2.

52. Johnson, *The Feminist Difference*, 193.

53. Johnson, *The Feminist Difference*, 173.

54. Johnson, *The Feminist Difference*, 81.

55. Johnson, *The Wake of Deconstruction*, 22.

56. Johnson, *The Feminist Difference*, 174.

57. Johnson, *The Feminist Difference*, 174, 175.

58. Johnson, *The Feminist Difference*, 75.

59. Johnson, *The Feminist Difference*, 85.

60. Morrison, *Sula*, 105.

61. Morrison, *Sula*, 60.

62. Redfield, *Theory at Yale*.

63. Johnson, *The Feminist Difference*, 83.

64. Johnson, *The Feminist Difference*, 86.

65. Wiegman, *Object Lessons*, 13.

66. Johnson's calculated use of the first-person plural is not unique, especially within identity knowledge fields. To cite but three examples out of many: Leo Bersani rehearses a similar anxiety to Johnson, devoting the entire preface of *Homos* to the question of the "we" in gay and lesbian studies (1–10). Saidiya V. Hartman, too, frequently uses the first-person plural, especially in the introduction to *Scenes of Subjection*—a choice that dialogues with her discussions of the meaning of "we the people" (65). More recently, Cameron Awkward-Rich explores what he calls the "terrible we"—a mode of theorizing collectivity that "insist[s] on recognizing—without romanticizing—various kinds of injury and repairment" (Awkward-Rich, *The Terrible We*, 22).

67. Alexander, "'Can You Be BLACK,'" 90.

68. Alexander, "'Can You Be BLACK,'" 81.

69. Womack, "Can You Be Black."

70. Johnson, *The Feminist Difference*, 86; Hartman, *Scenes of Subjection*, 20.

71. Hartman, *Scenes of Subjection*, 20.

72. Douglass, *Narrative of the Life of Frederick Douglass*, 96.

73. Sharpe, *Monstrous Intimacies*, 7.

74. Johnson, *The Feminist Difference*, 158.

75. Johnson, *The Feminist Difference*, 141.

76. Johnson, *The Feminist Difference*, 157.

77. Johnson, *The Feminist Difference*, 141.

78. Johnson, *The Feminist Difference*, 158.

79. Gallop, "Reading Johnson as a 'as a,'" 40.

80. McEleney, "Queer Theory and the Yale School," 159, 154, 160, 161.

81. Johnson, *The Feminist Difference*, 157.

82. Johnson, *The Feminist Difference*, 142.

83. Johnson, *The Feminist Difference*, 145.

84. Johnson, *The Feminist Difference*, 145.

85. Caughie, "Example of Barbara Johnson," 178.

86. Johnson, *The Feminist Difference*, 145.

87. Johnson, *The Feminist Difference*, 143.

88. Johnson, *The Feminist Difference*, 160.

89. Johnson, *The Feminist Difference*, 142.

90. D. A. Miller, "Call for Papers," 368.

91. Robinson, "It Takes One to Know One," 719; Frye, *The Politics of Reality*, 173.

92. Johnson, Review, 3.

93. These authors include McEleney: "How do we read the brief parenthetical (and exclamatory) anecdote that interrupts Johnson's quotation of de Man's study?" ("Queer Theory and the Yale School," 150), "Given Johnson's insistence on her personal erotic life throughout the essay, it is intriguing to note the parenthetical 'my' in this sentence—especially because the two subsequent uses of the pronoun in the same sentence are not parenthetical" (157); Caughie: "He does, however, discuss the meaning of the epigraph in some detail, noting that 'yes and no' are 'three words that would be expected from a deconstructionist'—though [the parenthetical] 'what else?' I would suggest is what we expect from Barbara Johnson" ("Example of Barbara Johnson," 180); Avital Ronell: "Why does the writer parachute parentheses at the end of this description? . . . On the face of it, there may be no rhetorical justification for the parenthetical annexation, for it follows no quotation or recognizable expository reasoning" ("Surrender and the Ethically Binding Signature," 133); and Gallop: "Yes-and-(then)-no is so frequent in this text that we might hear the parenthetic '(what else?)' as a recognition of predictability" ("Reading Johnson as a 'as a,'" 154), "We should certainly connect this 'reading otherwise' with Johnson's preference for questions over answers. . . . Which may be why in the anecdote that begins the book, when asked a question by Jeffery Nealon, she ultimately (if parenthetically) replies with a question: what else?" (160).

94. Johnson, *Mother Tongues*, 9.

95. Johnson, "Bringing Out D. A. Miller," 3.

96. Johnson, *Mother Tongues*, 9.

97. Johnson, *Mother Tongues*, 176.

98. Johnson, *Mother Tongues*, 175.

99. Johnson, *Mother Tongues*, 176.

100. Johnson, *Mother Tongues*, 15.

101. Johnson, *Mother Tongues*, 177.

102. Johnson, "Bringing Out D. A. Miller," 7.

103. D. A. Miller, "Call for Papers," 365.

104. Johnson, *Mother Tongues*, 5.

105. Johnson, "Apostrophe, Animation, and Abortion," 37.

106. Johnson, "Apostrophe, Animation, and Abortion," 36.

107. Spillers, "Mama's Baby," 80.

108. Edelman, "Future Is Kid Stuff," 22–23.

109. Edelman, "Future Is Kid Stuff," 22; Edelman, *No Future*, 14.

110. Johnson, "Apostrophe, Animation, and Abortion," 36.

111. Tanne, "US Pro-Life Groups Tell Black Women."

112. Roberts, *Killing the Black Body*.

113. Christian, *New Black Feminist Criticism*, 129.

114. Hong, *Death Beyond Disavowal*, 129.

115. Holland, *Erotic Life of Racism*, 75.

116. *Oxford English Dictionary*, s.v. "midwife (n.), Etymology," September 2024, https://doi.org /10.1093/OED/5618839815.

117. Ellerby-Brown et al., "African American Nurse-Midwives."

118. Bonaparte, "Physicians' Discourse for Establishing Authoritative Knowledge."

119. Morrison, *Beloved*, 82.

120. The numerous posthumous remembrances of Johnson produced by the gay men in her academic orbit might constitute another instance of cross-identification. These cross-identifications interestingly mirror Eve Kosofsky Sedgwick's more notorious eulogies of gay men, outlined in chapter 4 (thanks to anonymous manuscript reader number three for this provocative observation).

121. Edelman, "Unknowing Barbara," 93.

122. Nash, *Black Feminism Reimagined*, 104.

123. Berlant, "Intimacy," 281.

124. Voglar, "Sex and Talk," 365; Bersani, "Is the Rectum a Grave?," 222.

125. Edelman, "Unknowing Barbara," 90.

THREE. SHOCK THERAPY

1. Reid-Pharr, *Black Gay Man*, 9.

2. Reid-Pharr, *Black Gay Man*, 9–10.

3. Reid-Pharr, *Black Gay Man*, 10.

4. Reid-Pharr, *Black Gay Man*, 10.

5. Reid-Pharr, *Black Gay Man*, 85.

6. Reid-Pharr, *Black Gay Man*, 86.

7. Hemphill, "Now We Think," 155.

8. Thank you to Carly B. Boxer for pointing out the German aspect of this pun, which I originally missed.

9. Holland, *The Erotic Life of Racism*.

10. Brinkema, "Irrumation, the Interrogative."

11. Jacobellis v. Ohio, 378 U.S. 184 (1964).

12. The assumption that porn is nonrepresentational influences the study of gay porn in ways that are both similar to and different from the study of mainstream heterosexual porn. For more on the particularities of how debates about surface reading and paranoid reading play out in queer porn studies, as well as for good examples of how one might apply close reading practices to gay pornography, see Stadler, "Pornographesis."

13. Best and Marcus, "Surface Reading," 12.

14. Stadler, "Pornographesis"; L. Williams, *Porn Studies*.

15. Ruszczycky, *Vulgar Genres*, 1.

16. Ruszczycky, *Vulgar Genres*, 3.

17. L. Williams, *Porn Studies*, 3.

18. Ruszczycky, *Vulgar Genres*, 2.

19. Ruszczycky, *Vulgar Genres*, 2.

20. Ruszczycky, *Vulgar Genres*, 2.

21. C-SPAN, "User Clip: Helms on Mapplethorpe."

22. Ruszczycky, *Vulgar Genres*, 4.

23. Ruszczycky, *Vulgar Genres*, 79.

24. Lang and Lang, "Public Opinion and the Helms Amendment."

25. As a former radio worker, the "shock" also reminds me of shock jocks—DJs who attain fame and popularity because they push the envelope past the bounds of on-air decency. In this way, the word *shock* pairs obscenity and orality. (In the United States at least, most legal decisions about obscenity do not concern print media but rather focus on radio and television broadcasts. I still treasure a small button I received from my college radio station, in which the Federal Communications Commission [FCC] logo is surrounded by George Carlin's seven dirty words.) The oral nature of the radio broadcast hints at a link made later in this chapter between orality, racism, and obscenity. Consider, for example, that current FCC regulations define "obscene, indecent, or profane" content three different ways, all predictably vague. Additional broadcasting guidelines prohibit "profane" or "indecent" content to be broadcast between 6 a.m. and 10 p.m., "when there is a reasonable risk that children may be in the audience" (Federal Communications Commission, "Obscene, Indecent and Profane Broadcasts"). This specific reasoning hints at the ways on-air profanity, and perhaps profanity in general, might carry with it its own antisocial, antichild queer stigma (Edelman, *No Future*). Because the FCC covers broadcasting, the spoken obscenity becomes the controversial obscenity—although, notably, the FCC does not count racial, ethnic, or homophobic slurs that might constitute hate speech as "indecent" and therefore worthy of censure in its current policy (Farhi, "Wait, Wait").

26. See the following excerpts from Mercer, "Looking for Trouble" (emphasis added): "To *shock* was always the key verb in the avant-garde vocabulary. Over the past year, the *shocking* eroticism of Robert Mapplethorpe's exquisite and perverse photography has been at the center of a major controversy in the United States concerning public funding of con-

temporary art" (184); "We cannot assume that Black audiences are somehow exempt from its modernist 'shock effect,' although it seems Black voices have been curiously silent and muted in the recent furor" (184); "I can still quite vividly recall my first encounter with Mapplethorpe's Black male nudes precisely because I was so *shocked* by what I saw" (184); "Despite its value in cultural criticism, the residual moralistic connotation of the term fetishism tends to flatten out the affective ambivalence that viewers of Mapplethorpe's work experience as its characteristic 'shock effect'" (189); "He throws the binary structure of the question back to the spectator, where it is torn apart in the disruptive 'shock effect.' The *shock* of recognition of the unconscious sex-race fantasies is experienced precisely as an emotional disturbance which troubles the spectator's secure sense of identity" (189); "But now I am not sure whether the perverse strategy of visual fetishism is necessarily a bad thing, in the sense that as the locus of the destabilizing 'shock effect' it encourages the viewer to examine his or her own implication in the fantasies that the images arouse" (191); "I should emphasize that I've changed my mind about Mapplethorpe's *shocking* eroticism not for the fun of it, but because I have no particular desire to form an alliance with the New Right" (196).

27. Musing on the "shock effects" of *Black Book* (1986), a photo collection of Black male nudes by white gay photographer Robert Mapplethorpe, Mercer examines the implications of his initial shock from his own embodied authorial position as not only a Black gay man but a Black gay man who, he admits in the later piece, desires and eroticizes Mapplethorpe's Black subjects. In his article, Mercer details the circumstances of a change of heart and mind. Having previously panned *Black Book* for its racial fetishism, Mercer revisits his conclusions to make room for an alternate reading: "I should come out with regard to the specificity of my own subject-position *as a Black gay reader* in Mapplethorpe's text.... I am forced to confront the unwelcome fact that as a spectator I actually inhabit the same position in the fantasy of mastery which I said earlier was that of the hegemonic white subject" (Mercer, "Looking for Trouble," 191, emphasis added). Mercer's own desire implicates him in the very structures he had previously critiqued, a realization that leads him to a more complicated set of conclusions. It is hard not to hear Mercer's "my own subject-position as a Black gay reader" echoed in Reid-Pharr's own phrase "as a Black man."

28. Thomas, *Down These Mean Streets*, 61.

29. Reid-Pharr, *Black Gay Man*, 119.

30. Reid-Pharr, *Black Gay Man*, 116.

31. Reid-Pharr, *Black Gay Man*, 100.

32. Reid-Pharr, *Black Gay Man*, 101.

33. Here and elsewhere, Reid-Pharr refers to academic discourse as "polite," an adjective that carries with it classed and racial implications. See Ross, "The Politics of Politeness," 145.

34. V. A. Young, "Should Writers Use They Own English?," 110.

35. Reid-Pharr, *Black Gay Man*, 102–3.

36. Reid-Pharr, *Black Gay Man*, 101–2.

37. Scott, *Extravagant Abjection*, 256

38. Scott, *Extravagant Abjection*, 230.

39. Butler, *Bodies That Matter*, 223.

40. Eve Kosofsky Sedgwick's self-diagnosis as "oral sadistic, anal masochistic" in her ground-

breaking essay "A Poem Is Being Written" further clues us in to a longer genealogy of orality in queer criticism that has yet to be fully explored (136). Though the rest of her essay chooses to elaborate on the latter "anal masochistic" diagnosis, Sedgwick's critical verbosity performs the former "oral sadistic" diagnosis, raising questions about the place of oral sadism in the relations of cross-identification and "homosexual reading" that she outlines in the piece.

41. Edelman, *Homographesis*, 58.
42. Scott, *Extravagant Abjection*, 27.
43. Ruszczycky, *Vulgar Genres*, 44.
44. Scott, *Extravagant Abjection*, 224.
45. Love, *Underdogs*, 26.
46. Reid-Pharr, *Black Gay Man*, 118.
47. Reid-Pharr, *Black Gay Man*, 118.
48. Huffer, *Are the Lips a Grave?*; Rohy, *Impossible Women*.
49. Brinkema, "Irrumation, the Interrogative," 15.
50. Reid-Pharr, *Black Gay Man*, 133.
51. Reid-Pharr, *Black Gay Man*, 134.
52. Reid-Pharr, *Black Gay Man*, 157.
53. Reid-Pharr, *Black Gay Man*, 157.
54. Reid-Pharr, *Black Gay Man*, 153.
55. Smith, "Toward a Black Feminist Criticism," 25; Radicalesbians, "The Woman Identified Woman," 1; Rich, *Compulsory Heterosexuality and Lesbian Existence*, 135.
56. Reid-Pharr, *Black Gay Man*, 11.
57. Reid-Pharr, *Black Gay Man*, 163.
58. Reid-Pharr, *Black Gay Man*, 162.
59. Lavery, "Egg Theory's Early Style," 387.
60. Lavery, "Egg Theory's Early Style," 384. Lavery is writing about Eve Kosofsky Sedgwick, but her argument could easily be applied to Reid-Pharr as well. "Living as a Lesbian" describes—in a near mirror image—a way of identifying across gender and sexuality for which Eve Kosofsky Sedgwick is also infamous. Reid-Pharr and Sedgwick share several points of connection beyond their *as if!* critical tendencies: Both have several theoretical and intellectual shared points of interest. Sedgwick and Reid-Pharr are both queer theorists, and both are queer public intellectuals who attempt to disrupt heterosexual frameworks in their theoretical and literary critical writing. Sedgwick's name makes an appearance in the acknowledgments of *Black Gay Man*; Reid-Pharr lived in Chapel Hill as an undergraduate student at the University of North Carolina until moving to Yale for his PhD in 1989, and Sedgwick became a professor one town away, at Duke University in 1988. As Sedgwick herself acknowledges throughout her career, both her scholarship and her personal life are structured by her identification across gender and sexuality as a heterosexual married woman writing about gay men and living in a homosocial community of gay male activists and academics. In other words, Sedgwick is living as a gay man in a similar way that Reid-Pharr is "living as a lesbian" (see chapter 4).
61. Aptheker, "Audre Lorde, Presente!"; Ferguson, "Of Sensual Matters"; N. Young, "'Uses of the Erotic.'"

62. Lorde, "Uses of the Erotic," 59.

63. McBride, "Lesbians in the Twentieth Century."

64. L. Williams, *Porn Studies*, 6.

65. Reid-Pharr, *Black Gay Man*, 10.

66. Reid-Pharr, *Black Gay Man*, 158.

67. Crawford, "Perfume," 152.

68. Madeleine Atwood, "Perfume and the Camp Aesthetic, or, Camp Scent-sibilities," unpublished manuscript, December 7, 2020; Crawford, "Perfume," 152.

69. Crawford, "Perfume," 152.

70. De Lauretis, *Figures of Resistance*; Halberstam, *Female Masculinity*; Love, *Feeling Backward*; Newton, "The Mythic Mannish Lesbian"; Prosser, *Second Skins*.

71. Reid-Pharr, *Black Gay Man*, 158; Hall, *The Well of Loneliness*, 187; Love, *Feeling Backward*, 187.

72. Reid-Pharr, *Black Gay Man*, 158.

73. Reid-Pharr, *Black Gay Man*, 163.

74. Bersani, "Is the Rectum a Grave?," 14.

75. Stockton, *Beautiful Bottom, Beautiful Shame*; Scott, *Extravagant Abjection*.

76. Walcott, "Reconstructing Manhood," 77.

77. Reid-Pharr, *Black Gay Man*, 161.

78. Currah and Stryker, "General Editors' Introduction," 159. Just as Roderick A. Ferguson points out that Black sexuality cannot be heteronormative, so too do these theorists help us see that Black masculinity has a different relation to normative gender than white masculinity (Ferguson, *Aberrations in Black*, 126). Marquis Bey reads Hortense Spillers for her work's trans potential, arguing that Black subjects are, in some ways, already positioned outside of or opposed to normative gender binaries set up under white supremacy (Bey, "The Trans*-ness of Blackness," 282). Working in a similar vein, C. Riley Snorton draws on the work of the Combahee River Collective to argue that their famous manifesto, aimed at white lesbian separatists, raises several questions, including: "How can black (cisgender or non-transgender) men be feminists? . . . What opportunities are made possibly [sic] by black feminisms' radical inclusivity, and how does that shape the study of masculinities within black women's studies and Women's Studies more generally?" (Snorton, "Transfiguring Masculinities in Black Women's Studies"). These questions are also vitally important to "Living as a Lesbian."

79. Reid-Pharr, *Black Gay Man*, 161.

80. Snorton, "Transfiguring Masculinities in Black Women's Studies."

81. Reid-Pharr, *Black Gay Man*, 143.

82. Reid-Pharr, *Black Gay Man*, 143.

83. Reid-Pharr, *Black Gay Man*, 139.

84. Snorton, "Transfiguring Masculinities in Black Women's Studies."

85. Baker, *Fabulosa!*, 93.

86. Reid-Pharr, *Black Gay Man*, 139.

87. Reid-Pharr, *Black Gay Man*, 144–45.

88. Reid-Pharr, *Black Gay Man*, 159.

89. Baldwin, *Evidence of Things Not Seen*, 39.

90. Nash, *Black Feminism Reimagined*, 27.

91.   Hong, *Death Beyond Disavowal*, 125–26.

92.   Reid-Pharr, *Black Gay Man*, 98.

93.   Reid-Pharr, *Black Gay Man*, 98.

94.   Reid-Pharr, *Black Gay Man*, 86.

95.   Reid-Pharr, "This Useful Death."

96.   Reid-Pharr, "This Useful Death."

97.   Sedgwick, *Tendencies*, 257.

98.   Hong, *Death Beyond Disavowal*, 15; Christian, "Diminishing Returns," 173.

99.   Edelman, *No Future*, 117.

100.   Sharpe, *Monstrous Intimacies*, 135.

101.   Fisher, *Gary in Your Pocket*, 231.

FOUR. GAY-MALE-ORIENTED AND NOW

1.   Sedgwick, *Tendencies*, xi.

2.   Sedgwick, *Tendencies*, xii.

3.   Fawaz, "'Open Mesh of Possibilities,'" 19.

4.   Fawaz, "'Open Mesh of Possibilities,'" 20.

5.   Fawaz, "'Open Mesh of Possibilities'"; Bradway, *Queer Experimental Literature*; Ahmed, "Sensitivity to Stigma"; Muñoz, "Race, Sex, and the Incommensurate."

6.   Sedgwick, *Tendencies*, 209.

7.   Sedgwick, "A Poem Is Being Written," 110.

8.   Berlant and Edelman, "What Survives," 39.

9.   Sedgwick, "A Poem Is Being Written," 177. I borrow the phrase "theater of embarrassment," as well as the idea of "making a scene," from Joseph Litvak's "Making a Scene: Henry James's Theater of Embarrassment," an essay that profoundly influences Sedgwick's later work on shame. In particular, Litvak's chapter on James inspired the *Touching Feeling* chapter "Shame, Theatricality, and Queer Performativity: Henry James's *The Art of the Novel*" (35–66).

10.   Sedgwick, "A Poem Is Being Written," 137.

11.   Litvak, "Sedgwick's Nerve," 254.

12.   Sedgwick, "A Poem Is Being Written," 132.

13.   Another embarrassment: Because her essay showcases her juvenilia—namely, the lyric poems that she wrote as a preteen, quoted at length—her readers quickly learn that the young Sedgwick, though precocious, simply is not that good at writing. At the very least, she does not write from the position of "professional success and hyperconscious virtuosity" that Sedgwick attributes to herself in 1987, and her flagrant display of such bad writing reveals a vulnerable childhood self, one prone to melodrama, lyric verse, and hyperbole. As Jane Gallop points out, "A Poem Is Being Written" stages an encounter between Sedgwick and her younger self, what Gallop calls "a passionate, queer identification," one that is also "fairly uncanny; in that the worldly writer and the young innocent are both Sedgwick" (Gallop, *Anecdotal Theory*, 116). That Sedgwick can experience a botched identification in this way, across temporal selves, squares with the general anti-identitarian ethos of "A Poem Is Being Written."

14.   Sedgwick, "A Poem Is Being Written," 132.

15.   Sedgwick, "A Poem Is Being Written," 132.

16.   Solomon, "Flaming Iguanas, Dalai Pandas, and Other Lesbian Bardos"; Litvak, "Sedg-wick's Nerve"; Berlant and Edelman, "What Survives."

17.   Sedgwick, "A Poem Is Being Written," 113, 129.

18.   Sedgwick, as quoted by herself in "A Poem Is Being Written," 127. While "The Warm De-cembers" was published in *Fat Art, Thin Art* in 1994 (89–152), it was written over decades and is sometimes described as unfinished (159).

19.   Sedgwick, "A Poem Is Being Written," 134.

20.   Sedgwick, "A Poem Is Being Written," 134.

21.   *Oxford English Dictionary*, s.v. "tortuous (adj.), Etymology," June 2024, https://doi.org/10 .1093/OED/1143738905; *Oxford English Dictionary*, s.v. "queer (adj. 1), Etymology," June 2024, https://doi.org/10.1093/OED/3759958359.

22.   Sedgwick, "A Poem Is Being Written," 133.

23.   Sedgwick, *Epistemology of the Closet*, 16.

24.   Edelman, "Unnamed," 185.

25.   Wiegman, "Eve's Triangles," 50.

26.   Sedgwick, "A Poem Is Being Written," 129.

27.   I am grateful to Calvin Hui for this observation.

28.   Sedgwick, "A Poem Is Being Written," 141n18.

29.   Sedgwick, "A Poem Is Being Written," 133.

30.   Sedgwick, "A Poem Is Being Written," 133.

31.   Solomon, "Flaming Iguanas, Dalai Pandas, and Other Lesbian Bardos," 210.

32.   Solomon, "Flaming Iguanas, Dalai Pandas, and Other Lesbian Bardos," 208.

33.   Sedgwick, "A Poem Is Being Written," 133–34.

34.   Sedgwick, preface to *Epistemology of the Closet*, xv.

35.   Radicalesbians, "The Woman Identified Woman," 3.

36.   Radicalesbians, "The Woman Identified Woman," 1.

37.   Gallop, *Anecdotal Theory*, 159.

38.   Love, *Underdogs*, 169.

39.   Love, *Underdogs*, 169.

40.   Wiegman, "Eve's Triangles," 58.

41.   Sedgwick, "A Poem Is Being Written," 140–41n15.

42.   Holland, *Erotic Life of Racism*, 38.

43.   "The Champagne Incident" refers to the photo otherwise known as "Carolina Beau-mont, New York, 1976," taken by the white French photographer Jean-Paul Goude and featured in his 1982 photo collection *Jungle Fever*. The photo depicts the Black model Car-olina Beaumont naked and spilling the contents of a bottle of champagne over her head and onto her exposed and exaggerated buttocks. Using Goude's signature "French Cor-rection" method, the photograph cuts together multiple images to create the illusion of the impossible pour. Goude later paid homage to this image in his infamous portrait of Kim Kardashian for *Paper* magazine's winter 2014 "break the internet" issue (Thompson, "Break the Internet").

44.   Crawford, "Slender Trouble."

45. Person, *On Freud's "A Child Is Being Beaten."*

46. Sedgwick, "A Poem Is Being Written," 134.

47. Sedgwick, "A Poem Is Being Written," 131.

48. Sedgwick, *Epistemology of the Closet*, 75.

49. Sedgwick, *Epistemology of the Closet*, 75.

50. Somerville, "Feminism, Queer Theory, and the Racial Closet," 197.

51. Sedgwick, "Socratic Raptures, Socratic Ruptures," 127.

52. Sedgwick, *Tendencies*, 11.

53. Sedgwick, *Tendencies*, 8.

54. Sedgwick, "Socratic Raptures, Socratic Ruptures," 125.

55. Holland, *Erotic Life of Racism*, 61.

56. Sedgwick, *Touching Feeling*, 129.

57. Sedgwick, *Touching Feeling*, 132.

58. *Oxford English Dictionary*, s.v. "displacement (n.), sense 2.a," June 2024, https://doi.org/10.1093/OED/2588737716.

59. Sedgwick, *Tendencies*, 256.

60. Sedgwick, *Tendencies*, 256.

61. Sedgwick, *Tendencies*, 257.

62. Sedgwick, *Tendencies*, 255.

63. Sedgwick, *Tendencies*, 255.

64. Eng, *Racial Castration*, 142.

65. Lavery, "Egg Theory's Early Style," 388.

66. Lavery, "Egg Theory's Early Style," 390.

67. Lavery, "Egg Theory's Early Style," 395.

68. Lavery, "Egg Theory's Early Style," 385.

69. Lavery, "Egg Theory's Early Style," 390.

70. Sedgwick, *Tendencies*, 257.

71. Hong, *Death Beyond Disavowal*, 8.

72. Sedgwick, *Tendencies*, 11.

73. Hansen, "The Future's Eve," 107.

74. Fisher, *Gary in Your Pocket*, 231.

75. Hanson, "The Future's Eve," 109.

76. Sedgwick, *A Dialogue on Love*, 179.

77. Fisher, *Gary in Your Pocket*, 279.

78. Muñoz, "Race, Sex, and the Incommensurate," 152.

79. Bradway, *Queer Experimental Literature*, 211.

80. Ahmed, "Sensitivity to Stigma." Heather Love, following Ahmed, also writes on "sensitivity to stigma" as Sedgwick's main mode of queer solidarity. Love helpfully points out that not only Sedgwick's identification with gay men but also her earlier fascination with the Holocaust and the US civil rights movement "[rearticulate] the guiding principle of queer politics: that the experience of stigma awakens you to its wider effects and that mass assumption of stigma . . . is an effective political strategy." Love, *Underdogs*, 168.

81. Sedgwick, *Touching Feeling*, 30. Here, Sedgwick writes about observing a picket line as an early lesson in "the then almost inconceivable willed assumption of stigma" and also ex-

plores the differences between "voluntary stigma" and what she calls "the nondiscretion-ary stigma of skin color." Sedgwick initially makes this differentiation while reflecting on her early introduction to protests as a white person growing up in the 1950s and 1960s—a time when, for her, "'protest' itself implied black civil rights protest" (30).

82. Ahmed, "Sensitivity to Stigma."
83. Recently, Love, writing on Ahmed and Sedgwick, similarly argues that "the challenge to White queer studies concerns this failure to address the imbrication of race and sexuality. But it also responds to the queer belief in the ability to work across or athwart difference, to forge coalition in spite of disagreement." Though this strategy, she writes, has largely disappointed, "the idea that a politics might be founded on shared stigma and a wide-spread antagonism to normativity remains vital, central to continuing investments in the possibility of queer politics." Love, *Underdogs*, 169.
84. Fawaz, "'I Cherish My Bile Duct.'"
85. Sedgwick, *Tendencies*, 261.
86. Nunokawa, "Queer Theory."
87. Sedgwick, "Socratic Raptures, Socratic Ruptures," 128, emphasis added.
88. Holland, *Erotic Life of Racism*, 70.
89. Ahmed, "Sensitivity to Stigma."
90. Sedgwick, *Tendencies*, 264.
91. Sedgwick, *Tendencies*, 265.
92. Bailey, *Many Hands Make a Quilt*, 4.
93. Nash, *Black Feminism Reimagined*, 107.

CONCLUSION

1. Eliot, as quoted in Gill, "Introduction," xxxvii.
2. Cain, "Malorie Blackman."
3. Kidd and Castano, "Reading Literary Fiction Improves Theory of Mind," 377.
4. Bader, "The Right Is Passing Bills That Ban the Teaching of Empathy."
5. Castillo, *How to Read Now*, 30.
6. Anderson, "'Could I Decide I Was an Asian Man?'"
7. Lai, *Asian American Connective Action*, 70.
8. Ahmed, *Living a Feminist Life*, 251.
9. Green, "'Race and Gender Are Not the Same!'"
10. D. A. Miller, "Hitchcock's Hidden Pictures," 127.
11. Johnson, "Bringing Out D. A. Miller," 5, quoting D. A. Miller, *Bringing Out Roland Barthes*, 3.
12. D. A. Miller, *Bringing Out Roland Barthes*, 4.
13. The essay also enacts a split between Miller and Sedgwick themselves: Holding Miller up as the paragon of paranoia allows the already quite paranoid Sedgwick to become a cham-pion of the reparative mode. Whenever I read this essay, I cannot help but remember that Sedgwick and Miller were, at one point, friends. They attended graduate school at Yale at the same time. They thanked each other in their first book's acknowledgments. Sedg-wick dedicates the first published version of "A Poem Is Being Written" to "two Davids,"

her brother David Kosofsky and David Miller. Their personal, public, and intellectual falling out—indicated in the introduction to *Novel Gazing* but also in the pointed dedication
of the *Tendencies* reprint of "A Poem Is Being Written" to *one* David, just Kosofsky—lends
even more affective charge to "Paranoid Reading and Reparative Reading," which no
doubt gets much of its power from the personal history and field-wide gossip that sur-
rounds it.

14. See the age-old joke, common in lesbian coming out stories, that early gay desire often
confuses wanting to be someone and wanting to sleep with them.

15. Sedgwick, "Paranoid Reading and Reparative Reading," 21, 3, 31, 32.

16. Sedgwick, "Paranoid Reading and Reparative Reading," 33.

17. Sedgwick, "Paranoid Reading and Reparative Reading," 34.

Bibliography

Abel, Elizabeth. "Black Writing, White Reading: Race and the Politics of Feminist Interpretation." *Critical Inquiry* 19, no. 3 (1993): 470–98.

Abel, Elizabeth, Barbara Christian, and Helene Moglen, eds. *Female Subjects in Black and White: Race, Psychoanalysis, Feminism*. University of California Press, 1997.

Ahmed, Sara. *Living a Feminist Life*. Duke University Press, 2017.

Ahmed, Sara. "Sensitivity to Stigma: Eve Sedgwick and Queer-of-Color Critique." *Feministkilljoys* (blog), October 20, 2013. https://feministkilljoys.com/2013/10/20/sensitivity-to-stigma/.

Alexander, Elizabeth. "'Can You Be BLACK and Look at This?': Reading the Rodney King Video(s)." *Public Culture* 7, no. 1 (1994): 77–94.

Amin, Kadji. "We Are All Nonbinary: A Brief History of Accidents." *Representations* 158 (2022): 106–19.

Anderson, Daniel. "'Could I Decide I Was an Asian Man?': Sen. Ted Cruz's Question During SCOTUS Nominee Hearing Goes Viral." *NextShark, Yahoo News*, March 24, 2022. https://news.yahoo.com/could-decide-asian-man-sen-233409211.html.

Aptheker, Bettina. "Audre Lorde, Presente!" *Women's Studies Quarterly* 40, nos. 3–4 (2012): 289–94.

Awkward, Michael. "Response." In *Afro-American Literary Study in the 1990s*, edited by Houston A. Baker Jr. and Patricia Redmond. University of Chicago Press, 1989.

Awkward-Rich, Cameron. *The Terrible We: Thinking with Trans Maladjustment*. Duke University Press, 2022.

Bader, Eleanor J. "The Right Is Passing Bills That Ban the Teaching of Empathy and Care in Schools." *Truthout*, December 17, 2023. https://truthout.org/articles/the-right-is-passing-bills-that-ban-the-teaching-of-empathy-and-care-in-schools/.

Bailey, Jess. *Many Hands Make a Quilt: Short Histories of Radical Quilting*. Common Threads Press, 2022.

Baker, Paul. *Fabulosa! The Story of Polari, Britain's Secret Gay Language*. Reaktion Books, 2019.

Baldwin, James. *The Evidence of Things Not Seen*. Holt, Rinehart and Winston, 1985.

Berlant, Lauren. "Intimacy: A Special Issue." *Critical Inquiry* 24, no. 2 (1998): 281–88.

Berlant, Lauren, and Lee Edelman. *Sex, or the Unbearable*. Duke University Press, 2014.

Berlant, Lauren, and Lee Edelman. "What Survives." In *Reading Sedgwick*, edited by Lauren Berlant. Duke University Press, 2019.

Berlant, Lauren, and Michael Warner. "What Does Queer Theory Teach Us About *X*?" *PMLA: Publications of the Modern Language Association of America* 110, no. 3 (1995): 343–55.

Bersani, Leo. *Homos*. Harvard University Press, 1995.

Bersani, Leo. "Is the Rectum a Grave?" *October* 43 (1987): 197–222.

Bersani, Leo. *Is the Rectum a Grave? And Other Essays*. University of Chicago Press, 1989.

Best, Stephen, and Sharon Marcus. "Surface Reading: An Introduction." *Representations* 108, no. 1 (2009): 1–21.

Bey, Marquis. "The Trans*-Ness of Blackness, the Blackness of Trans*-Ness." *TSQ: Transgender Studies Quarterly* 4, no. 2 (2017): 275–95.

Bloom, Harold. *The Anxiety of Influence: A Theory of Poetry*. 2nd ed. Oxford University Press, 1997.

Bonaparte, Alicia D. "Physicians' Discourse for Establishing Authoritative Knowledge in Birthing Work and Reducing the Presence of the Granny Midwife." *Journal of Historical Sociology* 28, no. 2 (2015): 166–94.

Bradway, Teagan. *Queer Experimental Literature: The Affective Politics of Bad Reading*. Palgrave Macmillan, 2017.

Brim, Matt. *Poor Queer Studies: Confronting Elitism in the University*. Duke University Press, 2020.

Brinkema, Eugenie. "Irrumation, the Interrogative: Extreme Porn and the Crisis of Reading." *Polygraph* 26 (2017): 130–64.

Brooks, Gwendolyn. "the mother." In *Selected Poems*. Plume, 1992.

Browne, Rembert, Brittney Cooper, Allison P. Davis, et al. "Watching White People: The Year's Dark Comedy of Manners." *The Cut*, May 25, 2021. https://www.thecut.com/2021/05/when-people-are-suddenly-forced-to-confront-race.html.

Butler, Judith. *Bodies That Matter: On the Discursive Limits of "Sex."* Routledge, 1993.

Butler, Judith. "Critically Queer." *GLQ: A Journal of Gay and Lesbian Studies* 1, no. 1 (1993): 17–32.

Butler, Judith. "Imitation and Gender Insubordination." In *Inside/Out: Lesbian Theories, Gay Theories*, edited by Diana Fuss. Routledge, 1991.

Butler, Judith, and Biddy Martin. "Cross-Identifications." *Diacritics* 24, nos. 2–3 (1994): 3.

Cain, Sian. "Malorie Blackman: 'Children's Books Still Have a Long Way to Go Before They Are Truly Diverse.'" *Guardian*, August 23, 2014. https://www.theguardian.com/childrens-books-site/2014/aug/23/malorie-blackman-teen-young-adult-fiction-diversity-amnesty-teen-takeover-2014.

Castillo, Elaine. *How to Read Now: Essays*. Penguin, 2022.

Caughie, Pamela L. "The Example of Barbara Johnson." *differences* 17, no. 3 (2006): 177–94.

Caughie, Pamela L. *Passing and Pedagogy: The Dynamics of Responsibility*. University of Illinois Press, 1999.

Centers for Disease Control and Prevention. "HIV and AIDS—United States, 1981–2000." *Morbidity and Mortality Weekly Report*, August 6, 2001. https://www.cdc.gov/mmwr/preview/mmwrhtml/mm5021a2.htm.

Christian, Barbara. "Diminishing Returns: Can Black Feminism(s) Survive the Academy?" In *Multiculturalism: A Critical Reader*, edited by David Theo Goldberg. Boston: Blackwell, 1994.

Christian, Barbara. *New Black Feminist Criticism, 1985–2000*. Edited by Gloria Bowles, M. Giulia Fabi, and Arlene R. Keizer. University of Illinois Press, 2007.

Clarke, Cheryl. "*But Some of Us Are Brave* and the Transformation of the Academy: Transformation?" *Signs* 35, no. 4 (2010): 779–88.

Clarke, Cheryl, Jewelle L. Gomez, Evelynn Hammonds, Bonnie Johnson, and Linda Powell.

"Conversations and Questions: Black Women on Black Women Writers." *Conditions* 3, no. 3 (1983): 88–137.

Cleaver, Eldridge. *Soul on Ice*. Dell, 1968.

Clifton, Lucille. "The Lost Baby Poem." *Good News About the Earth*. Random House, 1972.

Cohen, Cathy J. "Punks, Bulldaggers, and Welfare Queens: The Radical Potential of Queer Politics?" *GLQ: A Journal of Lesbian and Gay Studies* 3, no. 4 (1997): 437–65.

Cohen, Cathy. "The Radical Potential of Queer? Twenty Years Later." *GLQ: A Journal of Lesbian and Gay Studies* 25, no. 1 (2019): 140–44.

Crawford, Lucas. "Perfume." *TSQ: Transgender Studies Quarterly* 1, nos. 1–2 (2014): 151–52.

Crawford, Lucas. "Slender Trouble: From Berlant's Cruel Figuring of Figure to Sedgwick's Fat Presence." *GLQ: A Journal of Lesbian and Gay Studies* 23, no. 4 (2017): 447–72.

Crimp, Douglas. "Right On, Girlfriend!" *Social Text* 33 (1992): 2–18.

C-SPAN. "User Clip: Helms on Mapplethorpe (September 14, 1993)." c-span.org. Accessed November 19, 2024. https://beta.c-span.org/clip/senate-proceeding/user-clip-helms-on -mapplethorpe/4665361.

Currah, Paisley, and Susan Stryker. "General Editors' Introduction." *TSQ: Transgender Studies Quarterly* 4, no. 2 (2017): 159–61.

Daly, Kathleen. "Different Ways of Conceptualizing Sex/Gender in Feminist Theory and Their Implications for Criminology." *Theoretical Criminology* 1, no. 1 (1997): 25–51.

Delany, Samuel R. *The Mad Man*. Masquerade Books, 1994.

De Lauretis, Teresa. *Figures of Resistance: Essays in Feminist Theory*. Edited by Patricia White. University of Illinois Press, 2007.

Douglass, Frederick. *Narrative of the Life of Frederick Douglass, an American Slave*. Broadview, 2018.

Doyle, Laura. "Transnational History at Our Backs: A Long View of Larsen, Woolf, and Queer Racial Subjectivity in Atlantic Modernism." *Modernism/Modernity* 13, no. 3 (2006): 531–39.

Dreisinger, Baz. *Near Black: White-to-Black Passing in American Culture*. University of Massachusetts Press, 2008.

Edelman, Lee. "The Future Is Kid Stuff: Queer Theory, Disidentification, and the Death Drive." *Narrative* 6, no. 1 (1998): 18–30.

Edelman, Lee. *Homographesis: Essays in Gay Literary and Cultural Theory*. Routledge, 1994.

Edelman, Lee. "Learning Nothing: *Bad Education*." *differences* 28, no. 1 (2017): 124–73.

Edelman, Lee. *No Future: Queer Theory and the Death Drive*. Duke University Press, 2004.

Edelman, Lee. "Unknowing Barbara." *Diacritics* 34, no. 1 (2004): 88–93.

Edelman, Lee. "Unnamed: Eve's 'Epistemology.'" *Criticism* 52, no. 2 (2010): 185–90.

Ellerby-Brown, Anitra, Trickera Sims, and Mavis Schorn. "African American Nurse-Midwives: Continuing the Legacy." *Minority Nurse* (2008): 46–49.

Ellison, Treva, K. Marshall Green, Matt Richardson, and C. Riley Snorton. "We Got Issues: Toward a Black Trans*/Studies." *TSQ: Transgender Studies Quarterly* 4, no. 2 (2017): 162–69.

Eng, David L. *Racial Castration: Managing Masculinity in Asian America*. Duke University Press, 2001.

Eng, David L., Jack Halberstam, and José Esteban Muñoz. "Introduction: What's Queer About Queer Studies Now?" *Social Text* 84/85 (2005): 1–18.

Farhi, Paul. "Wait, Wait—Can You Say That on Air? There's a Debate on Cursing at NPR." *Washington Post*, August 31, 2017. https://www.washingtonpost.com/lifestyle/style/wait-wait

-can-you-say-that-on-air-theres-an-internal-debate-on-cursing-at-npr/2015/07/29/61f7e4cc-35
47-11e5-8e66-07b4603ec92a_story.html.

Fawaz, Ramzi. "'I Cherish My Bile Duct as Much as Any Other Organ': Political Disgust and the Digestive Life of AIDS in Tony Kushner's *Angels in America.*" *GLQ: A Journal of Lesbian and Gay Studies* 21, no. 1 (2015): 121–52.

Fawaz, Ramzi. "'An Open Mesh of Possibilities': The Necessity of Eve Sedgwick in Dark Times." In *Reading Sedgwick*, edited by Lauren Berlant. Duke University Press, 2019.

Federal Communications Commission. "Obscene, Indecent and Profane Broadcasts." January 13, 2021. https://www.fcc.gov/consumers/guides/obscene-indecent-and-profane-broadcasts.

Ferguson, Roderick A. *Aberrations in Black: Toward a Queer of Color Critique.* University of Minnesota Press, 2004.

Ferguson, Roderick A. "Of Sensual Matters: On Audre Lorde's 'Poetry Is Not a Luxury' and 'Uses of the Erotic.'" *WSQ: Women's Studies Quarterly* 40, no. 3 (2013): 295–300.

Fisher, Gary. *Gary in Your Pocket: Stories and Notebooks of Gary Fisher.* Duke University Press, 1996.

Fournier, Lauren. *Autotheory as Feminist Practice in Art, Writing, and Criticism.* MIT Press, 2021.

Freud, Sigmund. "A Child Is Being Beaten." *International Journal of Psycho-Analysis* 1 (1920): 371–95.

Frye, Marilyn. *The Politics of Reality: Essays in Feminist Theory.* Crossing, 1983.

Furlonge, Nicole Brittingham. *Race Sounds: The Art of Listening in African American Literature.* University of Iowa Press, 2018.

Fuss, Diana. *Identification Papers.* Routledge, 1995.

Gallop, Jane. *Anecdotal Theory.* Duke University Press, 2002.

Gallop, Jane. "Reading Johnson as a 'as a': Yes and No." *differences* 17, no. 3 (2006): 151–66.

Gallop, Jane, Marianne Hirsch, and Nancy K. Miller. "Criticizing Feminist Criticism." In *Conflicts in Feminism*, edited by Marianne Hirsch and Evelyn Fox Keller. Routledge, 1990.

Gates, Henry Louis, Jr. and James Engell. "Barbara Johnson Memorial Service." YouTube, March 30, 2013. 2 hr., 7 min., 55 sec. https://www.youtube.com/watch?v=9L-Md6QLTmE.

Gill, Stephen. Introduction to *Adam Bede*, by George Eliot. Penguin, 1985.

Goffman, Erving. *Stigma: Notes on the Management of Spoiled Identity.* Simon and Schuster, 1986.

Gomez, Jewelle. "Repeat After Me: We Are Different. We Are the Same." *New York University Review of Law and Social Change* 14, no. 4 (1986): 935–41.

Goude, Jean-Paul. *Jungle Fever.* Xavier Moreau, 1981.

Gray, Jeffery. "Identity Cards: Autobiography and Critical Practice." In *Selves in Dialogue: A Transethnic Approach to American Life Writing*, edited by Begoña Simal González. Rodopi, 2011.

Green, K. Marshall. "'Race and Gender Are Not the Same!' Is Not a Good Response to the 'Transracial'/Transgender Question or We Can and Must Do Better." *Feminist Wire*, June 14, 2015. https://thefeministwire.com/2015/06/race-and-gender-are-not-the-same-is-not-a-good-response-to-the-transracial-transgender-question-or-we-can-and-must-do-better/.

Halberstam, Jack. *Female Masculinity.* Duke University Press, 2018.

Hall, Radclyffe. *The Well of Loneliness.* Pocket Books, 1950.

Halperin, David M. *How to Be Gay.* Belknap Press of Harvard University Press, 2012.

Hanson, Ellis. "The Future's Eve: Reparative Reading After Sedgwick." *South Atlantic Quarterly* 110, no. 1 (2011): 101–19.

Hartman, Saidiya V. *Scenes of Subjection: Terror, Slavery, and Self-Making in Nineteenth-Century America.* Oxford University Press, 1997.

Hemphill, Essex. "Now We Think." In *Ceremonies: Prose and Poetry*. Plume, 1992.

Henderson, Mae G. "Speaking in Tongues: Dialogics, Dialectics, and the Black Woman Writer's Literary Tradition." In *Changing Our Own Words: Essays on Criticism, Theory, and Writing by Black Women*. Rutgers University Press, 1989.

Holland, Sharon Patricia. *The Erotic Life of Racism*. Duke University Press, 2012.

Hong, Grace Kyungwon. *Death Beyond Disavowal: The Impossible Politics of Difference*. University of Minnesota Press, 2015.

Huffer, Lynne. *Are the Lips a Grave? A Queer Feminist on the Ethics of Sex*. Columbia University Press, 2013.

Huffer, Lynne. *Mad for Foucault: Rethinking the Foundations of Queer Theory*. Columbia University Press, 2010.

Hurston, Zora Neale. *Mules and Men*. Harper Perennial, 2008.

Hurston, Zora Neale. *Their Eyes Were Watching God*. Negro Universities Press, 1969.

Jagose, Annamarie. *Queer Theory: An Introduction*. New York University Press, 1996.

Johnson, Barbara. "Apostrophe, Animation, and Abortion." *Diacritics* 16, no. 1 (1986): 29–47.

Johnson, Barbara. "Bringing Out D. A. Miller." *Narrative* 10, no. 1 (2002): 3–8.

Johnson, Barbara. *The Feminist Difference: Literature, Psychoanalysis, Race, and Gender*. Harvard University Press, 1995.

Johnson, Barbara. *Mother Tongues: Sexuality, Trials, Motherhood, Translation*. Harvard University Press, 2003.

Johnson, Barbara. Review of *The Critical Difference*, by Roland Barthes. *Diacritics* 8, no. 2 (1978): 2–9.

Johnson, Barbara. "Thresholds of Difference: Structures of Address in Zora Neale Hurston." *Critical Inquiry* 12, no. 1 (1985): 278–89.

Johnson, Barbara. *The Wake of Deconstruction*. Blackwell, 1994.

Johnson, Barbara. *A World of Difference*. Johns Hopkins University Press, 1994.

Jones, Alethia, Virginia Eubanks, and Barbara Smith, eds. *Ain't Gonna Let Nobody Turn Me Around: Forty Years of Movement Building with Barbara Smith*. State University of New York Press, 2014.

Kidd, David Comer, and Emanuele Castano. "Reading Literary Fiction Improves Theory of Mind." *Science* 342, no. 6156 (2013): 377–80.

Krafft-Ebing, Richard von. *Psychopathia Sexualis: With Especial Reference to Contrary Sexual Instinct: A Medico-Legal Study*. F. A. Davis, 1892.

Lai, James S. *Asian American Connective Action in the Age of Social Media: Civic Engagement, Contested Issues, and Emerging Identities*. Temple University Press, 2022.

Lang, Gladys Engel, and Kurt Lang. 1991. "Public Opinion and the Helms Amendment." *Journal of Arts Management and Law* 21 (2): 127–40.

Larsen, Nella. *"Quicksand" and "Passing."* Rutgers University Press, 1986.

Lassila, Kathrin Day. "Why They Call Yale the 'Gay Ivy.'" *Yale Alumni Magazine*, July 2009. https://yalealumnimagazine.org/articles/2494-why-they-call-yale-the-gay-ivy.

Lavery, Grace. "Egg Theory's Early Style." *TSQ: Transgender Studies Quarterly* 7, no. 3 (2020): 383–98.

Litvak, Joseph. "Making a Scene: Henry James's Theater of Embarrassment." In *Caught in the Act: Theatricality in the Nineteenth-Century English Novel*. University of California Press, 1992.

Litvak, Joseph. "Sedgwick's Nerve." *Criticism* 52, no. 2 (2010): 253–62.

Litvak, Joseph. *Strange Gourmets: Sophistication, Theory, and the Novel*. Duke University Press, 1997.

London, Bette. *Writing Double: Women's Literary Partnerships*. Cornell University Press, 1999.

Lorde, Audre. "Uses of the Erotic." In *Uses of the Erotic: The Erotic as Power*. Out and Out Books, 1978.

Love, Heather. *Feeling Backward: Loss and the Politics of Queer History*. Harvard University Press, 2007.

Love, Heather. *Underdogs: Social Deviance and Queer Theory*. University of Chicago Press, 2021.

Lowder, J. Bryan. "Joan Crawford's Cream Pantsuit: How Camp Rescues the Sublimely Beautiful from Unfair Obscurity." *Slate Magazine*, April 3, 2013. https://slate.com/culture/2013/04/rescuing-joan-crawfords-cream-pantsuit-from-unfair-obscurity.html.

Macharia, Keguro. "Queering Helga Crane: Black Nativism in Nella Larsen's *Quicksand*." MFS: *Modern Fiction Studies* 57, no. 2 (2011): 254–75.

Mapplethorpe, Robert. *Black Book*. Schirmer/Mosel, 2010.

McBride, Andrew. "Lesbians in the Twentieth Century, 1900–1999: The Sex Wars, 1970s to 1980s." OutHistory, 2008. http://outhistory.org/exhibits/show/lesbians-20th-century/sex-wars.

McDowell, Deborah E. "Boundaries, or Distant Relations and Close Kin." In *Afro-American Literary Study in the 1990s*, edited by Houston A. Baker Jr. and Patricia Redmond. University of Chicago Press, 1989.

McDowell, Deborah E. *"The Changing Same": Black Women's Literature, Criticism, and Theory*. Indiana University Press, 1995.

McDowell, Deborah E. Introduction to *Passing*, by Nella Larsen. Rutgers University Press, 1986.

McDowell, Deborah E. "'It's Not Safe. Not Safe at All': Sexuality in Nella Larsen's *Passing*." In *The Lesbian and Gay Studies Reader*, edited by Henry Abelove, Michèle A. Barale, and David M. Halperin. Routledge, 1993.

McDowell, Deborah E. "New Directions for Black Feminist Criticism." In *The New Feminist Criticism: Essays on Women, Literature, and Theory*. Pantheon, 1985.

McEleney, Corey. "Queer Theory and the Yale School: Barbara Johnson's Astonishment." GLQ: A *Journal of Lesbian and Gay Studies* 19, no. 2 (2013): 143–65.

Mercer, Kobena. "Looking for Trouble." *Transition* 51 (1991): 184–97.

Mercer, Kobena. "Skin Head Sex Thing: Racial Difference and the Homoerotic Imaginary." *New Formations* 16 (1992): 1–24.

Miller, D. A. *Bringing Out Roland Barthes*. University of California Press, 1992.

Miller, D. A. "Call for Papers: In Memoriam Barbara Johnson." GLQ: A *Journal of Lesbian and Gay Studies* 17, nos. 2–3 (2011): 365–69.

Miller, D. A. "Hitchcock's Hidden Pictures." *Critical Inquiry* 37, no. 1 (2010): 106–30.

Miller, D. A. *Jane Austen, or The Secret of Style*. Princeton University Press, 2003.

Miller, D. A. *The Novel and the Police*. University of California Press, 1988.

Miller, D. A. *Place for Us: Essay on the Broadway Musical*. Harvard University Press, 2000.

Miller, Nancy K. *Getting Personal: Feminist Occasions and Other Autobiographical Acts*. Routledge, 1991.

Morrison, Toni. *Beloved*. Penguin, 1987.

Morrison, Toni. *Sula*. Alfred A. Knopf, 1972.

Moten, Fred. *In the Break: The Aesthetics of the Black Radical Tradition*. University of Minnesota Press, 2003.

Muñoz, José Esteban. *Disidentifications: Queers of Color and the Performance of Politics*. University of Minnesota Press, 1999.

Muñoz, José Esteban. "Race, Sex, and the Incommensurate: Gary Fisher with Eve Kosofsky Sedgwick." In *Reading Sedgwick*, edited by Lauren Berlant. Duke University Press, 2019.

Murray-García, Jann, and Melanie Tervalon. "The Concept of Cultural Humility." *Health Affairs* 33, no. 7 (2014): 1303.

Nash, Jennifer C. *Black Feminism Reimagined: After Intersectionality*. Duke University Press, 2019.

Newton, Esther. "The Mythic Mannish Lesbian: Radclyffe Hall and the New Woman." *Signs* 9, no. 4 (1984): 557–75.

Nunokawa, Jeff. "Queer Theory: Postmortem." *South Atlantic Quarterly* 106, no. 3 (2007): 553–63.

Person, Ethel Spector, ed. *On Freud's "A Child Is Being Beaten."* Karnac Books, 2013.

Prosser, Jay. *Second Skins: The Body Narratives of Transsexuality*. Columbia University Press, 1998.

Radicalesbians. "The Woman Identified Woman." In *The Second Wave: A Reader in Feminist Theory*, edited by Linda J. Nicholson. Routledge, 1997.

Rand, Erin J. *Reclaiming Queer: Activist and Academic Rhetorics of Resistance*. University of Alabama Press, 2014.

Redfield, Marc. *Theory at Yale: The Strange Case of Deconstruction in America*. Fordham University Press, 2016.

Reid-Pharr, Robert F. *Black Gay Man: Essays*. New York University Press, 2001.

Reid-Pharr, Robert. "Living as a Lesbian." In *Sister and Brother: Lesbians and Gay Men Write About Their Lives Together*. Harper San Francisco, 1994.

Reid-Pharr, Robert. "This Useful Death." *Feminist Wire*, February 15, 2014. https://thefeministwire .com/2014/02/this-useful-death-audre-lorde/.

Rich, Adrienne. *Compulsory Heterosexuality and Lesbian Existence*. University of Chicago Press, 1980.

Rich, Adrienne. "To a Poet." In *The Dream of a Common Language: Poems, 1974–1977*. Norton, 1978.

Roberts, Dorothy E. *Killing the Black Body: Race, Reproduction, and the Meaning of Liberty*. Vintage Books, 1999.

Robertson, Pamela. "Mae West's Maids: Race, 'Authenticity,' and the Discourse of Camp." In *Camp: Queer Aesthetics and the Performing Subject: A Reader*. Edinburgh University Press, 1999.

Robinson, Amy. "It Takes One to Know One: Passing and Communities of Common Interest." *Critical Inquiry* 20, no. 4 (1994): 715–36.

Rohy, Valerie. *Impossible Women: Lesbian Figures and American Literature*. Cornell University Press, 2000.

Ronell, Avital. "Surrender and the Ethically Binding Signature: On Johnson's Reparative Process." *differences* 17, no. 3 (2006): 129–50.

Ross, Sabrina N. "The Politics of Politeness: Theorizing Race, Gender, and Education in White Southern Space." *Counterpoints* 412 (2013): 143–59.

Ruszczycky, Steven. *Vulgar Genres: Gay Pornographic Writing and Contemporary Fiction*. University of Chicago Press, 2021.

Ryan, Katy. "Falling in Public: Larsen's *Passing*, McCarthy's *The Group*, and Baldwin's *Another Country*." *Studies in the Novel* 36, no. 1 (2004): 95–199.

Saler, Michael. *As If: Modern Enchantment and the Literary Prehistory of Virtual Reality*. Oxford University Press, 2011.

Scott, Darieck. *Extravagant Abjection: Blackness, Power, and Sexuality in the African American Literary Imagination*. New York University Press, 2010.

Sedgwick, Eve Kosofsky. *Between Men: English Literature and Male Homosocial Desire*. Columbia University Press, 1989.

Sedgwick, Eve Kosofsky. *A Dialogue on Love*. Beacon, 1999.

Sedgwick, Eve Kosofsky. *Epistemology of the Closet*. University of California Press, 1990.

Sedgwick, Eve Kosofsky. *Fat Art, Thin Art*. Duke University Press, 1994.

Sedgwick, Eve Kosofsky. "Paranoid Reading and Reparative Reading; or, You're So Paranoid You Probably Think This Introduction Is About You." In *Novel Gazing: Queer Readings in Fiction*. Duke University Press, 1997.

Sedgwick, Eve Kosofsky. "A Poem Is Being Written." *Representations* 17 (1987): 110–43.

Sedgwick, Eve Kosofsky. Preface to *Epistemology of the Closet*. University of California Press, 2008.

Sedgwick, Eve Kosofsky. "Socratic Raptures, Socratic Ruptures: Notes Toward Queer Performativity." In *English Inside and Out: The Places of Literary Criticism*, edited by Susan Gubar and Jonathan Kamholtz. Routledge, 1993.

Sedgwick, Eve Kosofsky. *Tendencies*. Duke University Press, 1993.

Sedgwick, Eve Kosofsky. *Touching Feeling*. Duke University Press, 2002.

Sharpe, Christina E. *Monstrous Intimacies: Making Post-Slavery Subjects*. Duke University Press, 2010.

Smith, Barbara. "Toward a Black Feminist Criticism." In *All the Women Are White, All the Blacks Are Men, but Some of Us Are Brave: Black Women's Studies*, edited by Akasha (Gloria T.) Hull, Patricia Bell Scott, and Barbara Smith. Feminist Press, 1982.

Snorton, C. Riley. "Transfiguring Masculinities in Black Women's Studies." *Feminist Wire*, May 18, 2011. https://thefeministwire.com/2011/05/transfiguring-masculinities-in-black-womens -studies/.

Solomon, Melisa. "Flaming Iguanas, Dalai Pandas, and Other Lesbian Bardos (a Few Perimeter Points)." In *Regarding Sedgwick: Essays on Queer Culture and Critical Theory*, edited by Stephen M. Barber and David L. Clark. Routledge, 2002.

Somerville, Siobhan B. "Feminism, Queer Theory, and the Racial Closet." *Criticism* 52, no. 2 (2010): 191–200.

Spillers, Hortense J. "'All the Things You Could Be by Now If Sigmund Freud's Wife Was Your Mother': Psychoanalysis and Race." *Boundary 2* 23, no. 3 (1996): 75–142.

Spillers, Hortense J. "Mama's Baby, Papa's Maybe: An American Grammar Book." *Diacritics* 17, no. 2 (1987): 64–81.

Stadler, John. "Pornographesis: Sex, Media, and Gay Culture." PhD diss., Duke University, 2018.

Stockton, Kathryn Bond. *Beautiful Bottom, Beautiful Shame: Where "Black" Meets "Queer."* Duke University Press, 2006.

Stockton, Kathryn Bond. "Rhythm." In *Queer Times, Queer Becomings*, edited by E. L. McCallum and Mikko Tuhkanen. State University of New York Press, 2011.

Stoever, Jennifer Lynn. *The Sonic Color Line: Race and the Cultural Politics of Listening*. New York University Press, 2016.

Stoler, Ann Laura. *Race and the Education of Desire: Foucault's History of Sexuality and the Colonial Order of Things*. Duke University Press, 1995.

Stowe, Harriet Beecher. "Sojourner Truth, the Libyan Sibyl." *Atlantic*, April 1863, 473–81.

Tanne, Janice Hopkins. "US Pro-Life Groups Tell Black Women That Abortion Is Genocide." *BMJ: British Medical Journal* 340, no. 7746 (2010): 556–56.

Thomas, Piri. *Down These Mean Streets*. Knopf, 1967.

Thompson, Elizabeth. "Break the Internet: Kim Kardashian." *PAPER*, June 2, 2021. https://www.papermag.com/break-the-internet-kim-kardashian-cover.

Voglar, Candace. "Sex and Talk." In *Intimacy*, edited by Lauren Berlant. University of Chicago Press, 2000.

Walcott, Rinaldo. "Reconstructing Manhood; or, The Drag of Black Masculinity." *Small Axe: A Caribbean Journal of Criticism* 13, no. 1 (2009): 75–89.

Walker, Alice. *Gathering Blossoms Under Fire: The Journals of Alice Walker, 1965–2000*. Edited by Valerie Boyd. Simon and Schuster, 2022.

Walker, Rafael. "Nella Larsen Reconsidered: The Trouble with Desire in *Quicksand* and *Passing*." *MELUS: Multi-Ethnic Literature of the United States* 41, no. 1 (2016): 165–92.

Washington, Eric. "The AIDS Epidemic Has Always Been Defined by What We Don't Know." *Colorlines*, December 1, 2010. https://colorlines.com/article/aids-epidemic-has-always-been-defined-what-we-dont-know/.

Washington, Mary Helen. "Barbara Johnson, African Americanist: The Critic as Insider/Outsider." *differences* 17, no. 3 (2006): 167–76.

Weiner, Joshua J., and Damon Young. "Queer Bonds." *GLQ: A Journal of Lesbian and Gay Studies* 17, no. 2 (2011): 223–41.

Wiegman, Robyn. "Eve's Triangles, or Queer Studies Beside Itself." *differences* 26, no. 1 (2015): 48–73.

Wiegman, Robyn. "Heteronormativity and the Desire for Gender." *Feminist Theory* 7 (April 2006): 89–103.

Wiegman, Robyn. *Object Lessons*. Duke University Press, 2012.

Wiegman, Robyn, and Elizabeth A. Wilson. "Introduction: Antinormativity's Queer Conventions." *differences: A Journal of Feminist Cultural Studies* 26, no. 1 (2015): 1–25.

Williams, Linda. *Porn Studies*. Duke University Press, 2004.

Williams, Patricia J. *The Alchemy of Race and Rights*. Harvard University Press, 1991.

Womack, Autumn. "Can You Be Black and Listen to This?" *Los Angeles Review of Books*, June 1, 2020. https://lareviewofbooks.org/short-takes/can-black-listen/.

Wright, Richard. *Native Son*. Harper Perennial Modern Classics, 2008.

Young, Nikki. "'Uses of the Erotic' for Teaching Queer Studies." *WSQ: Women's Studies Quarterly* 40, no. 3 (2013): 301–5.

Young, Vershawn Ashanti. "Should Writers Use They Own English?" *Iowa Journal of Cultural Studies* 12, no. 1 (2010): 110–17.

Index

Clarke, Cheryl, 16, 26, 29, 96, 108; McDowell and, 23–24, 33, 38, 44; Walker and, 26, 151n14

class, 6, 12–14, 20–21, 37, 84, 88; academic inquiry and, 149n46; differentiation, 87; formation, 13, 28

Clueless, 7, 143

color line, 6, 56, 67, 125

Combahee River Collective, 95, 161n78

communism, 54–55, 112

comparative literature, 7, 75; departments, 4

Conditions journal, 23, 25–27, 29–31, 37–38, 96

Crawford, Lucas, 99

Crimp, Douglas, 5–6

critical theory, 19–20, 22, 29–31, 37–38, 44; canon, 99; conference, 48

critical writing, 15, 38, 115; *as if!*, 15, 68, 141; Johnson's, 50, 57, 68; queer, 4; Reid-Pharr's, 160n60; Sedgwick's, 125–26, 160n60

cross-identification, 4–6, 8, 10, 15–18, 83, 111, 141–43, 145; critical, 53; Johnson and, 57, 65, 68, 78, 81, 157n120; Reid-Pharr and, 88–89, 102, 108–9; Sedgwick and, 11–12, 118, 122, 127–31, 133–35, 137, 160n40; in *Tendencies* (Sedgwick), 114, 129, 137

Cruz, Ted, 141–42

culture wars, 13, 44, 88

deconstruction, 5, 59–60, 81; American, 149n48; deaths of, 63; de Manian, 77; of gender, 59; Yale University and, 150n48

defensiveness, 27, 45, 82, 131–32

Delany, Samuel R., 91–93

de Man, Paul, 62–63, 150n48, 156n93

desire, 12, 60, 68–71, 82, 101, 103, 120, 150; Black gay male, 128; of the critic, 25; cross-class, 88; cross-racial, 71, 88, 94, 107; early gay, 166n14; embodiment and, 106–7; fear and, 40; female, 40; Gallop and, 34, 36; gay male structures of, 55, 117; homosexual, 119;

identity and, 106; intimacy and, 1–53; Johnson and, 61, 65, 71, 73; lesbian structures of, 25, 38, 44, 72; problematic, 86, 101; queer, 145; recognition and, 8; same-sex, 34, 39, 41–42; sexual, 86, 96, 101; shock of, 89; structures of, 25, 68, 71, 74; transsexual, 98, 132; white, 71, 85. *See also* lesbian desire

differences journal, 49–50, 69

dissatisfaction, 15, 20–22, 24, 28, 37, 45

Douglass, Frederick, 66–67

drag, 10–11; bans, 56; organizational, 88; performance, 17; queens, 104; sophisticate, 13

Edelman, Lee, 78, 80–82, 92, 108, 117–18, 128, 132, 150n48

egg theory, 98, 131–32

embarrassment, 10, 15, 143; Sedgwick and, 16, 113–14, 117–20, 162n13; theater of, 113, 162n9

embodiment, 19, 97, 101–2, 106–7, 126–27, 130, 132

empathy, 5, 67–68, 140–41, 143–44; white, 15

Eng, David L., 4, 130

Engell, James, 48–50, 52, 82

English departments, 4

eroticism, 158–59n26; anal, 89, 114, 123; auto-, 32; gynocentric, 98; oral, 89, 93

erotics, 97, 107–8, 115; lesbian, 72–73; of slavery, 103; of voyeurism, 72

ethnicity, 124–25

exhibitionism, 12, 114

Facebook, 1–2

Fawaz, Ramzi, 111, 135

femaleness, 116, 120, 124

feminism, 33, 63, 121, 127; Black, 45, 104, 161n78; Black lesbian, 28; lesbian, 96; male, 104; pornography and, 98; postmodern, 61; queer theory and, 117; white, 155n51; woman of color, 45

feminist criticism, 34, 51, 71; materialist,

60; white, 61. *See also* Black feminist criticism

Feminist Difference, The: Literature, Psychoanalysis, Race, and Gender (Johnson), 16, 43, 49, 60–61, 63, 66, 74, 77; Gallop and, 151n34; McDowell and, 152n46; Spillers and, 154n46

Ferguson, Roderick A., 28, 148n11, 161n78

fetishism, 159n26; racial, 12, 89, 134, 159n27

Fisher, Gary, 102–6, 109, 133–35; *Gary in Your Pocket*, 102–3, 134

Floyd, George, 1, 67

Freud, Sigmund, 8; "A Child Is Being Beaten," 124, 152n38

Frug, Mary Joe, 62–63

Furlonge, Nicole Brittingham, 56–57

Fuss, Diana, 8, 10

Gallop, Jane, 116, 121, 151n34; Johnson and, 61, 69–70, 156n93; McDowell and, 32–37, 42, 44; Sedgwick and, 162n13

Gates, Henry Louis, Jr., 48–53, 56–57, 59–60, 65, 81, 150n48

gay and lesbian studies, 4, 41, 122, 155n66

gay men, 5, 94, 97–98, 145; Black, 107–8, 126–28; divas and, 11; femme, 104; Johnson and, 157n120; Sedgwick and, 5, 16, 111–12, 115–18, 122–24, 127–28, 131–32, 139, 157n120, 160n60, 164n80

gayness, 3, 53, 55, 101, 122, 124, 127; Lynch's, 130

gender, 3, 6, 11, 20, 37, 83–84, 98–101, 106, 115, 117, 120, 127–28, 150n63, 153n77; binary, 99–100, 161n78; categories of, 20–21, 93, 99, 104; class and, 149n46; equality, 71; essentialism, 98; identifications, 10, 88, 100, 103, 109, 111–12, 122, 125, 132–34, 136, 160n60; identity, 4, 89, 98, 104, 113, 124, 136, 149n43, 160n60; ideologies of, 140; Johnson and, 51, 59; normative, 161n78; oppression, 125; oral rape and, 92; policing, 98, 100; profiling, 56; queer studies and, 147n7; race and, 141–42; roles, 85; self-determination, 131–32; sexuality

and, 132; Spillers and, 78; subordination, 39; transition, 98, 131

genocide, 17, 79

Gomez, Jewelle L., 17, 23

Halberstam, Jack, 4

Halperin, David M., 11, 38

Hanson, Ellis, 133–34

Harlem Renaissance, 40–42

Hartman, Saidiya, 35, 67–68, 155n66

Helms, Jesse, 87–88

Hemphill, Essex, 85, 108

Henderson, Mae G., 58

heteronormativity, 85, 88

heterosexism, 18, 101

heterosexuality, 63, 99, 130

HIV, 105–7, 128, 134

Holland, Sharon Patricia, 47, 52, 80, 86, 123, 127, 136

homophobia, 17, 24, 38, 45, 76, 92, 125, 131

homosexuality, 3, 27, 55, 87–89; male, 119, 124

homosexual reading, 115–17, 127, 160n40

homosexual writing, 115–16

Hong, Grace Kyungwon, 18, 45, 80, 106, 108, 133

Hughes, Ted, 75–76

Hurston, Zora Neale, 24, 49, 57–60, 82

identification, 2, 7–12, 15, 68–69, 72, 142–43, 147n10, 150n52; alloidentification, 112, 122, 132; cross-class, 13; cross-racial, 125, 129, 154n12; easy, 7, 37; gender and, 10, 88, 100, 103, 109, 111–12, 122, 125, 132–34, 136, 160n60; identity and, 86; inconsistency of, 39; Johnson and, 52–54, 58–60, 66–67; McDowell and, 25, 30, 34, 37, 39, 41–45, 44–45; queer, 18, 145, 162n13; Reid-Pharr and, 95, 98–104, 106, 109; Sedgwick and, 111–14, 116–25, 127–32, 135–37, 139–40, 160n60, 162n13, 164n80; self-identification, 12, 43, 116; tragedy and, 17; unalienated, 25; white, 67. *See also* cross-identification identity, 2–13, 15–18, 55, 103, 107, 117, 141–42, 147n10, 149n43, 159n26; activism based on, 149n48; authorial, 43, 57, 63, 104; Black, 25, 55, 57, 66, 104; Black lesbian, 23, 96; Black racial, 57; critical, 16, 20, 22, 42, 44, 50, 90; Delany and, 93; difference and, 20, 22; embodiment and, 102, 106; ethnic, 11; female, 25, 100; French theory and, 31; gay, 125; gay male, 99; gender, 89, 98, 104, 136; health and, 106; homosexual, 51; ideologies of, 150n48; Johnson and, 50–51, 57, 59, 63, 66, 69–70, 74, 80; lesbian, 43, 69, 99–100; McDowell and, 16, 22, 34, 36–38, 42, 44; nonlesbian, 118; policing, 43, 88, 142; racial, 92, 104, 125, 129, 136, 142, 155n46; racialized, 47; Reid-Pharr and, 84, 86, 88–91, 93, 99–102; Sedgwick and, 112–13, 118, 122, 124–25, 126–33, 135–37, 140; sexual, 92, 96, 142; Smith and, 27–28, 43

identity categories, 7–9, 12, 25, 36, 88, 90, 129; academic discourse of, 102; AIDS and, 5–6, 106–7; critical, 16, 20, 22; fixed, 16, 128, 147n10, 150n63; of gender, 104, 113, 142; racial, 113, 142; sexual, 113, 142

identity knowledge, 5, 27, 47, 125, 149n46, 150n48; fields, 3, 10, 124, 142

identity politics, 6, 17, 55, 69–70, 73, 85; American left and, 83; anti-identity politics, 28; co-option of, 142; neoliberal, 47; the obscene and, 88

inauthenticity, 37, 118

interruption, 15–16, 70, 105, 109, 112, 143; bodily, 98; intratextual, 108; of language, 92; pornographic, 95, 100, 102; queer, 90; of racial hate speech, 91; sexual, 102; of systems of logic, 94–95; textual, 84, 102

intersectionality, 45, 47

intimacy, 15–16, 57, 60–61, 71, 81–82, 85, 138, 143; Johnson and, 16, 51–53, 65, 67–68, 81–82

intuition, 55; maternal, 76

Jackson, Ketanji Brown, 141

Johnson, Barbara, 5–8, 14, 16–18, 48–82, 117, 143–44, 155n46, 155n56; "Apostrophe, Animation, and Abortion," 77–79; on Benjamin, 46; Blackness of, 49, 53, 71; "Bringing Out D. A. Miller," 50–51, 53, 55, 57, 75–76, 144; class and, 13; cross-identification and, 57, 65, 68, 78, 81, 157n120; desire and, 61, 65, 71, 73; "Double Mourning and the Public Sphere," 62, 69; on feminism, 155n51; Gallop and, 61, 69–70, 156n93; gay men and, 157n120; gender and, 51, 59; identification and, 52–54, 58–60, 66–67; identity and, 50–51, 57, 59, 63, 66, 69–70, 74, 80; intimacy and, 16, 51–53, 65, 67–68, 81–82; "Lesbian Spectacles: Reading *Sula, Passing, Thelma and Louise,* and *The Accused,*" 42–43, 63, 68, 71–74, 79; McDowell and, 35, 42–44; Miller and, 148–49n33; *Mother Tongues: Sexuality, Trials, Motherhood, Translation,* 74–77; passing and, 11, 61, 65, 74, 76, 81; race and, 49, 53–54, 58–60, 67, 79; "The Re(a)d and the Black: Richard Wright's Blueprint," 54, 57–58, 60; sexuality and, 52–53, 73; "Thresholds of Difference: Structures of Address in Zora Neale Hurston," 57–60, 63, 65; Yale University and, 150n48. See also *Feminist Difference, The: Literature, Psychoanalysis, Race, and Gender*; lesbianism; queerness; *Sula* (Morrison); whiteness

King, Rodney, 66

kinship, 31–32, 95, 97

knowledge, 2–3, 5, 9, 21, 45, 58, 84, 120, 124–25, 142; affect and, 120; cultural, 105; expert, 96; field, 20; historical, 36; insider, 52; limits of, 81; ontological, 57; production, 114, 121. *See also* identity knowledge

Larsen, Nella, 15, 38–42; *Quicksand,* 37–42, 69. See also *Passing*

Lavery, Grace, 98, 131–32, 160n60
legitimacy, 21, 26–27, 124, 129; feminist, 121
lesbian criticism, 23, 74; Black, 24, 28
lesbian desire, 5, 68–70, 73; Black feminism and, 25; Johnson's, 50, 70; *Passing* (Larsen) and, 38, 42, 71–72
lesbian gap, 61–63, 82
lesbianism, 24–25, 63, 119; Black, 96, 105; Johnson's, 50–51, 53; motherhood and, 75, 77; radical political, 38; Reid-Pharr's, 8, 96–97, 101–2
lesbian writing, 5, 119
literary criticism, 4, 13, 22, 75, 84, 143–44, 148n21; African American, 30–32; Black, 54; feminist, 34; gay, 88; Johnson's, 68; from lesbian vantage point, 43; McDowell's, 20, 47; Miller's, 72; Reid-Pharr and, 87–88; Sedgwick and, 114; white, 66. *See also* queer literary criticism
literary studies, 44–46; queer studies and, 4
literature, 4–5, 20, 34, 36; Black/African American, 30–31, 40, 52, 54, 90; Black gay male, 103; classical, 75; comparative, 4, 7, 75; identities in, 144; lesbianism and, 96; oral sex scenes in, 92; pornography and, 87; queer, 85; queer theory and, 147n7; vernacular, 54–55
Litvak, Joseph, 13, 113, 150n48, 162n9
Lorde, Audre, 9, 18, 26, 95, 98, 101, 105, 107–8
Love, Heather, 93, 100, 122, 148n11, 164n80, 165n83

maleness, 104, 124
Mapplethorpe, Robert, 12, 87–88, 158–59nn26–27
marriage, 32, 39–42; Boston, 133; heterosexual, 31, 38, 40–41
McDowell, Deborah E., 5, 6, 11, 13, 15–47, 69, 71, 74, 143, 151–53; Black feminist criticism and, 37, 42; "Boundaries: Or Distant Relations and Close Kin," 29–32; Clarke and, 23–24, 33, 38,

44; identification and, 25, 30, 34, 37, 39, 41–45, 44–45; identity and, 16, 22, 34, 36–38, 42, 44; "'It's Not Safe. Not Safe at All': Sexuality in Nella Larsen's *Passing*," 38, 40–41; Johnson and, 35, 42–44; "The 'Nameless . . . Shameful Impulse': Sexuality in Nella Larsen's *Quicksand* and *Passing*," 38–41, 43, 69, 153n77; "New Directions for Black Feminist Criticism," 23–25, 27–28; rereading, 15, 19, 22, 121; revising, 15, 19, 22, 30, 38, 47; sexuality and, 19–20, 25, 29–31, 37–38, 42. *See also* *"Changing Same, The": Black Women's Literature, Criticism, and Theory*; queer literary criticism; queer theory; *Sula* (Morrison)
McEleney, Corey, 14, 70, 150n48, 156n93
Mercer, Kobena, 6, 11–12, 88–89, 158–59nn26–27
midwifery, 80–81
Miller, D. A., 52–56, 65, 70, 73, 75–78, 80–82, 143; *Bringing Out Roland Barthes*, 50–51, 53, 144; "Call for Papers: In Memoriam Barbara Johnson," 50–51, 68, 72; *The Novel and the Police*, 144; *Place for Us: Essay on the Broadway Musical*, 144; Sedgwick and, 165–66n13; Yale University and, 150n48, 165–66n13
Miller, Nancy K., 9, 32, 68, 121, 148–49n33
misunderstanding, 2, 15, 18
Morrison, Toni, 15, 24, 35, 65–67, 104; *Beloved*, 35, 60, 81, 92. *See also* rememory; *Sula*
motherhood, 19, 31–32, 40, 46, 75, 77–80
Muñoz, José Esteban, 4, 9, 134

Nash, Jennifer C., 34, 45–47, 81, 106, 138
neoliberalism, 14, 17

obscenity, 88–90, 109, 158n25; Baudelaire's trial for, 75; law, 86–87; Mapplethorpe's art and, 89
oppression, 6, 92, 125, 141; incommensurate systems of, 137; structural, 2

pain, 92, 109, 114

passing, 10–11, 55, 57, 73, 141; bad, 10, 13, 112–13, 118, 128; Johnson and, 61, 65, 74, 76, 81; racial, 6, 38, 40–42, 71, 142, 152n55; sexual, 38, 42, 55

Passing (Larsen), 6, 15, 37–43, 68–73; Butler and, 153n77. *See also* Johnson, Barbara: "Lesbian Spectacles: Reading *Sula, Passing, Thelma and Louise,* and *The Accused*"

Plath, Sylvia, 75–76

pleasure, 64–65, 94, 109, 114, 117, 120; anal, 124; carnal, 84; danger and, 40; degradation and, 93; deviant, 127; domination and, 104; homosexual, 93; knowing and, 56; masochistic and sadistic, 113; queer and, 6; queer identification and, 18; self-pleasure, 32; sexual, 32, 89

"Poem Is Being Written, A" (Sedgwick), 114–16, 119, 124, 149n33, 162n13, 165–66n13; identification and, 114, 116, 118, 122, 125, 127, 139; orality and, 160n40

poetry, 4, 77, 80, 108, 115–16; ancient, 75–76; by Lorde, 95; lyric, 76, 81; Sedgwick's, 114

pornography/porn, 83, 86–89, 91, 98, 155n51, 158n12

poststructuralism, 20, 31

qualification, 15–16, 21–23, 27, 32, 39, 45, 123

queer literary criticism, 4–5, 13, 17, 83, 92, 147n7; McDowell and, 29, 37; Miller and, 143; Sedgwick and, 139, 144; Smith and, 28

queerness, 15, 78, 85, 89, 91, 130, 132–33, 148n11; Johnson's, 50, 53, 56

queer politics, 125, 134–35, 164n80, 165n83; of positionality, 16

queer reading, 114, 145

queer studies, 2–4, 122, 147n7, 147n10; white, 165n83

queer theory, 4, 13, 15, 132, 139, 143–44, 147n7; as academic field, 46; antisocial

turn of, 78; Black feminism and, 148n11; bodies and, 85; deconstructive, 70; early, 28, 38, 98, 117; identity and, 112; McDowell and, 28, 153n76; queer body and, 106; Reid-Pharr and, 90; reproduction and, 80; Sedgwick and, 117–18, 130, 132; white, 47; Yale and, 149n48

race, 3–4, 10–11, 73, 78, 141–42; as category, 20–21, 30, 53, 142; class and, 149n46; critical race theory, 103; Delany and, 93; embodiment and, 101; erasure of, 29; fantasies, 159n26; feminists and, 62; Gallop and, 32, 37; identity and, 149n43, 150n63; ideologies of, 140; Johnson and, 49, 53–54, 58–60, 67, 79; oppressions of, 6; queer and, 153n77; queer theory and, 106; Reid-Pharr and, 84–85, 88, 90–92, 97, 106, 109; relations, 88; Sedgwick and, 16, 112–13, 122–25, 127–28, 130, 134; sound and, 56; white feminists and, 32–33; white queer theorizing and, 86, 165n83

racial categories, 6, 142, 152n55

racial hierarchies, 6, 53, 92

racism, 45, 62, 90, 125, 158n25; erotic life of, 136; state, 108

rape, 52; crisis centers, 131; oral, 92–93

Reagan, Ronald, 6, 17

real, the, 85, 113, 128, 136

recognition, 27, 112, 117, 133, 135, 150n52; death and, 108; de-recognition, 128, 136; desire and, 8; mutual, 51, 57; N-word and, 91; queer, 145; shock of, 159n26; *Sula* (Morrison) and, 64

Reid-Pharr, Robert, 5, 7–8, 11, 13, 16–18, 83–109, 159n27, 159n33, 160n60; cross-identification and, 88–89, 102, 108–9, 143; "Dinge," 84–86, 98, 106–7; identification and, 95, 98–104, 106, 109; identity and, 84, 86, 88–91, 93, 99–102; "Living as a Lesbian," 16, 95–103, 105–8, 160n60, 161n78; race and, 84–85, 88, 90–92, 97, 106, 109; sex and, 84–89, 92–93, 95, 97–98, 100,

107; sexuality and, 84, 88, 103, 160n60; "The Shock of Gary Fisher," 88, 102–3, 105, 108; "Tearing the Goat's Flesh," 89–90, 92, 105, 109; "This Useful Death," 107; white partners of, 13; Yale University and, 150n48. See also *Black Gay Man: Essays*; lesbianism

rememory, 35–36

reproductive futurism, 38, 78

Rich, Adrienne, 77, 96, 99

Robinson, Amy, 55, 57, 72–73

Ronell, Avital, 50, 156n93

Rose, Jacqueline, 75–76

Ruszczycky, Steven, 86–88, 92

Sappho, 75–76

Scott, Darieck, 91–92

Sedgwick, Eve Kosofsky, 5, 11–14, 16–18, 55–56, 102–3, 110–45, 159–60n40; AIDS and, 135–37; *Between Men*, 117, 122; cross-identification and, 11–12, 118, 122, 127–31, 133–35, 137, 160n40; death and, 108; *A Dialogue on Love*, 134; Duke University and, 126, 160n60; *Epistemology of the Closet*, 2, 8, 55, 117, 121, 125; Gallop and, 162n13; gay men and, 5, 16, 111–12, 115–18, 122–24, 127–28, 131–32, 139, 157n120, 160n60, 164n80; humiliation and, 113–14; identification and, 111–14, 116–25, 127–32, 135–37, 139–40, 160n60, 162n13, 164n80; identity and, 112–13, 118, 122, 124–25, 126–33, 135–37, 140; Love on, 164n80, 165n83; Miller and, 148–49n43; *Novel Gazing: Queer Readings in Fiction*, 89, 144–45, 166n13; "Paranoid Reading and Reparative Reading; or, You're So Paranoid, You Probably Think This Introduction Is About You," 12, 144–45, 166n13; "Queer and Now," 126, 133; race and, 16, 112–13, 122–25, 127–28, 130, 134; sexuality and, 111–12, 115, 117, 122–25, 132–33, 160n60; shame and, 162n9; smuggling and, 126–27; "Socratic Raptures, Socratic Ruptures: Notes Toward Queer Performativity" ("Interlude, Peda-

gogic"), 125–29, 131, 135–36; spanking and, 114–15, 124; stigma and, 135–37, 164–65nn80–81, 165n83; *Touching Feeling: Affect, Pedagogy, Performativity*, 125, 162n9; "The Warm Decembers," 116, 163n18; "White Glasses," 129–33, 135–37; Yale University and, 150n48. *See also* embarrassment; Fisher, Gary; Miller, D. A.; "Poem Is Being Written, A"; queer theory; *Tendencies*; whiteness

sentimentalism, 35, 37

sex, 19–20, 30, 42, 83, 139; anal, 115–16; fantasies, 159n26; Fisher and, 134; oral, 89, 92–94; Reid-Pharr and, 84–89, 92–93, 95, 97–98, 100, 107; soliciting, 124; in *Sula* (Morrison), 29, 32, 64, 96

sexuality, 3–4, 10, 15, 21, 69, 78, 82–83, 91, 113; Black, 161n78; Black female, 40–41, 123; butch, 101; camp and, 149n43; Delany and, 93; Fisher and, 134; gender and, 132; ideologies of, 140; Johnson and, 52–53, 73; lesbian, 52, 61, 96, 119; McDowell and, 19–20, 25, 29–31, 37–38, 42; as mutable, 142; in *Passing* (Larsen), 40; Plath's, 75; queer, 52, 153n77; queer studies and, 147n7, 165n83; queer theory and, 147n7; race and, 165n83; Reid-Pharr and, 84, 88, 103, 160n60; Sedgwick and, 111–12, 115, 117, 122–25, 132–33, 160n60; in *Sula* (Morrison), 29–30, 38

sexual politics, 38; of the asshole, 123–24

shame, 85, 113, 118–19, 126, 162n9

Sharpe, Christina, 52, 67–68, 71

slavery, 35–36, 68, 78, 102–3, 108; transatlantic, 35, 52, 80

smell, 99–100

Smith, Barbara, 16, 24–25, 29, 32, 39, 43, 74, 95–97, 101–2; Miller and, 149n33; "Toward a Black Feminist Criticism," 25–28, 69, 96, 149n33

Smith, Bessie, 123–24

Snorton, C. Riley, 102, 104, 161n78

Solomon, Melissa, 120

Somerville, Siobhan B., 125

www.ingramcontent.com/pod-product-compliance
Lightning Source LLC
Chambersburg PA
CBHW030839270326
41928CB00007B/1123